HOW TO BUILD Cobra
KIT CARS
+ Buying Used

D. Brian Smith

S-A DESIGN

CarTech®

CarTech®

CarTech®, Inc.
838 Lake St S
Forest Lake, MN 55025
Phone: 651-277-1200 or 800-551-4754
Fax: 651-277-1203
www.cartechbooks.com

Edit by Paul Johnson
Layout by Monica Seiberlich

ISBN 978-1-61325-387-8
Item No. SA202P

Library of Congress Cataloging-in-Publication Data

Smith, D. Brian.
 How to build Cobra kit cars + buying used / by D. Brian Smith.
 p. cm.
 ISBN 978-1-934709-43-6
1. Automobiles, Home built. 2. A.C. automobile–Design and construction--Amateurs› manuals. I. Title. II. Title: How to build Cobra kit cars plus buying used.

 TL240.2.S65 2012
 629.222'2–dc23

 2012011038

Printed in U.S.A.

Title Page:

Backed by a Tremec TK0-500 5-speed manual transmission, the Engine Factory 351-ci Windsor V-8 mill in Mr. Wayne's FFR roadster makes 425 hp. A Mass Flo fuel injection system provides free-flowing fuel for the fine Factory Five Racing ride.

Back Cover Photos

Top Left:
There's no mistaking that sleek Cobra body. For all those destined to build a Cobra replica, your body will be delivered and look like this. Factory Five has mounted the body of the Mk4 to the chassis for safe delivery. The Stewart Transport driver and one of our intrepid builders unload the body/chassis from the truck.

Top Right:
After connecting the fan switch wire at the fan, wire and install the fan toggle switch in the dash. This is a manual switch. You can install a thermostat that automatically turns on the fan, which needs to be retrofitted. The fan comes on automatically, via the thermostat in the aluminum radiator. The fan can also be manually activated if, say, you're sitting in traffic.

Middle Left:
With the hood now fitting as it should, Jorge used the air grinder to sand off just a smidgen of the hood on the driver's side. He has 30+ years of experience working with fiberglass on boats, catamarans, and, the past 10 years on Porsche replicas at Thunder Ranch.

Middle Right:
Here is how a properly installed Simpson racing safety harness should be installed. Notice that the passenger side could use some adjustment. I wound up having to re-install the passenger side harness to get the shoulder straps to be the same length.

Bottom Left:
The panel-marking procedure includes drilling those aluminum panels that overlap each other prior to removal. Drill the passenger-side trunk wall. Look closely at this wall and you see we've also marked openings that need to be filed or trimmed. These panels fit well, but precise trimming in high spots enables them to fit perfectly, which the ultimate Cobra deserves.

Bottom Right:
Pass the shock body through the upper control arm with the shock body facing up, and hang the shock by temporarily running a long Philips screwdriver through its upper attachment holes. Do this to attach the .43-inch shock spacers that are supplied for the lower control arm in the FFR Mk4 Complete Kit.

CONTENTS

CONTENTS

ACKNOWLEDGMENTS

Building a kit car, taking photography of all the work involved and writing a book about the process is quite a challenge. Without my dad, Dan Brian Smith, Sr., by my side every step of the way, the project would not have been nearly as fun and fulfilling. Indeed, I would have also taken far too long to get everything done.

From an early age Dad instilled a love of all things automotive in both my brother Kevin and me. Had it not been for him, I probably would not have such a passion for cars, and I possibly would have never embarked on creating a Factory Five Racing Mk4 Cobra roadster replica. When it comes to building cars the right way, he knows his way around a garage and is a persevering perfectionist. Thank you so much Dad for working on this project with me. We now have a Cobra replica and a book that honors the original vintage sports cars and all the replicas.

Kevin was also monumentally helpful in the creation of our FFR Mk4. He provided expert advice all the way from Suwannee, Georgia, where he and his wife Agnes live. Kevin visited us in California at several critical stages of the build and did everything from turning wrenches and riveting aluminum panels to assisting us in rescuing the car from a body and paint shop. He is also an accomplished car builder and is an adept amateur race car driver, in addition to being the marketing and public relations director for Lotus Cars U.S.A.

We relied on family and friends throughout the project, both for emotional support and for expert collaboration. My cousin Kenny Smith has several years under his belt racing first-generation Ford Broncos and campaigning off-road trucks for a couple seasons for Mickey Thompson's Racing Team. At any given moment in time, he has several of his own enthusiast car and truck projects underway. When we needed to mate the Dart aluminum 427-stroker mill to the Tremec T56 Magnum 6-speed transmission and install the drivetrain in our Mk4 chassis, his expertise helped make the installation a reality. Kenny also provided our professionally built engine and our homebuilt kit car project with first-class transport home from the engine shop and to the bodywork and paint shop, when the car was getting close to being finished. Despite having a multi-million dollar appraisal business and an earthmoving equipment rental business to run, Kenny took time out to be a guest expert Cobra builder on several occasions. He has earned the right to drive the roadster as if it were his own, as has my brother. But, we won't let Kenny take the roadster off road.

Deciding which Cobra replica to build is likely the single biggest choice you have to make; it was with us. We are so very thankful that we chose to assemble a Factory Five Racing Mk4 roadster. At the time that we were investigating all the manufacturers kits, we contacted Dave Smith, president and owner of Factory Five Racing (FFR). He let us in on a little secret, which he didn't make public until later. Dave informed us that FFR would be releasing the company's fourth-generation Cobra car replica. He explained that the all-new Mk4 body was closest to the original AC Cobra 427SC shape because a digital rendering was made of Dick Smith's record-shattering 198 mph 1966 Shelby Cobra 427SC. Equally compelling, numerous improvements were made to the chassis, the suspension, and even the interior foot boxes. What sold us was the fact that the Mk4 would be available at the same time that we needed to commence work on building our Cobra dream car. Dave, thank you so much for letting us in on your little secret. To you and your talented crew at

ACKNOWLEDGMENTS

Factory Five Racing, we greatly appreciate being able to build the most sold Cobra car replica in the world. Working with you and your team at FFR was (and is) always a pleasure.

Once you determine which kit to create, the drivetrain is a close second in terms of importance, especially with a sports car/race car that has the reputation of the Cobra. Original Cobras earned the title of "world's fastest production sports car." After talking to several crate engine companies and engine builders, we selected a Dart Manufacturing 351 Windsor aluminum block and Dart Pro CNC aluminum cylinder heads to form the basis of our engine. Jack McInnis, Dart's director of advertising, didn't have to do any sort of sales job to convince us that his company's engine components form the basis of a very solid foundation to build a stout powerplant. We thank him for also recommending pro-engine builder, QMP Racing Engines to balance, blueprint, and build our mill.

That engine is stuffed with the best components that we could afford, most of which were purchased from Summit Racing. From the Holley Avenger EFI and Weiand aluminum intake manifold to the Comp Cams valvetrain assembly all the way to the custom Moroso windage tray and aluminum 7-quart-capacity oil pan, we have a lightweight, engine dyno proven mill that produces 516 hp and 492 ft.-lbs. of torque. It's a good thing that we have a Tremec T56 Magnum 6-speed manual transmission to back it up.

We spent an enormous amount of time trying to figure out what colors to paint our Mk4 replica. The auto finish was an easy choice. If you've ever been to the SEMA Show and seen the House of Kolor exhibit, you know why the paint manufacturer selection was simple. Fortunately, our racy and rich Stratto Blue with Galaxy Gray Le Mans stripes and Re-Entry Red team stripes paint scheme looks great. I guess we're not color blind after all.

To all the manufacturers that worked with us on this project, we owe a debt of gratitude. Thank you one and all.

There are so many other friends to thank. I can't possibly mention everyone, but I'd be remiss, if I didn't thank Thomas Mauldin, owner of Texas Venom. Tom builds Factory Five Racing kits for his clients as a second business and for fun. He knows more about the various FFR kits than just about anyone, and he was never too busy to help us when we called with questions. James Yale is another buddy, who has many years in the kit car hobby. Like Thomas, he has a second business building Backdraft Racing roadsters for clients. Both of these guys are so knowledgeable about Cobra replicas; they were an invaluable resource throughout our build.

Though James and Thomas live in Texas, we also had plenty of help right in Oceanside where we live. Our next-door neighbor, Mike Wilson, loaned us tools and his time throughout the project. Jim Warner, owner of Warner's Mufflers is mentioned throughout the book. With the custom work that we undertook on our Mk4, he was instrumental in our success. If truth be told, he's currently creating a top radiator hose out of polished stainless steel, while I'm singing (or more accurately, typing) his praises.

Last but by no means least, my family and extended family, which includes my sister Melinda, my brother-in-law Cris Lehman, my nephew Travis, and nieces Maddy and Lacey all offered words of encouragement and attaboys to Dad and me. The extended family part goes out to my good buddies, who are more like brothers and sisters. Dr. Larry Yao, Carl Nearey, Mark Williamson, Jeremy Rice, Ben Moment and my good friends at Marlado Highlands Park. All of you listened to my tales of woe and triumph on an almost daily basis, and yet none of you unfriended me on Facebook.

Of course, Paul Johnson, one of CarTech Books visionary acquisitions editors, realized that a book like this would have broad appeal, as it had never been done before. I appreciate the fact that he sought me out to write this book, and have had the honor and pleasure to work with him on the project as my editor.

Without mentioning my canine companion Samantha the Champion Stunt Labrador retriever, this Acknowledgments page would be incomplete. Sammie patiently watched Dad and me as we toiled away. She was a faithful shop dog throughout this two-year project. In fact, she's by my side right now, ready to go for a ride in our new roadster.

Marlado Highlands Park here we come!

BIRTH OF THE COBRA KIT CAR

The Shelby Cobra burst onto the racing scene in the early 1960s and seared its way into automotive enthusiasts' hearts and souls from that moment on. Everything about the sports car is intoxicating: a curvaceous aluminum exterior, a lightweight and strong tubular chassis, disc brakes, and an all-independent suspension. And that all-powerful Ford V-8 under the hood gave the Shelby Cobra all the elements it needed for racing success in its time.

Carroll Shelby's Shelby American Racing Team won the Fédération Internationale de l'Automobile (FIA) World Grand Touring Championship in 1965. They had a cadre of Cobra roadsters and six aerodynamic Cobra Daytona Coupes for the longer, more demanding high-speed European road circuits. The Shelby Team bested Enzo Ferrari and the Ferrari Racing Team that dominated FIA racing in the 1950s and 1960s.

Young Shelby engineer Peter Brock, with help from the Shelby American crew, designed and developed the rakish Cobra Daytona Type 65 Coupe in just 90 days in 1964.

Virtually from the start, the Type 65 was about 40 mph faster on long straights than the Cobra roadsters. The Daytona Coupes were so swift and rock steady that co-drivers Dan Gurney and Bob Bondurant placed first in class in 1964 at Le Mans and fourth overall in the Type-65's first racing season of development!

It is amazing to think that all these racing successes began because of the diminutive Shelby Cobra. The Cobra is a sports car that first came into existence as a Bristol straight-6 British AC Cars Limited AC Ace roadster that dates to 1951. But in February 1962, Carroll Shelby and Dean Moon, in Moon's shop in Southern California, spent just 8 hours changing auto racing. They removed the 2-liter Bristol six-cylinder and 4-speed manual transmission from a 1962 AC Ace and replaced it with a Ford 260-ci V-8 and Toploader 4-speed manual transmission. The first Shelby Cobra was basically a hot-rodded AC Ace.

From 1962 through 1967, a total of 1,003 Shelby Cobra roadsters, street cars, and race cars were produced. The first 75 were 260-ci-powered Shelby Cobras. The next 580 cars were 289-ci machines and finally 348 of the 427-ci big-block cars that ended the Cobra's production run. Many regard the Shelby Cobra as the greatest production sports car ever built, but as these numbers indicate, not many of these legends are available for purchase. A number of elements go into whether an automobile goes down in history as being legendary and collectible. The Shelby Cobra has all of these components, rarity, glorious racing history, and Spartan form-follows-function design.

Ironically, Cobras didn't sell so well during the five-year production run. Their chief American competition, the Chevrolet Corvette, cost a bit less than the Cobra and was abundantly more civilized.

From the start, the Shelby Cobra was a no-frills race car for the street, even in its initial 260-ci and wire-wheeled form. The Cobra was lightweight, a well-balanced road burner, and weighed almost 1,000 pounds less than the Corvette. Genuine 1960s vintage Cobras and Corvettes are highly prized by collectors. As when they both were new, Shelby Cobras still cost more than Corvettes.

A few years after Shelby Cobra production ended, an inevitable void formed. But a vacuum never stays empty for very long. Vintage sports and race car collectors began to snap up the genuine Cobras, and the value of these Anglo/American land rockets has continued to escalate ever since.

In the mid to late 1970s, kit car manufacturers began to produce Cobra replicas. Unique Motorcars opened its doors for Cobra kit creation in 1977 and is still manufacturing high-quality Cobra replicas today. ERA Replicas and Contemporary Classics followed Unique's lead a short time later. Several other kit-car companies followed suit, bringing out their own replica kits, all seeking a slice of the business for the seemingly ever-growing demand for Cobras.

CHOOSING A KIT

Before buying your own kit you need to decide whether you'll be using all-new components or whether you wish to start with a donor car.. For the project in this book I chose the Factory Five Racing Mk4 Cobra kit. We'll be building our Cobra replica with all-new components.

Select a Donor Car

There are many things to take into consideration when you are looking for a donor car. Here are some important questions to ask yourself:

- How much does it cost?
- How many miles does it have? Most cars were designed to last only 120,000 miles so you would then buy a new one.
- Are you going to re-use or replace important items the brake hoses, master cylinder, and calipers?
- How long the car has been sitting? (calipers can seize)
- How much wear is on the rotors?
- What kind of shape are the bushings on the control arms?
- What condition is the radiator, rear end, and gas tank in?

- If the donor car has fuel injection, can the kit manufacturer supply the wire harness to include the computer system that runs the fuel injection system?

What you should do is make a list of all the items you have to remove and re-use from the donor car. These are the items you should examine when purchasing the donor car.

Second, when you are comparing donor cars here are some items to consider:

- How well does it handle and how good is the ride? (determined by the design of the chassis)
- Does it have an adequate brake system? In a car like this you want the best brake system available. Is there an option for a better brake system? You cannot just take a brake system out of another car and re-use it on a car that is completely different. Weight distribution, total weight, spring rates, tire size, and much more are important factors in choosing the right brake system.
- Have you considered power

Factory Five Racing offers the Mk4 as a Base Kit that requires a donor car, but we assembled a Mk4 Complete Kit, which includes the components to build the entire car.

- brakes? How strong are your legs?
- What about power steering? How strong are your arms and how fast can you move them? Remember you will be compelled to drive with two hands at low speeds and shift at the same time. How close to the door does the steering wheel come?
- Does the donor car have a safety fuel cell? Is it an option? Where is it located? Why is the fuel filler not on the fender?
- Does the roll bar come as standard equipment, or is it an option? Is the roll bar attached to the frame? If not, how much would it cost to do it? Does it come painted or chrome plated?
- How strong is the frame? Will it twist? Which engine is recommended? That suggests what the frame is designed to take.
- Chrome door sills?
- Chrome all the way around the engine compartment?
- Light under the hood & trunk?
- Grilles in front?
- Ten gauges rather than five? Why a dash panel rather than mounting directly to dash?
- Stereo and speakers included?
- On the cooling system, why is the radiator vertical? Why is it that big?
- Enough support under the nose along with a skid plate?
- Are the bumpers included or are they an option?
- Do the headers/side pipes come un-coated, chrome plated, or S/S?
- Why a full interior?
- Why are WCC seats more comfortable than original design?
- Why are there trim moldings around the cockpit?
- Why are there return lips on the wheel wells?

- Why do you sit low in the car?
- Measure the distance from the bottom of the steering wheel to the seat and floor. Is it enough? Should it be wider? Or longer?
- Why are the seat belts bolted to the frame?
- Why is the trunk so big?
- Why is the battery in the trunk?

Factory Five Racing

When it came time to decide which kit to build for this project, Factory Five Racing was at the top of our list, with its Mk4 Base Kit, Challenge Kit, and Complete Kit. We chose the Mk4 Complete Kit. After all, Factory Five Racing (FFR) is the market leader of new Cobra kit cars. The company offers one of the best Cobra kit cars on the market today. Beyond that, a thorough and detailed Cobra assembly manual is included with every kit to help the novice assembler through the entire Cobra build-up process. And the company even offers an assembler school where the customer learns how to assemble the car, so when they return home, the customer is able to competently assemble his or her own car. No other company matches Factory Five for customer support and service.

Brothers Dave and Mark Smith founded Factory Five Racing in 1995. It employs 30 full-time staff members and has become the largest manufac-

turer of component car kits. Everyone who works at the company is very knowledgeable and passionate about the automotive enthusiast hobby in general and Factory Five Racing in particular. Critics and competitors have called FFR a cult. This claim is embraced by Factory Five right on the company's Web site: "We won't ask you to drink Kool-Aid or wear a brown shirt, rather, fellowship, kindness, gear-head knowledge, and a love for all things Motorsports are the only requirements in this club. Welcome to the cult of Factory Five!"

With component kits engineered and designed through a sophisticated CAD/CAM system and built using automotive robotics and skilled technicians, Factory Five Racing produces high-quality, affordable component car kits and provides exceptional customer service. FFR's customers are almost fanatical about the company and the component kits that the company manufactures and sells.

In addition to manufacturing three variants of the Cobra replica kit, FFR also produces the mid-engine GTM Supercar, the 1933 Hot Rod (a 1933 Ford convertible/coupe kit), and the Type-65 Coupe (Cobra Daytona Coupe kit). For more information on these component vehicles, visit Factory Five Racing's Web site. You can also join the popular independent web forum of FFR owners and enthusiasts.

Cobras were born for competition, and Factory Five holds true to that tradition with the Mk4 Challenge. Designed for many types of competition, owners typically campaign the car in road racing, and there's a race series specifically for this replica.

Factory Five Racing Complete Kit

The Factory Five Racing Mk4 Complete Kit costs $19,900 and includes:

Frame
- Complete jig-welded original-style 4-inch-round tube frame; includes all mounts ready to accept small-block Ford and 1987–2004 Mustang running gear; kit can be ordered to accept a wide variety of engines and suspensions
- Comes powdercoated in gloss black
- Three-point roll bar powdercoated to match
- Includes mounts to accept passenger-side roll bar

Body
- Hand-laid 3/16-inch laminate composite body and panels made with vinylester resin
- Driver and passenger doors with molded door liners
- Hood with molded hood liner, and centered hood scoop
- Trunk with molded trunk liner and improved mount face for license-plate light
- Secondary body fasteners assembly
- Adhesive-backed and foam weatherstrip
- C-channel door-edge trim and fasteners
- Plastic end-caps and body U-nut fasteners
- Trunk and engine bay seal and push-on rubber bulb seal
- Rubber hood and trunk bumpers
- Multi-adjustable door hinges with bronze bushings and fasteners
- Vintage trunk hinge kit, hinge support plates, and fasteners
- Hood hinge kit with hydraulic piston supports and fasteners
- Original-design Quickjack competition bumpers with stainless-steel sleeves and fasteners

Chassis Aluminum Panels
Includes more than 40 CNC-cut pre-formed 6061-T6 aluminum panels for cockpit, trunk, and engine bay

- 1,200 pre-packaged rivets: 1/8-inch short and long, 3/16-inch short and long
- Complete Mk4 cockpit aluminum with optional block-off plates and patch covers
- Engine bay aluminum assembly with aluminum nose sections and splash guards
- Molded trunk liner in place of aluminum

Complete Front Suspension
- Unequal-length A-arm control arms
- Koni high-performance mono-tube, rod-end shock absorbers
- Coil-over kit for Koni dampers, including spring hat, threaded seat, and 500-pound black powdercoated performance springs
- Adjustable upper control arms with ball joints and fasteners
- Lower tubular control arms with ball joints and fasteners
- Grade-8 mounting hardware

Complete Rear Suspension
- FFR Deluxe three-link suspension kit with rear-end brackets, upper link kit and fasteners, including Panhard bar kit with rod ends and grade-8 fasteners
- Koni-brand high-performance mono-tube, rod-end shock absorbers
- Coil-over kit for Koni dampers, including spring hat, threaded seat, and 350-pound black-powdercoated performance springs
- Factory Five tubular rear-lower control arms, with polyurethane bushings and fasteners

Complete Front Brake Kit
- S/N 95-style spindles and spindle adapter bracket with fasteners
- Front hubs, fasteners, and dust covers
- Ford GT 11-inch front rotors with twin piston calipers, brake pads, and fasteners
- Master cylinder (listed in pedal box assembly), front stainless braided brake line with mount clips, banjo bolts, and brake-line mounting fasteners
- Pre-flared 3/16-inch brake line and brake-line T-adapter
- OEM Ford Mustang emergency-brake handle, fasteners, and cable

Complete Steering System
- 15:1 manual-steering rack with inner and outer tie rod ends and fasteners
- Polyurethane steering rack bushings and fasteners
- Steering rack shaft adapter (9/16-26 spline)
- Nickel-plated lower steering shaft (fully welded U-joints)
- Collapsible upper steering shaft with friction washers
- Authentic wood and aluminum 14-inch steering wheel with boss and ceramic FFR center section and fasteners

- Steering bearings and hardware, including flange bearing, pillow block bearing, and fasteners

Complete Fuel System and Parts
- Works with carburetors or fuel injection systems; external fuel pump required.
- OEM-style fuel tank with mounting straps and hardware, vents, gaskets, pick-up, and fuel level sending unit
- Fuel lines, connectors, and filler neck and fasteners
- Pre-flared fuel lines (1/4- and 5/16-inch) with unions, barbs, hose clamps, and high-press flex lines and fasteners
- Aston Martin Le Mans-style polished-aluminum fuel cap with integral pressure cap, gaskets, ground strap, and fuel hose to tank with fasteners
- 3/8-inch-line fuel filter, connectors, and hose clamps

Complete Cooling System and Parts
- Electric cooling fan and mounting hardware, extensions for radiator hoses, and all necessary fasteners
- Electric cooling fan and mounting kit with connectors
- Aluminum radiator with cap and in-line filler neck
- Radiator mount kit and fasteners
- Stainless-steel radiator hose kit including adapter kit, fasteners, and hose
- Overflow tank with cap, hoses, hose clamps, and mounting hardware
- Thermostat (185 degree F) switch and wiring

Engine Accessories, Side Exhaust and Mounts
- The Mk4 Complete kit is configured to accommodate the engine of your choice
- Select from full tubular 4-into-4-into-1 headers and side exhaust
- Engine and Transmission mounts (select 302/351 or 4.6L, or 390/427/428, or 429/460), with fasteners
- Exhaust with gaskets and fasteners. Select from:
    - 1987–1995 straight pipes
    - 1996–2004 straight pipes
    - 302 Headers, ceramic coated
    - 351 Headers, ceramic coated
    - 390/427/428 Headers, ceramic coated
    - 429/460 Headers, ceramic coated
    - 1987–1995 Catalytic converters with air hose, check valve, T-hose fitting

- 1996–2004 Catalytic converters
    - 4.6L 2-Valve Headers, ceramic coated
    - 4.6L 4-Valve Headers, ceramic coated
- Side Exhaust (bare steel with rubber hanger brackets), gaskets, and fasteners

Driveshaft
- Select from one of three available driveshafts with fasteners to match engine/transmission:
- 28-spline, 10.375-inch driveshaft for T-5 or Tremec 3550s
- 31-spline, 10.375-inch driveshaft for Tremec TKO 500 or 600s
- 31-spline, 12.875-inch driveshaft for 4.6L engines with T-45s or 3650s

Gauges, Dash and Electrical Assembly
- Vintage/replica or modern/performance gauges
- Mk4 pre-cut original-style aluminum dashboard with fasteners
- Padded dash cover, black vinyl
- Custom-fit chassis wiring harness
- Ignition switch and FFR key, headlight switch, three-position turn signal switch, starter solenoid, and horn.
- Dash indicators, red, green, and blue dash lights
- Wiring harness mounting kit and hardware including fuse panel mount
- Insulated line clip hardware and fasteners
- Cable ties, wire loom, and flex grommets
- On/Off switch, horn button, flasher, and all connectors
- Battery ground strap
- Battery Box and Relocation Kit includes trunk-mounted battery box, cables, and hold-downs with fasteners
- Speedometer sending unit, pigtail, fasteners, and 3.55:1 gear
- Autometer Ultra-Light electronic gauges with connectors, terminals, and installation kit including:
    - Speedometer
    - Tachometer
    - Oil pressure gauge
    - Water temperature gauge
    - Fuel level gauge
    - Voltmeter

Factory Five Racing Mk4 Base Kit *CONTINUED*

Oil temperature gauge
- Or select complete set of seven vintage-style FFR replica gauges with connectors, terminals, and installation kit including:
    - Speedometer, reverse read
    - Tachometer
    - Oil pressure gauge
    - Water temperature gauge
    - Fuel level gauge
    - Voltmeter
    - Clock

Complete Interior Accessories
- Authentic original roadster metal-framed seats, black vinyl with fasteners
- Five-point Simpson harnesses (3-inch-wide driver and passenger), frame mounted with fasteners
- Complete cockpit carpet set, black all-weather
- Emergency-brake boot, black vinyl
- Authentic interior rearview mirror with fasteners
- Full seven-gauge electronic FFR Vintage gauges or Autometer Ultra-Lite gauges (listed in gauge assembly)
- Original-style door latches, fasteners, and leather check straps
- Authentic stainless shifter handle, shift knob, boot, polished ring, and fasteners
- 14-inch authentic wood and aluminum steering wheel (listed in steering assembly) with polished-aluminum boss and small center badge

Exterior Accessories and Lighting
- Chrome-on-brass vintage windscreen, tinted with side bars and fasteners (DOT safety glass compliant)
- Original-style three-lock set including T-trunk handle, L-shaped hood handles, matching keys, cam wedges, fasteners, latch pin sleeves, and plastic end cap
- License-plate light and bracket with fasteners
- 3.5-inch Aston roller gas cap, polished cast aluminum with adapter kit and all fasteners
- Competition hood pins
- High-quality laser-cut aluminum side louvers

- Ceramic FFR badging nose and tail
- Original-style headlamp assemblies, including buckets, halogen headlamps, trim rings, and fasteners (DOT approved)
- Original-style British front amber turn signals and red rear taillights (all DOT approved)

Complete Pedal Box and Components
- Wilwood pedal box and mounting hardware
- Master cylinders, clutch quadrant, clutch cable, and threaded firewall adjuster
- Accelerator pedal and cable, return spring and ball stud retainer with fasteners
- Brake-line adapters and T-fittings

Oil Filter Relocation and Alternate Drive Pulley Assemblies
- Oil-filter relocation kit with all hoses and hardware; other parts to help 302 EFI and Mustang engine users include:
    - Oil filter relocate mount with fittings, hoses, barbs, and fasteners
    - Spin-on engine block adapter
    - Alternate drive pulley, spacer, pulley wheel, and fasteners
    - Air filter, conical
    - Fan belt, six-rib

1987–1995 Mk4 Roadster Assembly Manual
- Bound, more than 200 pages

Fasteners
- 1,500 top-quality zinc-plated, chrome, and stainless-steel USS and SAE fasteners, numbered and packed individually by assembly

Parts Needed to Finish the Factory Five Racing Mk4 Complete Kit
- The following parts and assemblies are needed to complete the car:
    - Engine and transmission
    - Rear end with brakes
    - Wheels and tires
    - Paint
    - Fuel pump

BUYING A PRE-OWNED COBRA REPLICA

Most people know whether or not they have the do-it-yourself gene. If you're the sort of homeowner who always has ongoing home improvement projects, whether or not your spouse spurs you into action, you probably have it. If you're the sort who takes pride in getting your hands dirty and getting the job done and if you'd rather remodel your own kitchen, wash and wax your own cars, build the best science project with your kids, perform a brake job on your autos… if you have done or do any of these things, you could be a great candidate for assembling your own Cobra replica. It's great that you're good with your hands, you're creative, and you have the MacGyver sort of ingenuity to tackle such an immense undertaking. But, building a rolling, running work of art isn't for everyone.

If you'd rather take your Cobra cruising with other enthusiasts, participate in car shows, or race your replica on the track than meticulously build your car from scratch for months and months in your garage, you may be better suited to finding a pre-owned replica to purchase. There's nothing to be ashamed about realizing that you'd rather be enjoying your replica by driving and racing it than putting it together. Think of this chapter as your map to Cobra replica ownership.

Throughout the chapter, I provide photos of the various replica manufacturers' finished vehicles, some of which were purchased pre-owned and others that are still owned by their original builders/owners. In all cases, these cars have been superlatively and painstakingly constructed. Every one of these Cobras would be show-winning vehicles at almost any car show across the land, yet many of them are driven quite often and also see extensive track time.

In fact, one of the most notable aspects of replica ownership is the fact that the vast majority of Cobra owners drive their cars. Cobra replicas aren't just trailer queens and museum pieces. They're driven more than the original cars from the 1960s, because those roadsters are too valuable to drive. How ironic is

Dave Betts, of Blairstown, New Jersey, built a very nice Unique Motorcars 427SC, which Bruce Bunn painted Ford Red Fire Metallic.

that? The fastest production sports car of the 1960s isn't driven much these days. What's even more ironic, many replicas would blow the doors off original Shelby American 289 and 427 Cobras in every aspect of performance, except of course how much they cost to own.

Where To Look

A number of resources are available to find a Cobra replica. Many Web sites sell these vehicles, and you can learn a lot on various Web forums. The cars also appear at old-school places like auctions and car shows, plus in various newspapers, including your local publication. Don't leave any stone unturned in your quest.

Cobra Country

The "Cobras For Sale" section of the CobraCountry.com website provides an extensive and informative classified advertising section for enthusiasts looking to buy or sell Cobra replicas. Ad listings provide large images of the replicas for sale from different perspectives and include detail photos of the engine compartments and interiors. There are comprehensive descriptions of each Cobra replica for sale in all classified listings. Seller contact information is also provided.

Curt Scott, the originator of the site, has covered the Cobra replica hobby in particular and the kit car arena since 1996. He has also written a book called *The Complete Guide to Cobra Replicas: All-New 4th Edition.*

eBay Motors

On the day that I perused the eBay Motors website for Shelbys, there were no less than 233 cars listed up for auction. As you can imagine, many of these vehicles were Cobra replicas, Shelby Mustang re-creations, Daytona Coupe replicas, and Ford GT40 re-creations. It's not hard to figure out why. With the passage of time, the genuine cars from the 1960s are being increasingly held on to as an investment, or they're in museums.

ClubCobra.com

ClubCobra.com caters to the general Cobra replica and genuine Cobra hobby and includes authentic and kit Daytona Coupes, as well as GT40 replicas and authentic 1960s race cars. All of the various replica manufacturers products are covered on Club Cobra. There is a very good chance that the replica you're looking at is already known and well documented on the site.

Visit the forum, become a member (membership is free), and start doing searches. Members (well over 25,000) often times post a thread with full details of their replica when they wish to sell the vehicle.

Extracted from an early 1960s Ford Galaxie 500, Bill Parham, owner of Southern Automotive in McDonough, Georgia rebuilt, bored, and stroked the 427-ci side-oiler big-block Ford V-8 mill for Betts' Unique 427SC replica. The powerplant now produces 525 hp and delivers 560 ft-lbs of torque. If something doesn't seem quite right with the engine in the used Cobra you're inspecting, perform a leak-down test or a compression test. Should you not have the tools or the knowledge to perform such tasks, pay a local reputable mechanic to give the car a thorough inspection. If the seller balks, that's a red flag.

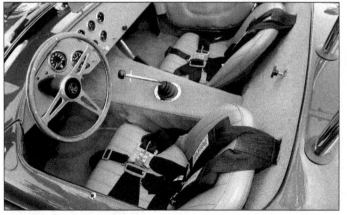

Black leather seats with black wool carpet are standard in Unique replica kits. This owner, however, opted for the optional tan leather and wool carpet, perhaps to complement the Red Fire Metallic exterior. Unique's kit includes first-quality interior components, whether in standard black or optional colors. You won't find a carpet gap/gaffe anywhere.

FFCars.com

Go to this Web site if you're seeking a Factory Five Racing (FFR) Cobra, an FFR Type 65 (original Shelby American code name for Daytona Coupe), an FFR GTM, a FFR Cobra Spec Racer, or a 1933 hot rod FFR. In other words, any Factory Five Racing vehicle that has ever been built or is under construction is probably written about (possibly from start to finish of the project) on this forum. There are even build logs of specific cars that include detailed notes and quality photos of the projects.

FFCars.com has well over 23,000 active members, most of them passionate Factory Five Racing replica owners and/or builders. If you're interested in purchasing a completed FFR roadster, this is the best place to start your search and the perfect place to learn all about Factory Five Racing. The company's website provides another excellent resource to learn all about its various vehicle kits.

Auctions

Going to a live auction can be a means to purchasing a Cobra replica or any other sort of enthusiast automobile, if you employ a viable strategy. You've no doubt heard of the major ones, Barrett-Jackson, Mecum,

Russo & Steele, Bonhams, Christie's, and RM Auctions. And you never know what you might find at smaller events. Typically replicas can be had for reasonable amounts of money.

At the start of week-long auctions, you usually see the low-cost sales leaders up for bid. In other words, you might snag a Backdraft Racing roadster for considerably less than what the owner paid for it, and it could be a low-mileage creampuff. The key is to get to the event at the very start of the auction and pore over the auction book, which shows all the cars up for sale with both photos and a reasonable description. Then look at the cars you wish to bid on.

In the case of Barrett-Jackson, the cars are in one of the immense temporary tent buildings or under the carnival tents (that's the more likely location for the replicas), barely shielded from the desert winter weather, typically cold and rainy. You may even get lucky and see the owner detailing his pride and joy. If so, you might convince him or her to fire it up. You may even have an opportunity to drive the car a short distance, if the owner thinks you're a serious buyer.

Remember that you need to have

your wits about you, should you wish to bid on a specific car. Don't get caught up in a bidding war. You could bid yourself broke.

Car Shows

Almost every major car show has an immense swap meet section, including used parts and new components. There is also often an old-car corral that's bound to have several road-going serpents for sale to a good home.

Hemmings Motor News

This automotive classifieds publication has been around since 1954. Its slogan is "World's Largest Collector-Car Marketplace." For many years, *Hemmings* was the only place to find pre-owned enthusiast automobiles for sale. The publication is available on newsstands and via subscriptions. You may find Cobra replicas for sale in three sections: Racing & Hi-Performance, Replica & Kit, and Shelby. You can also look up cars on hemmings.com.

Auto Trader

Auto Trader publishes various and sundry car classified magazines for specific marques. For enthusiast machines, the Web site is autotraderclassics.com. You can do various searches and discover Cobra replicas in several different categories and narrow your investigation to short distances from your home.

Local Newspaper

Before the Internet, automotive enthusiasts relied primarily on local newspapers for the Antiques & Classics section within the Automotive Classifieds. If I told you how many cars that I've found and acquired over the years from the Classifieds,

Dean Paquette selected an Engine Factory 393 stroker engine for his really well done FFR roadster. The powerplant's backed by a Tremec TKO-600 5-speed manual transmission utilizing the mid-shift location on the transmission and a Pro 5.0 shifter. If a car's built well, it shifts smoothly and easily. Also, the power should be prodigious, around 400 hp, so the roadster scoots along. If it's low on power, or clutch engagement is harsh, be suspicious and ask the owner a bounty of questions.

you might not believe me. Some of the larger newspapers also offer the Classifieds section online.

Which Car Is Right For You?

Chapter 18 includes a list of the various Cobra kit car companies and details the components in each manufacturer's product. One thing you are sure to learn is that no two companies offer the same kit. There is nuance in the way the cars appear, differences in how the frames, suspension systems, interiors, etc., are constructed and look. There are even various ways in which each kit is packaged, marketed, distributed, and sold.

Keep Your Head

Just as there are risks associated with buying used cars, there are also challenges to finding the right pre-owned Cobra replica. So before you get hot on the trail to hunt down a pre-owned Cobra kit car, I need to make this simple statement: Don't get emotionally attached to any car you're considering for purchase. You want to find the car of your dreams, of course. But you need to be analytical, methodical, and very deliberate about the process of buying a pre-owned Cobra. A potential owner who becomes excited about any one car will have clouded judgment, often overlook critical problems, commonly negotiate a poor deal, and many times end up buying a vehicle that doesn't fit his or her needs.

If you perform your due diligence in selecting the best used kit car, you will avoid getting stuck with a lemon, a car that needs extensive rework. In reality, it's more important to be skeptical, diligent, and

particular when buying a used Cobra than buying a factory-built car. You are interested in finding a Cobra kit that fits you physically, your style, performance, and budget. You also want one that's built well, is reliable, and is going to keep you and your passenger safe.

Know Your Intended Use

Manufacturers have built a variety of Cobra replicas over the years for various applications, such as high-performance street car, road racer, drag racer, stylish daily driver, weekend cruiser, and many variations in between. If you buy the ultimate 1,000-hp Cobra drag car

that runs on aviation fuel to power a full-race 13:1 compression engine, it's not suited for daily driving duties. A road race Cobra that develops its best power at 5,000 rpm or more and has incredible shocks and springs for racing does not make a great weekend cruiser. While these are extreme examples, they illustrate the point that you need to find a used Cobra replica that fits your particular application. Or, you need to take into consideration that you need to perform a certain amount of work to convert it to your particular application.

First and foremost, not all Cobra replicas are created equal. While all Cobra replicas feature the legendary

Mark Jackson is a pro E.R.A. builder, who has a famous uncle, none other than Mr. October, Reggie Jackson. In honor of his baseball-slugging uncle, Mark treated his E.R.A 289FIA replica to a Jackson-esque paint job, with New York Yankee Midnight Blue and Reggie's number 44 in the roundel. Some lucky buyer is probably driving the Jackson tribute E.R.A. 289FIA right now.

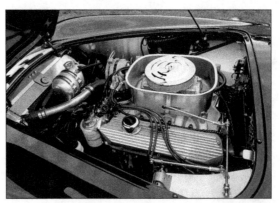

The Jackson E.R.A. 289FIA is actually equipped with a 351-ci Ford Windsor mill and has a small 427 competition-car air cleaner and a turkey pan, which may trick some Cobra fans into thinking the engine's a big-block instead of a small-block V-8. Evaluate things like the throttle linkage, notice how beautifully the aluminum radiator hose is run, consider the way that the remote oil filter is installed, see that there are spark plug wire looms in the middle of each valve cover (just as there was in the original Cobras), check out how sweet the wiring is installed. If you see items this well done, make the seller a good offer and hope for the best.

silhouette or body shape, the hardware or underpinnings make the difference. And there's been a wide variety of chassis, suspension, brakes, steering, etc. Over the past 40 years, more than 80 different companies have offered Cobra replicas kits, which run the gamut of quality and performance. The safest bet is to stick with one of the well-known companies with extensive enthusiast following and manufacturer support.

Factory Five Racing has built more than 7,000 Cobra replica kits since 1995, and ERA and Unique have also built thousands of Cobras. If you buy a used replica from a defunct manufacturer, you're taking a substantial risk because you won't be able to source information from the company, nor will you be able to get tech support and parts. I am not suggesting that it can't be done; and if you're a skilled mechanic and knowledgeable builder, it certainly is within the realm of possibly. But if you're a novice and you decide to buy an obscure, orphan Cobra, you may find a lot of hassle and expense to fix problems and fabricate parts.

Become an Expert

Once you determine the ideal Cobra replica for your budget, application, and taste, you need to become the expert on that particular make and model. Let's face it, the Cobra is a specialized vehicle and you may not be able to find the exact make and model you're looking for. Therefore, you need to define the car you're looking for and you may have to adjust that target during your search.

To become the expert, get all the information you can about that particular Cobra, which includes build sheets, illustrations, parts lists, and marketing information. This information is provided on some manufacturer Web sites. A premium-quality Cobra is not one with just a pretty body. It's the underpinnings. Some Cobras are built with Corvette, Jaguar, and other donor suspension parts. Factory Five Cobras utilize Ford Mustang chassis and suspension components while some use weaker common passenger car suspension, steering, and brake parts. Note all the details of your wish list.

In addition, join a Cobra replica club, such as the Ohio Cobra Club (OCC), and talk to members who own or know about the Cobra you want to buy. They may even have a lead on the specific replica you want to buy.

Visit popular Cobra replica sites and blogs. Ask the members questions and learn from their valuable information. But you also need to be skeptical and use creditable information. Anyone can write anything on a blog, so it doesn't mean that it's valid or accurate.

Review Component and Work Receipts

When contacting a potential Cobra seller, think of yourself as an investigative reporter. You want to know everything about this kit car. One of the first items you're going to want to know is who built the car. From there, you can formulate all your other questions and get the answers you need to make an informed decision.

If the builder and owner is the same person, ask whether all the receipts for the components purchased in the construction of the car are available. These receipts provide the DNA of what went into the car and how well it's built. Ask to look at these documents and study them carefully. A bunch of no-name automotive components on the receipts is a red flag. You want to see names such as Edelbrock, Finish Line, Holley, Demon, Hilborn, Smeding Performance, Roush, Keith Craft, Tremec, Ford Racing, Koni, Moto-Lita, Flaming River, ididit, Comp Cams, Bilstein, etc.

If engine or body and paintwork were performed on the replica, see whether you recognize the names of the shops on the invoices. In fact, if the engine was built by one of the professional crate engine builders, like Keith Craft or Smeding Performance, the engine may well still be under warranty, depending upon how old the vehicle is.

Location, Location, Location

If you live in a major metropolitan area, such as New York, Chicago, or Los Angeles, you may be able to find the right Cobra replica for you in your area. On the other hand, if you live in a less urban part of the country, chances are that you won't be able to conveniently see it. Therefore, it's important to do your homework.

When in contact with the seller, ask for detailed photos of every aspect of the car. Ask specific questions about any component of the car, build process, and ownership history. If the car is in a major metropolitan area and you do not live in that area, you can often hire a certified car appraiser and have him or her evaluate the Cobra. Typically, these appraisers compile a detailed report of the condition of the car and send it back to the perspective buyer.

Certainly, you can make arrangements, negotiate a price, buy the car sight unseen, and have the replica shipped to you. But many used Cobra replica buyers are not comfortable doing that, and they must see the Cobra before making a buying decision.

Inspection and Evaluation

You are buying a hand-built, rare super car, and that means you need to pay attention to specific details. But at the same time, you're buying a pre-owned or used car, and therefore, you're going to use the same time-honed techniques to inspect it. When buying any used car, you need to carefully inspect, analyze, and evaluate the function and condition of each major component group of the car.

To get a complete picture, get the car up on a hydraulic lift so you can look underneath it to see the frame, any collision repair, and other body work. I also recommend having a certified ASE mechanic inspect it at a shop. These guys work on cars for a living and can spot problems you may miss. Many professional service shops perform a basic inspection for about $100.

Of course, the test drive will reveal the Cobra's level of performance, problems, and current state of condition.

Engine
The engine should fire up and run smoothly once it has been primed. Allow the engine to reach operating temperature and listen for any usual sounds. If there is a clicking sound, this could mean worn lifters, push rod, or cam. Any loud tapping or knocking sounds indicate a serious valvetrain problem, and often the only solution is a rebuild.

From underneath, examine the entire engine, the block, oil pan, heads, and front timing cover. These should not have excessive oil leaks or grease build-up. If they do, it indicates poor maintenance and there may be some underlying issues. If there's oil between the head and block, then there is likely a leaking head gasket and possibly other problems.

To take a look at the engine oil, pull the dipstick. Ideally, the engine oil should be a caramel color or a little on the darker side. If the oil is milky, coolant has entered the engine, and a blown head gasket may be the culprit.

A compression test helps verify the health of the engine. Remove all the spark plug caps from the spark plugs and replace one spark plug with the compression tester and then proceed to test all eight cylinders. If the compression of all the cylinders is not within 10 pounds of one another, you may have a problem, such as a worn valve seat. Remember, an engine can't produce top performance if the cylinders do not have a good seal.

You can hook up a leak-down pressure gauge; using compressed air, you can see how much air enters the cylinder and how much is measured on the opposite end. Look for any fluid coming off the engine. If there is, you need to determine the source and ascertain the problem.

Transmission
Most Cobra replicas are equipped with a manual transmission for a true Cobra driving experience. Almost every iteration of manual transmission has been installed in Cobras—Toploader, Tremec, Muncie, Borg Warner, and others.

To get an indication of the transmission's health, pull the dipstick and examine the color of the fluid, or shine a flashlight in the fluid-leel hole after carefully removing the plug. Manual transmission fluid for most transmission is 80W/90, and the color is light brown or semi-transparent. If the color of your transmission fluid is dark brown or black, it needs to be replaced, and the gearbox may be fairly worn due to lack of proper maintenance.

If you find a transmission fluid leak, check to see if it's the base gasket or a more serious issue.

Since you're not going to be able to see inside the transmission, the road test is an important part of evaluation. The clutch should engage and disengage smoothly without stuttering or grabbing because that's a sign of a worn clutch or an out-of-adjustment cable. You should be able to smoothly and confidently find each gear, so you should not experience any gear grinding or significant resistance. In addition, it shouldn't take a lot of arm strength to do it. Once it's in gear, you should not hear excessive gear or bearing noise. If you do, the particular gear box may need to be rebuilt. Also it should always stay in gear and shouldn't fall out of gear and find a false neutral.

Differential
The most notable sign of a worn rear differential is that it makes a howling noise at speed. Often if you hear a clunk when you accelerate. The sound is because there's slop between these two components.

If the rear end is producing some sort of noise, most differentials with a Ford 9-inch or a Chevy 12-bolt are easy and relatively inexpensive to rebuild. While it's a consideration when making a purchasing decision, it should not be a deal breaker.

Chassis/Suspension
Once again, you need to get underneath the car. Inspect the suspension

arms, steering arms, steering arm ends, springs, torsion bar, and related front suspension equipment. There should be no damage, bends, or cracks, particularly on the welds. Also verify that everything aligns correctly.

If you compress the suspension by pushing on the nose of the car and you hear squeaking, then the front ball joints could be worn out, and replacing them will be an added expense.

If you ask the seller to push down on each corner, watch the rebound; if the suspension bounces repeatedly, expect to replace the shocks.

Make sure the car sits level or with the correct amount of rake. If it does not, this indicates a suspension or spring issue that needs to be resolved.

Steering and Brakes

As you view the brakes through the wheels, look for deep grooves, cracking (particularly from the cross-drilled holes and slots), and any other visible damage. Deep grooves mean that the pad doesn't sit on a uniform surface area and braking power is decreased. Also, the sur-face of the brake disc can warp, and then the rotor thumps or produces noise under braking. In addition, if a disc brake is cracked or damaged, it can break apart and fail. While not that common, this is a huge safety concern, so if this is the case, you need new calipers, rotors and pads, which can run $1,000 or more. But it depends on the equipment used.

Remove the wheel to examine the brake equipment and find out whether the pads are exceptionally worn. Sit in the driver's seat and press on the brake pedal to determine if it provides good brake pressure. Inspect the brake lines and fittings to determine if there are any leaks. If the system is leaking, you will see brake fluid on the ground when depressing the pedal.

Body and Paint

Kneel down at the front fender on each side and look down the length of the car. The bodywork should be clean and straight. If you see waves, ripples, or other abnormalities, often the body has been patched with filler and it was not done very well.

Look at the hood. Does it line up well with the fenders and are the gaps even on all sides? Do the fenders align evenly with the doors? Do the doors align with the trunk and runner boards? If fender, hood, and door alignments are off, these components can be adjusted and aligned. However, if the doors and rear quarter panels don't align, this can be a much more difficult proposition to bring into alignment because often the rear quarters and trunk are anchored to the body.

Look closely at the paint. It should have a deep, consistent luster from one edge to the other of each panel. And this means you should see no significant flaws in the paint. A paint job should have a smooth, glassy appearance from the application of the base color and clear coat. If the paint does not have a seamless and smooth appearance, the paint and/or primer may have been contaminated during application or was applied improperly.

Most Cobras should have an enamel or urethane paint job, which are very durable. Cobra replicas are not pre-painted, so owners must paint or have their cars painted. You need to determine if the car has a sound paint job because stripping and re-painting it is a major expense—$5,000 or more.

One of the best tests is to look at the reflection of an object in the paint; you want to see no waving or distortion. In some cases, painting hides poor bodywork and poor application of filler, particularly with the lighter colors. However, in some cases, poor filler application and contamination becomes apparent with darker colors.

Contamination and other preparation problems can create many other paint problems. These include fish eyes, wrinkling, bleeding,

Maggie Guillot, of Sterling, Virginia, convinced her husband Victor that he'd be better off building a Cobra replica than buying a Harley-Davidson. She was right. Victor bought and built a Shell Valley Cobra 427SC kit. He took his time building the Shell Valley roadster. All the gaps are great, the paint's first rate, and the drivetrain gets you down the road in short order, thank you very much.

checking, saggings, orange peeling, air trapping, scratches from sanding, and more. You need to recognize these common paint problems and take into consideration the ramifications of fixing them.

When the paint and/or primer are contaminated with oil, grease, or wax, you get paint-adhesion problems. Once the paint or primer is sprayed, fish eyes or circular imperfections form. In some cases, when new paint is not compatible with old paint, wrinkling can occur. Wrinkles develop when the new paint chemically reacts to the older paint underneath it. The new paint shrinks and it wrinkles.

Sags and runs are fairly common, especially with inexperienced painters. If the coat is applied too thick, the gun is held too close to the panel, or the painter does not move the gun fast enough, sags are often the result. Often, sags can be repaired by stripping the area and feathering in new paint, but this requires skill and experience.

Orange peel was prevalent in cars of the 1960s and 1970s and no longer exists on new cars. Orange peel is a paint texture that looks like the surface of an orange. If there is severe orange peel, the car may require repainting, but if it's mild orange peel, polishing and wet-sanding removes the imperfections.

Electrics

Although electrical problems can certainly be diagnosed and fixed, they sometimes take a great deal of work to pinpoint, and that can be very frustrating.

Test the headlights, turn signals, brake lights, dash lights, convenience lights (if any), and horn. The wiring under the hood must be correctly routed and anchored for safety; if it's not, it could melt or get caught and create a dangerous situation. All wiring throughout the car should be correctly fused and anchored. If you see wiring hanging below the dash, you know it was a poorly assembled car.

You need to examine the electrical connectors to verify they have been correctly crimped; if not, the rest of the wiring is suspect.

Examine how the wiring harness was installed and whether the fuse box has been properly anchored. A Cobra replica must have a professional-grade wiring harness and electrical component installation. If you look at the wiring diagram of the car and notice that the fuse box has higher-amp fuses than specified, this is a red flag. These circuits were designed for a specific amp load and if a high-amp fuse allows too much current to flow through the circuit, a fire could result. Frayed wires indi-

cate poor installation and maintenance, and often result in a short circuit, which in some cases leads to a fire. If the wiring has been spliced and spliced again, this indicates amateur installation and that you could have a difficult time sorting out the system.

Look at the battery ground straps and any chassis ground wires. These should be properly routed, properly installed terminals, and the grounds should be contacting bare metal.

Interior

The carpet should be correctly cut and oriented in the interior. In addition, it should extend under the rocker panels on each side of the car. Look for any unsightly gaps around the center console, footwells, seats, and other areas of the interior.

The gauges should be properly oriented with the steering wheel. The dash should be correctly mounted with no gaps between the windshield and the console. In addition, all the switches and convenience lights should be mounted in a logical and accessible location.

Look for any tears, abrasion, or damage to the dash, console, door panels, seats, and other items. Obviously, if there is damage, it requires time and money to repair, and that needs to figure into your decision making.

The seat tracks should be properly mounted in the correct location so you can adjust the seat to your preference. So sit in the drivers seat and adjust it until you're comfortable.

The door panels should be even and equally proportioned on each side.

Make sure all the lights, gauges, switches, and controls function properly.

The Kruegers installed a Corvette LS1/LS6 engine and utilized 1990 Corvette Lingenfelter IFS and IRS.

Wheels

Are the wheels balanced? Bolt-on wheels are a matter of personal preference. If you like what is on the car, great; if not, factor in a replacement some time down the road. Knock-offs should be checked to make sure they are tight. If the knock-offs are safety-wired on the car, that shows a good level of attention.

Owner Queries

Be sure to confirm what company produced the kit and whether it's a manufacturer that is held in high regard in the Cobra replica arena. Determine whether the current owner is the person who constructed the kit and get an idea of the person's technical skill level. Ask if a donor car was used in the car's construction and what used components went into the replica's build. Query what would have been done differently if the owner/builder were to build the project today. Find out how long ago the kit was built and how many miles are on the vehicle.

After these questions have been answered, ask some more. Just as with shopping for a used car, you need lots of information.

- Why are you selling it?
- Does it burn or leak oil?
- Has it ever been in an accident?
- Is it currently registered?
- How often do you drive it?
- Are you the original owner? etc.

All of these questions need to be answered before you ask if you can take the car for a test drive. Indeed, before you drive it, you need to thoroughly inspect every nook and cranny of the car, crawl under it, hover over it, and give it your best gearhead appraisal of how well it's constructed. Should you be a neophyte in the automotive and Cobra replica enthusiast arena, bring a Cobra expert buddy with you when you go to look at the car.

The Test Drive

When test driving the Cobra, remember that it's still not your car yet, so you need to be respectful and not abuse it. However, you need to verify the performance and operation of the Cobra, so you need to drive it aggressively. After all it's a Cobra, and it's meant to be driven in a certain way.

If you've never driven a Cobra before, start out conservatively and get acclimated to the car's power delivery and handling. Be gentle with your right foot. Remember how much power these cars make, how short the wheelbase is, how light they are, and respect that power-to-weight ratio. The laws of physics simply will not be denied.

Even if you're a Ferrari or Corvette C-6 owner, this is different. Those cars are refined. They're modern vehicles with traction control, ABS,

Superformance provides Cobra roadsters and all of its replicas as turnkey-minus cars. They come fully equipped, with the exception of the engine and transmission. Ted Soares, of Anaheim Hills, California bought his in PPG Monza Red with white stripes. With a Superformance or a Backdraft Racing roadster, you want to find out who installed the drivetrain. If it was professionally installed, the driveshaft angle to the engine/trans should be spot on, for instance. If the owner installed the powerplant, you want to really dig deep and try to discern how well the drivetrain is installed.

In a Superformance Cobra replica, as with the original Shelby Cobras from the 1960s, Smiths gauges fill the dash. A glovebox is also standard issue, just as it was back in the day. This car's owner had Carroll Shelby autograph the glovebox door. The leather wrapped steering wheel was ordered from Superformance as an option, since the standard wheels from Superformance are wood rimmed, as they were originally.

Street Beasts doesn't exactly have a stellar reputation in the kit car community. However, if one has been well constructed, as James Wagner built his, it can be a great pre-owned replica to purchase. James is a Diesel engine mechanic by profession. Sometimes, when you ask a Cobra replica owner what he or she does for a living, you may indeed get an idea of how well built their car is, should they be the builder.

and well-behaved driving characteristics. Find out how much torque and horsepower the test replica has before you plant your right foot from rest.

Once you've purchased the car, you can see how fast it will go. For now, "if you break it, you bought it."

Find a stretch of lightly traveled highway or freeway. Accelerate quickly through the gears and listen to the engine as you're doing it. Watch to see if it's burning blue smoke. If it is, this indicates poor ring seal or valve seal, and this often necessitates an engine rebuild.

Listen and feel the transmission as you shift through the gears. Accelerate aggressively, let off the pedal, and accelerate again. If you see blue smoke behind you, this indicates worn piston rings or valve seats because oil is getting into the combustion chamber and burning. You should continue to take it through a variety of conditions, highway, freeway, and city streets.

Find some chicanes and some winding roads, so you can get a sense of the car's handling capabilities and road holding. You should be able to select a line and the car should hold it. The steering should be smooth and precise through corners. The suspension should be firm yet compliant when driving over road bumps.

You should not hear any clunking or thumping noises from the front end. If the car bounces or keeps bouncing after going over bumps, the shocks have lost their damping and will need to be replaced.

Next brake aggressively but do not lock up the brakes and skid. You should not hear any grinding or unusual noises, pulling to one side or the other, thumping, or clunking. If you hear a squealing sound, the brake pads are likely worn down to the wear indicator. If you hear a grinding sound, you have metal-to-metal contact of the backing plate against the rotor.

Closely monitor the temperature gauge and make sure that the engine progressively warms up. During operation make sure it stays within the middle range. If it uses an electric fan, make sure it activates at the preset temperature.

More Owner Queries

The test drive is another crucial point in evaluating how well the Cobra is built and how much it has been driven. Just as with your daily driver, if you hear funny noises coming from the engine bay or the undercarriage, do some investigating. Should there be copious rattles, or you feel the chassis flex when you're driving over railroad tracks, make a mental note of all the anomalies and idiosyncrasies as you're cruising around in someone else's hand-built hot rod.

Be blunt with the owner and get him or her to divulge the cause of those peculiar noises, the frame flex, odd smells, etc. There may be an easy fix to the problem(s). Perhaps just the shocks need to be replaced to solve a soft ride or a rattle.

Maybe the remedy to an overheating problem is the simple replacement of the electric fans in front of the radiator. On the other hand, the block may have a crack in it. Or perhaps the car's been driven while hot for enough time that the aluminum heads are warped. New aluminum heads will set you back more than a thousand bucks.

A correctly identified problem is also a means to negotiate a lower price. Mind you, there are some things that could be too costly. If you see oil spots when the owner backs the vehicle out of the garage, that could be a deal killer. It's not good if there appears to be water in the oil. Listen to your gut. If you sense that something's just not right, walk away. There are always more Cobras out there for you to check out. Find the right car for you.

BUILD OPTIONS FOR COBRA KIT CARS

Living within your means—let's modify this concept and apply it to building a Cobra replica: creating the best possible Cobra roadster replica without going broke, getting a divorce, or sleeping in the doghouse outside for the next year while the project's underway in the home shop. On the other hand, don't be too much of a spendthrift when you build your Cobra. Just create a cool car that doesn't leave you homeless or spouseless. The last thing you want to do, when you get to the finish line in the project, is to regret the fact that you started the build in the first place. You, your family, and your friends all have the opportunity to enjoy in this build if you carefully plan how much you have to spend and then execute the plan.

This entire chapter is devoted to budgeting. It is possible to build a nice Cobra for $25,000. You can also spend more than $100,000 and have a wild replica. It all boils down to how little or how much money you have to spend, how much of the work you can do yourself, and what sort of dream machine you want to have when all the creating is complete and it's time to carve some corners at the wheel of your roadster.

Obviously, your budget determines whether you create your roadster with a mix of new and used components or all new parts. Over the years I've seen, heard, and even had the opportunity to pilot some spectacular Cobra creations that had inauspicious beginnings. The projects may have been started with an assortment of new and reconditioned components, or the entire build might have been a mix of a donor car with a barely started project that had been sitting for several years. Do not be dismayed if you have a paltry budget. It is amazing what you can create, even with very limited funds, especially if you're willing to invest your own sweat equity.

Apart from the Unique Motorcars' embossed floor mats in the cockpit, you are hard pressed to tell Tom Morgan's Unique 427SC from an original Shelby Cobra.

Using an FFR Mk3 Roadster Base Kit and a 2003 donor Mustang Mach 1, FFR engineer Jesper Ingerslev built an out-standing daily driver for a bit more than $26,000.

Jesper Ingerslev's Factory Five Racing Mk3 Roadster

When planning and creating a Cobra replica, it can certainly be beneficial to also be employed by a company that produces replica kits. Jesper Ingerslev works for Factory Five Racing as an engineer. He knows firsthand how well these kits are designed and manufactured. Can you imagine how frustrating it would be working for the leading kit-car company in the world and not building your own dream car? In the case of Ingerslev, his area of expertise revolves around designing, engineering, and building. And like many of us, he's an automotive enthusiast and

auto-racing fan. So, his vocation and avocation are in harmony. Creating his version of Cobra-car nirvana had to be an easy decision to make.

As a young family man, he also needed to be economical when plotting the financial course of his FFR build. He found a 2003 Mustang Mach 1 that had been totaled in a collision and dumped at a local wrecking yard. The Mach 1 had just 2,000 on the odometer with an engine and transmission that had barely been broken in.

You can guess what Ingerslev did. He was off to the races. Using the 2003 Mach 1's mill, the Tremec 3650 5-speed transmission, and as many of the other components that

he chose, Jesper built a super-nice FFR Mk3 roadster that is his daily driver. The top and side curtains are proudly stowed in the trunk. Those who have spent any time in New England or, more specifically, Massachusetts in the fall and winter, are aware how much rain, sleet, and snow that part of the country gets for much of every year.

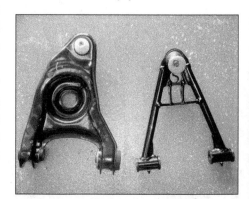

Rather than using the stock-donor lower control arms (left), Ingerslev splurged and purchased some lighter-weight, stronger, and higher-performance Factory Five Racing tubular lower control arms (right). The optional control arms yield a lower unsprung weight and enable the car to corner more firmly.

The 2003 Mustang Mach 1 engine had just 2,000 break-in miles when Ingerslev installed it in his Mk3 roadster chassis. This is a common donor vehicle for an FFR base kit. What is uncommon is the fact that Ingerslev found a 2003 Mustang Mach 1 with so few miles.

Jesper Ingerslev's Mk3 Roadster

Vehicle Manufacturer
Factory Five Racing

Owner
Jesper Ingerslev
Wareham, Massachusetts

Vehicle
Year and type/model: 2004 FFR Mk3 Roadster

Pricing
Price of kit: $12,990
Total price as tested: $26,817
Manufacturer estimate of hours to build/complete
    vehicle: 300

Donor
Year and type/model: Ford Mustang, 2003 Mach 1
Cost of donor car: $4,999
Profit from selling un-used Mustang parts: $2,054

Components Included In Kit

Chassis
Frame: FFR tubular space frame with integral backbone/
    aluminum paneled
Wheelbase: 90 inches
Rear end: Ford 8.8-inch solid axle from donor
Rear suspension: FFR three-link
Front suspension: FFR IFS
Shocks: Koni aluminum shocks, steel coil-over springs
Rear brakes: Ford Mustang donor 11.65-inch discs
Front brakes: Ford Mustang donor 13-inch discs with
    twin piston calipers
Brake lines: FFR
Master cylinder: Ford Mustang donor
Brake booster: Ford Mustang donor
Steering: Ford Mustang rack-and-pinion donor, FFR
    steering shaft
Front wheel make/size: Ford Racing, FR500, 18 x 9-inch

Rear wheel make/size: Ford Racing, FR500, 18 x 9-inch

Body
Paint brand/type: PPG Polyurethane Ford GT Silver
Windshield/glass: FFR
Roll bar: Structurally mounted to chassis, 2 x .120-inch
    wall
Bumpers: FFR optional
Lights: HiD
Mirrors: GT400 Bullett Fuel system; Ford Mustang
    donor
Fuel tank: Ford Mustang donor

Interior
Gauges: Auto Meter Ultra-Lite
Wiring: Ford Mustang donor
Steering wheel: Leather wrapped
Seating: FFR custom
Upholstery: FFR custom
Material: Vinyl seats, nylon carpet

Drivetrain
Engine Type: Ford Mustang donor, 4.6L, 281 ci
Water Pump: Ford Mustang donor
Radiator: FFR aluminum optional
Air cleaner: A&B
Ignition: Ford Mustang donor
Headers: Ford Racing shorty headers
Exhaust system: Custom
Transmission: Tremec 3650, 5-speed manual
Driveshaft: Ford Mustang donor
Shifter: Steeda Tri-ax
Battery: Ford Mustang donor
Engines brackets: Ford Mustang donor
Accessories: March underdrive pulleys
Customer upgrades: ABS brakes, Alpine stereo
FFR optional upgrades: Tubular front lower arms, three-
    link rear suspension, chrome roll bar, ceramic-coated
    exhaust, catalytic converters, stainless-steel bumper
    assembly, wind wings, and hood hinge

It is hard to tell Tom Morgan's Unique 427SC from an original Shelby Cobra. (The only difference is the Unique Motorcars' embossed floor mats in the cockpit.) Unique doesn't use donor cars for the basis of their Cobra kit cars.

Implementing the Mach 1's anti-lock braking system for handling the raucous New England climate was one of the many advantages to buying a FFR Mk3 Base Kit and going the donor car route for Jesper, along with the considerable financial savings.

Not long after Ingerslev completed his Mk3, he let me take the roadster for a spin. Being the editor of *KIT CAR* magazine had its perks. Despite the fact that it was created from a combination of new and barely used components, Jesper's Mk3 drives and handles like a brand-new, high-end sports car! When you consider that he spent a grand total of $26,817, does that give you hope

that you too can build a righteous Cobra replica on a budget? In my book, seeing, driving, and believing makes me one of the choir. I'll sing the praises of Ingerslev's Cobra creation, especially if he lets me take the roadster out on another spin sometime soon.

Tom Morgan's Unique Motorcars 427SC

Cobras are stunning in any color, with the possible exception of pink. The curvaceous lines of the car, often called the Coke-bottle shape, are the obvious reason these cars look so sweet wearing paint, in

brushed or polished aluminum, or even in fiberglass Gel-Coat. Concept cars are often sprayed silver because that's a hue that flatters any automobile's forms. It's also the color of steel and evokes a mechanical, substantial, and precisely built feel in the viewer.

Tom Morgan, of Mt. Juliet, Tennessee, had his Unique Motorcars 427SC roadster painted the color of pocket change, a Sterling Silver hue that's sublime in low light or sunlight. Because his car has a Ford big-block V-8 underhood that's detailed like an original Shelby Cobra's engine bay, it's a real challenge to discern that his roadster is a replica.

His Unique 427SC looks like it might go for maybe $500,000 to a million bucks, depending upon its ownership and potential race history as a 1960s original. Yet, Tom spent a very manageable $48,000 and an admittedly time-consuming 400-plus hours of labor on the build.

He didn't go the donor car route to help save money. Rather, he had an original Ford FE cast-iron big-block V-8 precisely machined by

Southern Automotive rebuilt the Ford FE big-block mill for Morgan's Unique Motorcars roadster. With the turkey pan and the Stelling & Hellings air cleaner, the FE engine's a dead ringer for a Cobra 427 powerplant.

Tom Morgan's Unique Motorcars 427SC

Vehicle Manufacturer
Unique Motorcars

Owner
Tom Morgan
Mt. Juliet, Tennessee

Vehicle
Year and type/model: Unique Motorcars 427SC

Pricing
Price of kit: $23,890
Unique accessories: $2,890
Dash-mounted mirror
Heater defroster kit
Adjustable Carrera-style coil-over rear shocks
Side-curtain ferrules
Removable hood scoop
Emergency-brake handle, cable, caliper
Ceramic-coated exhaust
Footbox heat shields
Thermotec insulation
Total price as tested: $48,000
Owner estimate of hours to build: 400+

Donor (if applicable)
Year and type/model: N/A

Components Included in Kit

Chassis
Frame: 2 x 4-inch rectangular tubing, MIG welded and Powdercoated
Wheelbase: 90 inches
Rear end: Jaguar Dana Spicer, 3:31 limited-slip
Rear suspension: Jaguar IRS with inboard disc brakes
Front suspension: custom tubular A-arms, 5/8-inch sway bar
Shocks: Front, adjustable coil-overs; Rear, four adjustable Carrere coil-overs
Rear brakes: Jaguar inboard disc
Front brakes: Wilwood Racing disc brakes

Master cylinder: Wilwood
Brake booster: N/A
Steering: MG rack-and-pinion
Front wheel make/size: Compomotive HB 15 x 8-inch three-piece wheel
Rear wheel make/size: Compomotive HB 15 x 10.5-inch three-piece wheel

Body
Body: Unique Motorcars hand-laminated fiberglass
Paint: Jodeco Auto Body, Bruce Bunn
Paint brand/type: PPG, Lexus Titanium with black stripes
Windshield: Unique Motorcars
Roll bar: Unique Motorcars chrome
Bumpers: Front and rear Quickjacks
Grille: N/A
Lights: Headlights, taillights, turn signals, and license-plate light
Mirrors: Dash mounted
Fuel system: Holley high-volume mechanical fuel pump, Holley fuel-pressure regulator
Fuel tank: 20-gallon aluminum tank

Interior
Gauges: Stewart Warner
Wiring: Custom wiring harness
Steering wheel: 15-inch, AC-style
Seating: Leather bucket seats, AC-style
Upholstery: Vinyl door panels and hinge covers
Material: Black wool carpet

Drivetrain
Engine brand: Ford
Engine type: FE 406
Edelbrock Performer FE 428 Cobra Jet Heads
Cam: Comp Cams
Comp Cams titanium adjustable rocker arms
Machining: Revolutionary Performance & Machine
Final assembly: Owner
Water pump: Edelbrock Victor Jr. aluminum
Radiator: Griffin aluminum with dual electric fans
Air cleaner: Stelling & Hellings with K&N filter

Tom Morgan's Unique Motorcars 427SC CONTINUED

Ignition: MSD billet aluminum distributor
Headers: Unique Motorcars ceramic coated
Exhaust system: Unique Motorcars ceramic coated
Transmission: Tremec TKO-600 5-speed, Lakewood
    bellhousing, Centerforce Flywheel, Keisler hydraulic
    release bearing
Driveshaft: Included
Shifter: Cobra replica bent shifter
Battery: Optima Red Top

Accessories
Unique Motorcars removable hood scoop
Crow five-point racing harness
Rear sway bar
Unique tonneau cover
Remote oil filter kit and braided steel lines
Stainless-steel surge tank
Canton overflow tank
Rear anti-sway bar
Lakewood driveshaft safety loop
Spal 16-inch puller radiator fan
Reverse 180-mph speedometer

Revolutionary Performance & Machine, conveniently located in his hometown. The V-8 was treated to some new speed-shop-quality engine components, like a Comp Cams valvetrain assembly, and backed the torque monster with a new Tremec TKO-600 manual transmission that can handle up to 600 ft-lbs of torque without breaking a sweat (or any of the gears). John then set to the task of stuffing the renewed block into the car. Bruce Bunn, the owner of Jodeco Autobody, in McDonough, Georgia, laid down the money-silver paint scheme, in PPG Lexus Titanium with black Le Mans stripes.

Considering that the owner saved 10 to 20 times what it could have cost him to buy an original Shelby Cobra 427SC, we say Tom budgeted well in the building of his Unique Motorcars Cobra. Depending upon how much savings you have and how good you are at turning wrenches, you could build something comparable to either Jesper or Tom. You just need to get your spreadsheet going so you can work out the details.

A Word to the Wise

With both of the above builds, the Cobra creators wound up achieving a happy ending while being able to save some money by reconditioning used components. In the case of Jesper Ingerslev, his good fortune began when he found a slightly used but thoroughly wrecked 2003 Mustang Mach 1 with just 2,000 miles on the odometer. Starting his FFR Mk3 build from such a strong foundation made perfect sense. The used components he installed didn't need to be reconditioned because they were almost brand new.

Tom Morgan, on the other hand, used an old Ford-FE big-block V-8 and had it professionally machined and reconditioned. He's lucky that the block was still usable and hadn't been bored and rebuilt too many times. Thankfully, he had some real pros providing the machining and reconditioning of the FE block.

When using old components, be careful that the parts aren't so worn that they can't be reconditioned. It's very possible to wind up spending more money on something that's not salvageable, when the initial goal was to save money. The word of caution here is to carefully inspect every used component to determine whether it can be reconditioned and reused. If you don't have the wherewithal to make that sort of determination, find an expert who you can trust. In the case of engine builders, there are a large number of reputable pro shops all over the country that can assist you with your engine rebuilding queries. For a nominal fee, they line-hone your engine block and determine if it is viable to re-build your old engine.

Several years ago, I had a used 1969 Ford 351W engine block that I bought from a wrecking yard for real cheap. The engine builder I was going to use determined that the block already had a 60 overbore and one of the cylinders needed to be sleeved. Rather than go that route, I wound up getting a brand-new engine from Smeding Performance a while later. That mill made 555 hp and 557 ft-lbs of torque on the engine dyno and ran like a NASCAR powerplant on steroids. Yes, I might have been able to get that much power out of the old block, but I might have also walked into a bunch of trouble and added engine headaches not far down the road.

If you wish to steer clear of any difficulties in renewing old components, you could take the sort of approach that Cobra caretaker Darren Friedman chose—spare no expense. He bought everything new and produced his version of a dream Cobra.

Darren Friedman's 2006 Kirkham 427SC

Darren Friedman, owner of the number-500 Kirkham 427SC, is no stranger to Cobra replicas. Several years ago, he had a side business called West Coast Dreams, where he and his business partner built and sold Cobra replicas to customers on demand.

You see, Mr. Friedman is an entrepreneurial sort of fellow with a couple of successful medical businesses to his credit. When the moment came to realize the Cobra replica of his

dreams, he contacted the Kirkham brothers, David and Thomas, in Provo, Utah. He ordered a polished aluminum Kirkham 427SC roadster with a removable Le Mans hardtop, a turnkey-minus car.

While waiting for the Kirkham's arrival, he ordered a Roush/Shelby 451 FE aluminum big-block V-8 and backed that mighty mill with an equally stout Tremec TKO 600 5-speed manual transmission. Because Darren enjoys taking the Cobra on cruises and displaying it at shows as much as he relishes track events in California, he has two sets of wheels and tires, one for the road courses and one set of four for the street.

Possibly because Kirkhams are crafted by former MIG fighter-jet engineers and fabricators, out of the same aluminum material that the original Shelby Cobras were comprised of back in the 1960s, many Kirkham owners order their Kirkham Motorsports cars in polished aluminum. Their badge of honor is to not wear paint. I imagine few polished aluminum roadsters see much track action. Darren's number-500 car has

dual badges, a bit of track rash from all the racing action, and enough polished aluminum bodywork to make anyone squint.

All of us Cobra replica builders are creating our own dream machines. The three vehicles discussed above illustrate different approaches to the same end result. The question is: How can you build the Cobra you choose? Keep dreaming, start planning, and get to the building. That's the fun part—the creating and building.

Engine Sources

Any automobile's heart and soul is the drivetrain. This is especially true with Cobra kit cars. Before Carroll Shelby approached AC Cars, Ltd. in England with the idea of transforming the Ace Bristol roadster into a fire-breathing race car, the Ace was a sweetly styled two-seater. Because the car was so light (1,950 pounds), the inline six-cylinder Bristol engine produced decent power for the Ace. Shelby's plan to drop an American V-8 engine in the Ace's spacious engine bay was a stroke of genius and

Darren Friedman's 2006 Kirkham 427SC

Vehicle Manufacturer
Kirkham Motorsports
Provo, Utah

Owner
Darren Friedman
Camarillo, California

Vehicle
Year and type/model: 2006 Kirkham 427SC
    number-500 with LeMans removable top

Pricing
Price of kit: $54,995 base
Total price as tested: $100,000
Manufacturer estimate of hours to build/complete
    vehicle: 300

Donor (if applicable)
No donor

Darren Friedman's 2006 Kirkham 427SC CONTINUED

Components Included In Kit

Chassis
Frame: Stainless steel
Wheelbase: 90 inches
Rear end: Dana 44 3.52:1
Rear suspension: Independent
Front suspension: Billet control arms
Shocks: Penske 7500 coil-over with 600-pound
    hyperlink springs
Rear brakes: Wilwood 1.250-inch rotors
Front: Wilwood Superlight with 1.250-inch rotor and
    brake scoops
Brake lines: Stainless
Brake Booster: None
Steering: Original rack-and-pinion
Front Wheel Make/Size: Trigo/15 x 8.5
Rear Wheel Make/Size: Trigo 15 x 9.5
Front Tire Make/Size: Avon CR6ZZ 245-60-15
Rear Tire Make/Size: Avon CR6ZZ 295-50-15

Body
Polished aluminum
Windshield/glass: Viracon laminated
Top: LeMans aluminum removable
Roll Bar: Stainless steel
Bumpers: Steel bumper jacks
Grille: NA
Lights: Wagner 7-inch
Mirrors: Raydot
Emblems and trim: none
Fuel System: Carb
Fuel Tank: 42-gallon

Interior
Gauges: Kirkham
Wiring: Kirkham
Steering Wheel: Moto Lita leather
Seating: Custom
Upholstery: Leather/Stingray
Material: Wool carpet

Drivetrain Installed in Vehicle
Engine brand: Roush/Shelby 451FE
Engine type: Aluminum-block Shelby
Water pump: High-volume Edelbrock
Radiator: Aluminum Kirkham
Air Cleaner: K&N
Ignition: MSD 6AL
Headers: Steel Kirkham
Exhaust system: Steel Kirkham
Transmission Type: TKO 600 short shaft
Shifter: Kirkham
Air-conditioning: None
Battery: Odyssey PC925
Engines Brackets: Steel
Accessories: See attached list

Additions, Modifications and Upgrades in the Tested Vehicle
Power: 506 hp 497 Torq Dyno 1/18/07
Make: Roush/Shelby Aluminum 451 FE
Crankshaft: Scat Nodular Iron 3.980-stroke
Pistons: Wiseco forged-aluminum 4.250-inch bore and
    10.0:1 compression ratio with plasma-moly file-fit
    rings
Camshaft: Roush proprietary hydraulic roller camshaft
    and lifters
Oil Pump: Melling high-volume
Radiator: Aluminum Kirkham
Alternator: 100-amp single wire
Heads: Edelbrock aluminum
Induction: Holley 770 with Edelbrock RPM dual-plane
    intake Manifold
Ignition: MSD 6AL
Headers: Steel Kirkham ceramic coated
Transmission: TKO 600 with short shaft
Flywheel: McLeod Clutch/throw-out bearing
Oil pan: 8-quart Canton fully baffled Road Race

Miscellaneous
Wheel-well foam, halon fire suppression system, fresh air ventilation system, battery cutoff switch, custom billet coolant tank, and driveshaft safety loop

was something that hot rodders had been doing with 1920s and 1930s vintage Fords and other American vehicles since the mid 1930s.

Installing a Ford V-8 mill in the AC Ace Bristol roadster and calling the new car a Shelby Cobra made all the difference. The Cobra was quicker, handled better, and had a top speed at least 40 mph faster than the AC Ace, and this was just the jump from the Ace to the 260-ci V-8 Ford engine that powered the first Cobras in 1962.

The current art of engine building provides small-block and big-block V-8s to choose from in either cast iron or aluminum. This enables Cobra replica builders to achieve significantly more horsepower and torque out of modern engines that are more reliable and weigh less than what was available when the Cobra was new, from 1962 through 1967.

There are many professional engine rebuilding companies in each of the 50 states that can build a top-quality, high-performance, and reliable powerplant for your Cobra project. Many of these shops offer computer-controlled engine building equipment that is state-of-the-art and also offer engine dyno and chassis dynamometer testing capabilities. Some of the companies only build engines using new components, and they provide solid multi-year warranties.

Some engine builders across the country specialize in a specific brand of American engine. There are Blue Oval builders, Bow Tie experts, and plenty of Mopar machinists. There are even pro shops, like Bill and Susan Parham's Southern Automotive, that focus only on Ford FE big-block mills.

To assist you with engine selection, here are several of the prominent U.S. Ford engine companies. They sell crate engines, are new engine specialists, and/or are rebuild experts. If you wish to put Mopar or Chevy power in your Cobra kits, you're on your own. I'm a Chevy-in-a-Chevy sort of guy and a Ford-in-a-Ford fan. What you choose is up to you.

QMP Racing Engines

The QMP stands for Quarter Mile Performance. This pro shop's specialty is building high-performance racing engines that can take whatever any drag strip dishes out in a 1/8-mile, 1/4-mile, or what have you. After we selected a Dart race-series aluminum Ford 351W engine block and Dart's Pro 1 CNC aluminum cylinder heads as the foundation on our engine build, we needed a top builder. Dart's Advertising Director, Jack McInnis, highly recommended QMP Racing Engines to build the engine for our Cobra replica. McInnis then kindly introduced us to Brad Lagman, the owner and founder of QMP Racing Engines.

All of the services that QMP performs are done in-house; no machining is ever farmed out. QMP offers a direct approach to building the best engines possible. That philosophy is summed up succinctly: "Tell us how fast you want to go, and we will make it happen." That's music to our ears and our three right feet.

Smeding Performance

Smeding Performance crate engines are designed from the ground up with value, reliability, and performance in mind. Only 100-percent new components, including the block, are used in Smeding-built engines. Every engine is individually balanced, engine dyno tested, and tuned with a lengthy break-in procedure. Smeding engines have one of the lowest warranty-return ratios in the industry.

The company, founded by pro engine builder Ben Smeding, specializes in Ford and Chevy engines ranging from 340 to 800 hp. And they all run on 91-octane filling-station fuel. Customization is available; the most popular are polish packages and multiple carburetion. Smeding Performance crate engines include carburetion, ignition with wires, and engine dyno tuning, providing a true turnkey package. Smeding guarantees their engines with a two-year, unlimited mileage warranty. An assortment of front-drive accessories for air conditioning, power steering, etc., are available installed as options.

As evidenced by a Ford 351W 427 stroker mill the company built for us that made 555 hp and 557 ft-lbs of torque, Smeding Performance builds reliable, proven, high-performance engines that last and get your vehicle going fast.

Keith Craft Performance Engines

Keith Craft, Inc., founded by Keith Craft, has been in business since 1984. I have several friends with Cobra replicas that are powered by Keith Craft's engines. They all swear by Craft's professionally built powerplants. These guys do have some sweet rides, and the mills inside them make prodigious power. Keith Craft Performance Engines builds and sells engines for street cars, performance cars, mud trucks, race cars, Cobras, restored vehicles, hot rods, show cars—just about any sort of vehicle you can imagine.

Roush engines are a popular choice for Cobra kits or any Ford-powered performance vehicle. Jack Roush has built a reputation for winning in various professional auto racing series, so it's easy to understand why many Cobra replica builders select Roush mills for their roadsters.

Ford Racing Performance Parts

Unless you've been living under a rock, you're aware that Ford Racing Parts recently introduced a new lineup of Boss 302 crate engines in two- and four-valve-per-cylinder varieties. Ford Racing also offers several of the venerable and reliable 351W crate engines, in displacements up to the magical 427 ci. They also offer modular engines in the 4.6L variety. If you favor dropping a Ford big-block V-8 mill in your 427SC roadster replica, there are two brand-new 521-ci Ford big-block V-8 engines to choose from.

Roush Engines

Jack Roush began his career in 1964 as an engineer for the Ford Motor Company. Roush was always interested in motorsports, so he eventually left Ford to pursue this passion. He first formed Jack Roush Performance Engineering, then Roush Industries in 1976, and Roush

Racing in 1988. With success in every race series, Roush became the only professional drag racer to venture into NASCAR, SCCA Trans-Am, and IMSA road racing and sports car racing.

Jack Roush is also very well-known for building a full lineup of Ford high-performance street and racing crate engines. His company manufactures and distributes an extensive array of small-and big-block Ford-based powerplants, from 327 ci all the way up to 588 ci. Whether you wish to run a carbureted mill or stack fuel injection in your Cobra, Roush Engines has an outstanding solution for your roadster.

Carolina Machine Engines

In business since 1984, Carolina Machine Engines (CME) has produced more than 40,000 remanufactured engines and has in excess of 40 years' racing experience and hot rodding passion. The company sells

street/strip, pump-gas high-performance, race, and stock OE replacement engines direct to consumers. CME's engines are available as complete, long-block and block assembly, from economy to high-end big-horsepower and big-torque versions. They offer Chevy and Ford powerplants.

Speed-O-Motive Racing Engines

With more than 60 years of producing high-performance engines, beginning with the Ford flathead V-8, Speed-O-Motive offers quite a bit of high-performance prowess to those seeking small- or big-block Ford V-8 power. The company offers a wide array of crate engines from various manufacturers. Whether you wish to go with the Blue Oval or some other make, Speed-O-Motive has been delivering the goods since 1946.

Summit Racing

Don't forget about Summit Racing Equipment. In 1968, the company started humbly and grew into the world's largest mail-order automotive-performance equipment company. Summit offers a complete line of Ford crate engines, as well as other American V-8s.

Southern Automotive

If you wish to rebuild an original Ford FE big-block mill, Southern Automotive provides rebuilt Ford Toploader 4-speed transmissions and Tremec transmissions.

Auto Parts Stores

Of course, the various auto parts stores across the country provide rebuilt engines. If you wish to go down this road, compare the warranties and price the best solution that fits your budget and power requirements.

McLeod produces blow-proof scattershields and high-performance clutches, while Tremec Transmissions offers spectacular manual transmissions for enthusiast automobiles. Many Cobra builders use the Tremec TKO 600 5-speed manual transmission. The transmission handles up to 600 ft-lbs of torque. It is precise, smoothly shifting, and offers multiple locations for the shifter, which comes in handy when building any enthusiast machine.

Transmissions, Clutches, Scattershields, Etc.

Whether you're installing an engine and transmission in a Backdraft Racing roadster or you're creating an ERA replica from the ground up, there are a number of drivetrain components for which you need to do some homework, determine what you want, and select where to purchase.

There are myriad decisions to make, including these:

- Do you want to use a hydraulic clutch or a cable-actuated clutch?

- Do you wish to install a manual or an automatic transmission?
- Do you want to really replicate an original Cobra as much as possible and install a Ford Toploader 4-speed with the reverse lockout T-shifter?
- Do you prefer to purchase a bulletproof and overdrive-equipped Tremec TKO 500 or 600 5-speed manual transmission?
- How about the top-of-the-line Tremec T56 Magnum 6-speed manual transmission that has overdrive in 5th and 6th gears and can handle up to 700 ft-lbs of torque?
- What bellhouse fits best?

- Whose clutch should you use?
- Would an aluminum flywheel or billet steel flywheel be better?

And so on. Don't be dismayed. Break it down into manageable components, get to work, and you begin to make progress bit-by-bit, step-by-step.

Properly planning your build to fit your budget and be the sort of Cobra replica you wish to create is a monumental challenge. But it's one that you can master. Two of us aren't too careful about planning. Yet, we did pretty well. You can make it to the finish line just as we did—step-by-step and bit-by-bit.

BUILDING YOUR COBRA ON TIME AND ON BUDGET

Many of the car- and motorcycle-building reality shows on cable television have crazy one-week, two-week, or month-long deadlines before the vehicles have to be finished and delivered to the customer. Accordingly, these projects are built in pro shops, whose staff of fabricators, engine maestros, electricians, body and paint pros, and interior artisans might number well into the double digits. If the shops have a stiff deadline in front of them, they can throw more people on the build tasks that aren't going as smoothly. The show's producers can add money into the seemingly bottomless pot of gold, so the shop can, for example, buy a big-block mill instead of rebuilding the existing powerplant to save time.

On the other hand, we don't have endless money or some media conglomerate paying to build an ultimate Cobra. What we do have is an endless amount of enthusiasm for the work with a pretty decent background of having owned and operated several enthusiast automobiles over the years. But our collective savings accounts, like many people in these challenging economic times, are stretched to the limit.

I suspect that you are faced with the same constraints and, therefore, a limited budget necessitates careful planning and attention to the details of the project. W get the job done one way or another because, in addition to being gearheads practically from birth, the three of us are pretty darn stubborn.

The problem is that at least two of us—the two doing the most work—also tend to procrastinate about being organized, fastidious, and proactive. Combine that with the fact that the Factory Five Racing Mk4 Roadster that we're building has a hard and fast deadline, and we may have a recipe for disaster.

It's not that we're lazy bums when it comes to working on cars. I actually do not put off writing most of the time. But planning and actually paying out the cash aren't too exciting for me. Perhaps if I had an immense bank account, I might have

Starting with the body on the chassis, the Stewart Transport driver and Dad began to unload our kit.

Our FFR Mk4 Complete Kit (22 boxes) was successfully loaded into the garage along with the body on the chassis.

I wonder if my wife would have permitted my storing all the engine components and some of the FFR Mk4 Complete Kit boxes in the living room. Perhaps I was lucky to be single at the time of the build.

a different perspective. But I don't, so I forced myself to write this chapter in sequence, rather than putting it off until after I had completed writing the more fun chapters.

The fun and easy part to this build project for us is working in the garage. But the building can only occur when you have all the components needed, coupled with the right tools for doing the job at hand. So proper planning means that we actually get to the fun and easy stuff—you know, turning wrenches and riveting aluminum panels in our three-car garage turned Cobra factory.

We had 14 months to finish our Factory Five Racing Mk4 Cobra roadster replica. Most of the kit arrived in April and we planned on being done with the project by the following June. Your overall time frame may be longer or shorter, and you may find some of the procedures more challenging than others. But hang in there; the prize is worth the work!

Develop a Plan

You've decided to build a Cobra kit car, and what an exciting prospect it is. Like most of us, you have visions of jamming through the gears with the top down, carving through a challenging set of turns, and listening to the sweet song of the V-8s exhaust notes exiting the side pipes. But between now and that moment, a considerable amount of work needs to be done.

While you will be assembling an entire car from the ground up, don't get overwhelmed because with proper planning, realistic goal setting, and good decision making, you simply build the car one task at a time. Therefore, you can reach your goal of a professional-grade assembly and do it on time and on budget.

Most of us know of avid enthusiasts who had grandiose dreams of restoring and building their own car. These people had the best intentions only to run out of time, money, and patience. In the end, the car sat in the garage for years, was never completed, and sold off to become someone else's project. This is something we want you to avoid. We want to see you complete your project and get your Cobra on the road because that's where it belongs.

You need to develop a cohesive assembly plan, set priorities, create project budgets, and project completion dates. While these aspects can adjust within reasonable parameters, establishing your priorities and assembly plan will see you through to completion of your kit.

The best and most effective way to plan, organize, and manage your project is with data and spreadsheet software. I am not suggesting that

Most FFR Cobra replica kits have a solid live rear axle. Though it costs more, we opted to go with an independent rear suspension, since original Cobra 427SCs all used IRS. Also, we wanted our car to accurately emulate the original. We were glad to spend about $3,500 more and several months' wait-time to get IRS.

Cool-looking upper rear control arms, half shafts, hub carriers, and hubs. We're glad that we went with the Ford IRS, though it took several months to track down these new components. You don't get wheel hop in tight corners with an IRS-equipped Cobra replica, but you could with a live-axle replica. Cornering is much better, and that's what Cobras are all about.

this takes learning a bunch of new programs, but rather that you make use of common programs on the market, such as Microsoft Excel.

It may seem that spending the time to organize all the information in these programs is taking away from the actual assembly time. But don't lose sight of the fact that you've embarked on a complex project, and while achievable, it demands thorough planning, competent task completion, and attention to detail. The reality is that time invested in planning and organization is going to save you time, money, and frustration down the road. Another reality is that you're going to develop or possess the mechanical, assembly, and problem-solving skills to get from one stage to another.

The assembly manual for any kit is a good guide to the entire assembly process, and therefore is an excellent resource for planning project task completion, setting critical procedures, projecting time deadlines, setting budgets, and other aspects of the project. Our Factory Five Cobra Mk4 manual proved to be invaluable throughout the project.

Although it's difficult to impossible to be super precise with every projection and goal, with the help of this book, other Cobra owners, Cobra club members, and support from the manufacturer of your kit, you can

develop a realistic plan. You can also consult directly with the manufacturer of your Cobra kit, for specific procedural, time budget, and money budget suggestions, so you can put together a strong assembly plan.

Evaluate Your Skills

A crucial part of the planning and budgeting process is determining your skill level, ambition, and limitations. Many enthusiasts have worked on engines, and some have rebuilt engines, transmissions, and other mechanical components. And these individuals are skilled at assembling the mechanical components of the car. Some enthusiasts have completed body work on a car, so they know how to trim and adjust body panels. They know how to hang a fender or install a quarter panel, and that includes welding in sheet metal, adding body filler, priming, and painting. Others have experience with installing interiors and reconditioning electrical components and installing a wiring harness.

If you're skilled in all the above areas and you can complete installation of every single component group, then you should be commended. If, on the other hand, you're like the majority of enthusiast builders, you have experience is one or several areas, but you're not skilled

in all areas. Therefore, you're going to subcontract some of the work to qualified professionals in a particular area.

For example, I had a good understanding of electrical theory and practice, but we installed a complete fuel injection system on our Ford Windsor-based engine, and the amount of wiring required for the system on the engine, the fuel pump, and the controls on the car seemed too much for us. While I possibly could have wired the system myself, the risk of making a mistake and damaging the system was too great. So I hired an automotive electrician.

Create a Spending Budget

1. Choose a spreadsheet program, such as Excel, and open a new file.

2. Set up three columns:

- Components
- Projected Cost
- Actual Cost

3. At the bottom of the columns, designate a cell for the total of each column. To arrive at the total use the AutoSum option in the pull down menu.

4. Input the name of each component you need to purchase.

5. Input the ballpark price you expect to pay for each.

6. As you buy a component, insert its actual cost.

This spreadsheet system tracks the spending on the project, letting you know how much you've already spent and how much is still in the budget. This is very helpful when it comes time to pay a credit card bill for parts.

Sample Spending Budget

This is our spending spreadsheet. Sure, we could spend much less, but we're building our version of the ultimate Cobra replica.

Component	Projected Cost	Actual Cost
FFR Mk4 Complete Kit	19,900.00	19,900.00
Chassis powdercoat	0.00	0.00
FFR electric gauges	0.00	0.00
351 headers, roadster	0.00	0.00
302-351 engine and transmission	0.00	0.00
31-spline 10.75-inch driveshaft	0.00	0.00
Body cut-outs	120.00	120.00
Black leather seats	499.00	499.00
IRS components	1,950.00	1,950.00
15-inch Vintage AC3 wheels	999.00	999.00
Drop ship cost for wheels	100.00	100.00
Stainless 4/4 exhaust and hardware	599.00	599.00
Wind wings	99.00	99.00
Mk4 LH chrome roll bar	290.00	290.00
Stewart Transport cost	1,700.00	1,700.00
Ford Racing IRS/rear brakes	3,284.00	3,284.00
IRS poly bushing set	35.00	35.00
Summit Racing Engine Parts:		
JE pistons, 8 of them	808.88	808.88
JE piston rings, set of 8	171.95	171.95
Scat 351 crankshaft	1,101.95	1,101.95
Scat H-beam connecting rods	541.95	541.95
Comp Cams camshaft	1,058.56	1,058.56
Comp Cams rocker arms	341.96	341.96
Comp Cams hydraulic lifters	551.52	551.52
Comp Cams timing set	191.29	191.29
Comp Cams pushrods	139.65	139.65
Comp Cams 10w30 synthetic oil 12 qts	86.52	86.52
Dart 351W aluminum engine block	5,746.27	5,746.27
Dart 351W aluminum heads, 2	1,197.07	2,394.14
MSD Digital 6AL ignition	226.60	226.60
MSD plug wires	86.80	86.80
MSD Blaster SS coil	44.50	44.50
MSD distributor	316.00	316.00
ARP engine assembly fastener kit SS	246.68	246.68
Fel-Pro gasket set for 351W	97.95	97.95
Fuel tank pickup and pump basket	110.00	110.00
Aeromotive fuel pump, fittings	600.00	600.00
Weiand intake manifold	199.95	199.95
Holley Avenger EFI TBI	1,999.00	1,999.00
March Performance pulleys/brackets	417.00	417.00
Moroso oil pan, 9-qt front sump	293.95	293.95
Moroso oil pump pickup	66.95	66.95
Moroso 351W windage screen	54.95	54.95
Moroso Stud-Kit windage tray	58.95	58.95
Moroso Stud-Kit oil pan	51.95	51.95
Kugel remote brake reservoirs	195.00	195.00
Powermaster mini starter	345.95	345.95
Powermaster alternator	244.95	244.95
Tremec T56 Magnum 6-speed	2,795.00	2,795.00
Hurst manual shifter	205.00	205.00
QuickTime bellhousing	555.95	555.95
Hays cable clutch	344.57	344.57
Hays billet aluminum flywheel	511.95	511.95
Ford Racing 427 valve covers	139.95	139.95
Fuel lines and connectors	50.00	50.00
K&N air filter and housing assy.	160.00	160.00
K&N oil filter	10.85	10.85
Tires	600.00	600.00
Paint job, including all materials	5000.00	5,000.00
Miscellaneous parts, tools, bolts, etc.	400.00	400.00
QMP Racing Engines, build fee	2,000.00	2,000.00
Sharkhide Aluminum Protectant, 2	140.00	140.00
Dynamat sound/heat protection	300.00	300.00
Total		**$61,580.04**

Create a Time Budget

I'm no computer whiz, but I did learn a thing or two that should make it easier for you to create your own budgets. Follow these steps and you'll have a simple but usable document to track your time during the project.

1. Choose a spreadsheet program, such as Excel, and open a new file.

2. Set up four columns:

- Component Group (this mirrors the order of tasks in your particular Cobra kit car assembly literature: Engine, Transmission, Drivetrain, Electrical, Interior, Chassis, Body, Suspension, Bodywork, Primer, and Paint)
- Task/Sub-Task
- Projected Hours
- Actual Hours

3. Input the name of each particular Task, such as "install front suspension."

4. Within each Task, input the name of each Sub-Task, such as "install the control arms," "install the shocks," "install the torsion bars," etc.

5. At the bottom each Sub-Task column, designate a cell for the subtotals. At the bottom of each Component Group, designate a cell for the total. To arrive at the totals, use the AutoSum option in the pull down menu.

6. Insert the Projected Hours for each Sub-Task.

7. After you finish each Sub-Task, insert the Actual Hours it took to complete.

If your actual hour figures are significantly off the projected numbers, then your projections were probably not that accurate. If you're

within 10 to 20 percent of the project numbers, your project is most likely proceeding in a reasonable time frame and reasonable progress is being made.

However, if your actual figures are 30 to 50 percent off (or more), it is an indication that the original projections were not accurate. Therefore, before you proceed to the next component group, you should revisit your Projected Hours and make the necessary adjustments.

Using a spreadsheet in this way allows you to make sure you're not forgetting any crucial steps along the way. For example, once you've completed the engine and transmission installation, you need to line up the bodywork and painting. This helps you organize and plan future stages of the project, so when one Component Group is completed, the work on the project does not grind to a halt.

Sample Time Budget

This is how you might set up spreadsheet to keep track of your time spent on various parts of the project. Other component groups to add are: Engine, Transmission, Electrical, Interior, Chassis, Body, Suspension, Bodywork, Primer, Paint, etc.

Component Group	Task/Sub-Task	Projected Hours	Actual Hours
Drivetrain	install front suspension		
	install the control arms	2	2
	install the shocks	1	2
	install the torsion bars	3	1
Subtotal		6	5
	install rear suspension		
	install the ...	4	2
	install the ...	2	1
Subtotal		6	3
Total		12	8

ORGANIZATION AND PREPARATION

It was a blue-sky Pacific-coast spring day in April 2010, when the Stewart Transport 18-wheeler backed up to our driveway with our precious cargo, the Factory Five Cobra Mk4. The shipment included the FFR Mk4 body on chassis and 22 carefully labeled boxes. The Stewart Transport driver helped us move all the boxes and the body/chassis to our home shop. He painstakingly had us confirm with the shipping manifest that we had received everything that Factory Five Racing had sent us. Within an hour, we had everything safely stowed away into two bays of our three-car garage. Some of the more fragile bits, like the seats, instruments, dashboard, etc., ended up in our living room for safe keeping.

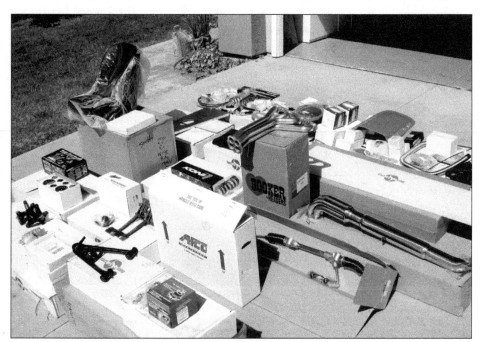

You could look at all these components and boxes and be dismayed that there's so much work to do. We were ecstatic.

Kit and Component Inspection

While you're inspecting and inventorying all the components that were shipped in your kit, it is a good idea to unpack your carpet and dashboard. This allows you to lay these items flat, so that they won't have stubborn wrinkles and creases when it's time to install them in your cockpit. If you don't have room to safely store them, you're probably best off leaving them in the boxes that they came in. That also holds true for the components that you've inspected and checked off your inventory list.

In the case of any FFR kit, the boxes are numbered from 1 to 22 according to when the components inside them are going to be used. Each box has a contents list.

The day after we loaded up our house and garage with FFR Mk4 components, we lined up all 22 boxes in chronological order in our driveway. We had two objectives in mind: take photos of the components for this book, and carefully inventory all of the parts before beginning the deconstruction/construction process.

We carefully inspected the Factory Five Racing Mk4 body, aluminum panels, and IRS-configured chassis on our first day. All the components appeared to be in brand-new condition.

Because the boxes had a large number of parts in them and we only had a finite amount of sunlight to work with to get the photos taken, we decided to remove just one or two prominent parts from each box for our photography. We gave each box a cursory inspection, but this approach proved inadequate. We didn't notice that one of the boxes had a new driver-side aluminum footbox panel in it that was to replace the old-style panel that was also pre-mounted on the chassis from the factory. We also didn't match up any backordered components with the complete listing of shipped and backordered items from Factory Five Racing. Kudos to FFR, the company provides a detailed and extremely well-organized listing of every shipped item, as well as the backordered components.

Our inspection/inventory oversights should serve as a forewarning for you to do a more thorough job than we did. The mistakes came back to haunt us later in the build, to the extent that we had to wait for some components we thought we had already received. In the other instance, we wound up replacing the pre-installed, old-style front footbox panel with the revised panel.

We could have left the old panel in place, if not for my brother Kevin. He reminded Dad and me that we're building the ultimate Cobra replica,

not some car with an obsolete footbox panel. Kevin insisted on removing the old panel and replacing it with the new one while Dad and I did other work, which made it an easy fix. That was an excellent display of teamwork. Kevin did the heavy lifting while we two procrastinators prepared other aluminum panels for being riveted to the cockpit by protecting them with Sharkhide.

Bear in mind that when we received our Mk4 Complete Kit, the fourth-generation Mk4 FFR Cobra replica was extensively re-designed and brand new. We received one of the first Mk4s in the world. So the fact that there weren't very many backordered components is testament to how professional and how thoroughly organized Factory Five Racing is and also to how great the company is at providing exemplary customer service. None of the components picked and packed by FFR and shipped via Stewart Transport were in any way damaged.

It was up to us to build our ultimate Cobra replica. In the coming months we found out firsthand whether or not the Smith men were up to the challenge.

Organization

The next thing to do is cross reference the parts manifest and project

assembly spreadsheet to determine if you have all the necessary parts and materials to start the assembly of a particular component group. Once you've determined you have all the parts for a particular component group, you should allocate a set of shelves and storage area for those particular parts.

One of the most effective methods I've used in the past is color coding the particular parts for a component group. Use colored duct tape to apply to the particular part or box. But keep in mind that duct tape leaves behind adhesive residue, so don't put it on sensitive parts. In addition, you can use a colored Sharpie pen to mark the boxes for a particular component group.

For color coding, you can mark interior parts green, suspension parts blue, chassis parts black, and so forth. This way, you can go to a specific area of your garage, see all the parts for a particular install, and then easily access those parts. Now you don't have to waste time looking through a bunch of boxes when it comes time to assemble a component group. You need at least one garage stall to store the parts and another garage stall to actually assemble the car. If you're working in a one-stall garage, you need to make some provisions for your situation. A large temporary shed to keep the parts organized and protected is one option, and be sure no animals can get into the area and damage your components.

Also be careful when storing your parts. We chose to store sensitive parts like gauges, glass, seats, and other parts in the house. We recognize that many builders may not have that option, but nonetheless, you need to store your parts wisely. Fragile and sensitive parts should not have anything resting on top of them and they should not be put around hazardous chemicals. I know this may seem like common sense, but people get in rush and make mistakes in complex projects. Thus, do not put oil or radiator fluid on top of the seats or make a similar mistake.

There are no substitutes for the correct storage containers and they should be used appropriately when you're working on your project. Want to minimize hassle and frustration? Use plastic Rubbermaid-type bins for large parts, and buy a large number of resealable freezer storage and sandwich bags for smaller parts. Also, zip ties come in handy to group particular fasteners or parts to a particular area. Permanent markers to label all the parts in the bags are required. Home painter's masking tape is good for labeling parts because it doesn't leave behind residue like regular masking tape.

Consult Your Build Manual

Before you begin your Cobra project, get into the habit of consulting the build manual that came with your kit. Whether you're building an E.R.A., Unique Motorcars, Shell Valley, Lone Star, Everett-Morrison, or Factory Five Racing Mk4 roadster like the one we're creating, make sure you carefully read each section of the

manual before you proceed to the work in your garage.

The Factory Five Mk4 Roadster Complete Kit manual is extremely thorough and very logically laid out. If you have an FFR Mk4, it is feasible to build your Cobra replica without this book. But having this book should make your job much easier. In addition, the descriptions in this book are more detailed. Also, having the advantage of more photos, and all in color, provides you with more ability to decipher exactly what you're supposed to be doing during each step of your Cobra project, no matter which kit you choose.

Maybe you can relate to how I used to be. I was one of those guys who said, "Who needs to read the darn manual? I'm a smart guy. I can figure this thing out." That sort of logic might work for putting together your daughter's bicycle before her birthday, or perhaps even hooking up your home network of laptops and desktops. But, it doesn't fly with building a car from scratch.

If you need more convincing, let's do some arithmetic. With the FFR Mk4 roadster, there are 22 boxes

filled with parts. We don't know exactly how many components, fasteners, wires, etc., are in those 22 boxes, never mind the body on the chassis and the 62 aluminum panels, but it's at least several thousand. Do you know how to assemble this kit completely so that it's a safe and reliably running car? If you answered yes, you're kidding yourself. Not even an automotive engineer could put a Cobra kit together without looking over the manual a time or two.

You actually have an advantage, because not only can you consult the instruction manual that came with your Cobra replica, you also have this book. Consulting your manufacturer's manual and this book gives you the best chance to avoid mistakes, which of course saves time and money.

If you've pored through both books and you're still having difficulty figuring out what to do next, you have other resources. There is a good chance that the manufacturer of your kit has its own online forum. You can also call your manufacturer's tech support line with questions. Use all the resources at your disposal so

Like the chassis, the front spindles are powdercoated in gloss black—first class all the way!

In the lower-right corner of this photo, you can see the Factory Five Racing Mk4 Complete Kit Assembly Manual. If you are also creating an FFR Mk4 Complete Kit, read this great resource often and carefully. Along with this book, it makes your build much easier. If you are creating some other manufacturer's Cobra replica, read that assembly manual. Because our Mk4 was just released, FFR also sent the Mk3 manual to supplement the just-printed Mk4 Complete Kit Assembly Manual. Kudos to FFR for being so thorough!

that you can build the best Cobra replica possible. If you avoid mistakes, you'll likely be saving time and money.

Tools and Supplies

You're creating a car from the ground up in your garage. So you're going to need a professionally equipped garage, with plenty of high-quality tools. Rather than using discount tools, make sure that your tool chests and workbench walls are equipped with tools that are guaranteed for life. Our garage is predominately a Sears Craftsman shop. We also use Snap-On and Home Depot Husky tools.

Your kit manufacturer's build manual may also specify automotive specialty tools. We had difficulty finding snap-ring pliers that worked well for us for more than a month. Instead, we made a couple visits to a local machine shop and a pro exhaust system shop to borrow tools. After checking with several auto parts stores in our area, we finally obtained an inexpensive set of four mini snap-ring pliers, both internal and external, that worked perfectly.

In the Factory Five Racing Mk4 Complete Kit assembly manual, there is a very helpful list of tools, which I don't copy here. Your assembly manual is likely to have a similar list. Just note that to create a quality kit car, you need to use first-class tools and supplies. Going cheap could prove much more costly than going first class.

Shop Safety

In every technical or how-to article I've written through the years, I have always stressed shop safety. I've actually been to pro shops and seen professional builders not being safe. That doesn't happen in my home shop.

Still, despite taking all kinds of safety precautions, accidents happen. Follow all of these safety guidelines to reduce the chance of making an unwanted trip to the emergency room:

- Be sure you have all the tools needed to do the job properly and safely. That includes eye protection, the right clothing, gloves, and enough space in which to work and store the car's parts.
- Remember that you're building a car that has more performance capabilities than most cars on the road. Only work on your Cobra when you're alert and full of energy.
- Make sure your kit is on sturdy jack stands when you're working under the car. Never use just a jack, no matter what.
- Have an up-to-date fire extinguisher at the ready at all times. Be sure that your car battery is disconnected whenever you're working on the vehicle's electrical or fuel system.
- Keep kids away from the work area.
- If your garage doors are open, don't leave your work area unattended. This is important both from a safety standpoint and also to prevent someone from wandering in and walking off with some of your Cobra components. And don't permit a bunch of people in your shop while you're working. They could get hurt. Shop safety is paramount.
- Make sure your cherry picker (engine hoist) has a load capacity that well exceeds the weight of your engine and transmission.
- Be sure that your electrical tools all have a proper ground. If you're working alone in the garage, have someone periodically check on you.
- Your shop needs to be well lit and well ventilated.
- If you are working under your chassis, use portable safety lights that have caged bulbs.
- Clean up spills as soon as they happen and dispose of any solvents or liquids in hazardous waste containers.
- Don't let a friend drive your car.
- Always wear your safety harness.
- Keep your build area clean at all times, especially after each work session. Put away your tools, fasteners, and components. Don't do as we did and place a box on top of a bag of rivets. We couldn't find those rivets for two months and had to buy more from a hardware store. Anyone need some rivets?

Use care and common sense at all times while you're working on your Cobra. If you do, it goes a long way toward preventing silly mistakes or having an accident.

CHASSIS, SUSPENSION AND BRAKES

As with many car builds, the construction can't start until the disassembly stops. You might not necessarily think that is the case with a brand-new kit. What makes this a necessity with the Factory Five Racing Mk4 Complete Kit, as well as for other variants of the FFR Cobra replicas, is the fact that the Mk4 kits are shipped with the bodies installed on the chassis.

Deconstruction Begins

Many of the 62 aluminum panels that comprise the cockpit, the trunk, the driver-side and passenger-side footboxes, and the engine bay, are pre-installed.

Typically, one fastener per panel holds each panel in place. So the aluminum panels are put in place, but they haven't been drilled and riveted yet. That's for you and your talented crew to perform. At first sight of all those loosely placed aluminum panels, you may feel overwhelmed. Never mind. When you're marking, drilling, and riveting them into their permanent locations, you feel as though you're building an airplane.

In a sense you are, these FFR Mk4 roadsters are veritable land rockets.

After safely storing away the carpet and the dash, you need to remove the hood, trunk lid, and doors from the chassis. A pair of gloves, 1/2-inch socket, ratchet, 5/8-inch wrench, pair of scissors, and three friends can make this job a snap. Use a secure place to store these body panels where they won't get trampled on or scratched. The gloves are to prevent you and your buddies from getting fiberglass cuts from any of the body's or panel's edges. Since the body is very light, it is possible for two people to lift it off the chassis. However, having a friend on either side to pull the sides of the body away from the frame rails is a big help.

After the doors are inside your house, or in the attic, or somewhere super safe, remove the hood. Our Cobra hood is under my bed. The fasteners are in a marked Ziploc bag with the other body fasteners in a box, and we actually know where that body fastener box is in the garage.

With the decklid stored safely, it's easy to appreciate that your Cobra is

nicely constructed. Before going on to the next step of unfastening bits, take a gander at those virgin aluminum body panels that have been formed by some real car craftsmen, whether they're Factory Five Racing employees, E.R.A. technicians, or whomever. Okay, that's enough of a break. The Quickjacks are next.

At this point, we believed we had all of the body fasteners and body panel bolts and nuts removed. With two neighbors standing by for doing light yet careful lifting, we attempted to remove the body off the chassis.

I should mention that just before this exciting step, we placed some wood floor panels on the garage floor. We formed a nice wood pad frame for our Factory Five Racing Mk4 roadster body to repose upon until we need to put it back on the chassis. The FFR assembly manual indicates that it's also okay to store the body outside. Since we had the garage space, we figured that this curvaceous form should stay inside. The daily drivers needed to be in the driveway for the coming months.

Since the body didn't separate from the chassis with our first lift

---

attempt, I lay on the creeper and rolled under the car. (The Mk4 chassis/body was on four sturdy jackstands, one at each corner of the frame. So, it was very safe for me to be under the car.) Sure enough, I found a small screw on each side of the body, which holds the back lip of the body to either frame-rail side, a little bit in front of where the openings are for the rear wheels. The FFR assembly manual didn't mention these screws. Perhaps they are just used in shipment. Regardless, I removed the screws and secured them in the Ziploc bag and box.

With all the fasteners and the Quickjacks in storage, the body lifted off easily. Unfortunately, I didn't get a photo since I was occupied lifting the nose of the fiberglass body.

Project 1: Disassembly

Unbolt Driver's Door

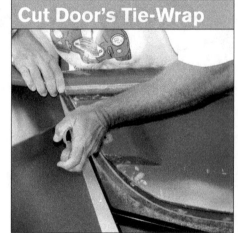

1 *You need to disassemble parts of the car before you can reassemble it. One of the first steps is to remove the doors. Using a wrench or socket and ratchet, remove the two bolts that hold the door to the hinge. The doors are fiberglass and weigh less than 10 pounds, so one person can do this job without a problem.*

Cut Door's Tie-Wrap

2 *Use a pair of scissors to cut the plastic tie-wraps that hold each door closed.*

Remove Doors

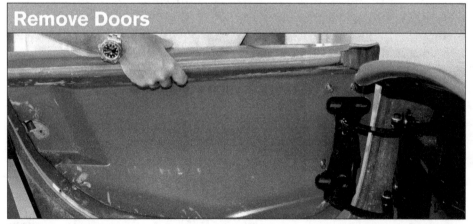

3 *After freeing the two bolts and the tie-wrap, the doors are light and easy to lift and store securely. Place the door fasteners in a Ziploc plastic bag and label the bag, before putting all the body fasteners in a box and storing in a memorable place. With the doors removed, you can see that there are component boxes everywhere. Because our three-car garage was filled with FFR Mk4 boxes and components and a 1934 Ford roadster pickup project in the third garage stall, we stored the doors, hood, and trunk lid in a spare bedroom. But keep in mind that you need a two-stall garage-type area to assemble the Cobra and the area of a single garage to properly store most of the parts.*

Remove Decklid

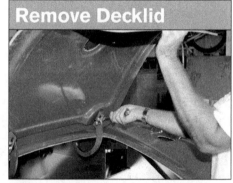

4 *There are two hidden hinges, one on either side of the trunk-lid, that hold the lid in place. Use the same socket and ratchet to remove the locknuts from the bolts and secure the fasteners in a marked Ziploc plastic bag, which in turn goes in the body fastener box. The decklid is light (fiberglass) and can be removed by one person, though two are preferable.*

Remove Rear Quickjacks

5 *Dad removes the rear Quickjacks with alacrity and places the fasteners and Quickjacks in the same Ziploc marked bag and box.*

Lift Body Off Chassis

6 *Lift the body off the chassis to begin installing the underpinnings of the car.*

Aluminum Panel Removal

When we lifted off the Mk4's fiberglass snakeskin, we were in form-follows-function design and engineering excellence. The aluminum panels nestled among the FFR's space frame tubular chassis are precision measured, cut, and folded, and fit together precisely. Upon inspection, we immediately recognized a challenge to our building prowess. Panel ends overlap each other. So if they were removed from the chassis, we wouldn't know where to drill certain panels for riveting. We were looking at an elaborate, 3-D jigsaw puzzle where every piece was the same silver-aluminum color.

In the Mk4 assembly manual, the directions say to mark the panels along the frame so you know where to drill the rivet holes for when the panels are riveted back onto the chassis.

That approach works great for the panels that don't overlap, but doesn't work at all for those that do. So, the Smith men made an executive decision to mark all the panels very painstakingly and also indicate where panel ends fit under or over each other. Also, where the panels overlap each other, we drilled the panels before removing them. According to the FFR manual, you can have rivets every 3 inches or every 2 inches. Factory Five Racing provides enough rivets for 3-inch spacing. They also provide a rivet-measuring/drilling tool that has holes in it every 3 inches. Going with the notion that more is better, we marked drill holes for the rivets every 2 inches.

Final installation of the aluminum panels was a rather complex process, very much like a 3D jigsaw puzzle with overlapping pieces. Therefore, we took great measures (pun intended) to accurately measure, mark, drill overlapping panels, and snap numerous photos showing how the panels go back together. We also used a blue Sharpie marker for the driver's side and a black Sharpie for the passenger's side. In hindsight, we really did have a well-engineered plan for ensuring these panels went back in and were relatively easy to silicone and rivet into place. Our master plan for careful aluminum panel fitment went well.

Project 2: Panel Removal

Mark Driver-Side Trunk for Drilling

1 *In this case, it is a good idea to work from the back to front, because the upper trunk floor requires drilling. Mark the trunk floor and place a dot every 2 inches. The only panels to be drilled now are the ones that overlap.*

Otherwise, remove the panels and drill them outside the car. FFR provides an aluminum drilling template that's pre-drilled with 2-inch-spaced holes on one side and 3-inch-spaced holes on the other side. You simply decide whether you want your rivets to be spaced 2 or 3 inches apart. Factory Five supplies enough rivets for having them spaced 3 inches apart.

Clamp Walls to Chassis Tubes

2 *The panel-marking procedure includes drilling those aluminum panels that overlap each other prior to removal. Drill the passenger-side trunk wall. Look closely at this wall and you see we've also marked openings that need to be filed* or trimmed. These panels fit well, but precise trimming in high spots enables them to fit perfectly, which the ultimate Cobra deserves.

Vacuum Clean Work Area

3 *It is very important to keep your work area clean. Make sure the cockpit rear walls align properly. We clamped them to the chassis square tubes prior to drilling, when we had panel overlapping panel. Using this approach ensures optimal aluminum panel fitment and alignment. Be sure to thoroughly mark these aluminum panels prior to removal and drill the panels that overlap. Take numerous photos also, so you can put this king-size jigsaw puzzle back together.*

Project 3: IFS Installation Preparation

Install F Panels

1 *Before installing the car's IFS, install the engine bay's F panels. Specifically, mark, remove, and silicone the back side of the panels where they meet with the frame, put back into place, clamp, drill, and rivet the panels into their permanent home in the engine bay. If you're not building an FFR, you probably don't have these panels.*

Inspect Components

Install Grease Fittings on Control Arms

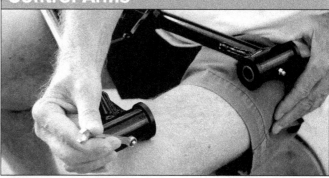

3 Each lower control arm has two Zerk (grease) fittings. Use a wrench to torque them as shown, but be careful not to overtighten and strip them. In the case of an FFR Mk4, use a 5/16-inch wrench. Here's a helpful tip: Dab your finger into the white lithium grease and spread it around the end of the neoprene/steel sleeve ends in the lower control arms before installation. The extra lube helps eliminate suspension squeaks. It may make the sleeves easier to install.

2 The IFS consists of the following: upper control arms, lower control arms, ball joints, Zerk fittings, and fasteners. Tools used include: a vise on a workbench, 13/16-inch socket, 5/16-inch wrench, 15/16-inch wrench, torque wrench, thread locker, 3/8-inch wrench, 3/4-inch socket, ratchet, and white lithium grease.

Tighten Lower Control Arm

4 After using lithium grease on the neoprene/steel sleeves, install the lower control arms. While holding the control arm parallel to the ground, torque the lower control arms to the specified torque setting indicated in your assembly manual. FFR's Mk4 lower control arm bolts are torqued to 100 to 110 ft-lbs. We used our shop stool and a box to hold the control arm parallel to the ground while torquing. I also held the box-end wrench while Dad applied force to the torque wrench. To accept OEM arms, the rear bushing mount is wider. Use the large shim washers to take up the additional space.

Prepare to Assemble Upper Control Arm

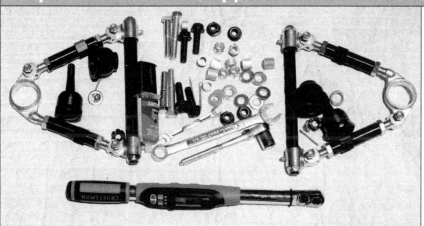

5 For assembling and installing the adjustable upper control arms, you need ball joints, ball joint boots or sleeves, upper control arms, fasteners, thread locker, a vise, 3/8- and 3/4-inch wrenches, a 3/4-inch socket, and a torque wrench.

Install Upper Control Arms

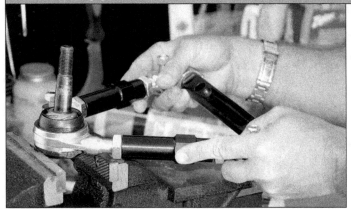

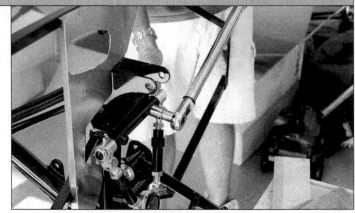

6 *After applying blue thread locker to the upper ball joint threads, place the ball joint in a bench vice, grab the upper control arm, and tighten it. Then use a 3/8-inch wrench to screw the Zerk grease fittings into the ball joints.*

7 *Using the two vertical-mount holes on the 2 x 3-inch tube, install the upper control arms to the chassis. Torque the bolts to 100 to 110 ft-lbs. The arms simply slide into the chassis brackets.*

Independent Front Suspension

This is where the fun begins!

Front Shock Absorbers
Factory Five Racing includes some pretty phenomenal shock absorbers in the Mk4 Complete Kit. Koni coil-overs have won many races on sports cars and racing machines all around the world. But before you can install the Konis on your front suspension, you need to assemble the coil-over springs onto the shock bodies.

This is where a high-quality pair of snap-ring pliers comes in handy. If you don't have a pair, borrow one from a local machine shop, or perhaps rent a pair from an auto parts retailer.

Project 4: Front Shock Absorber Installation

Prepare to Install Shock Absorbers

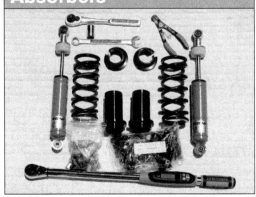

1 *To assemble and install the front Koni coil-over shock absorbers, use the following tools and components: snap-ring pliers, 3/4-inch wrench, 3/4-inch socket, ratchet, torque wrench, Koni front shock set, IFS components, and insulated clip hardware.*

Install Coil-Over Sleeve on Shock Body

2 *Place some white lithium grease on the shock bump stop before sliding the coil-over sleeve over and past the bump stop. Screw the spring seat on the coil-over sleeve, making it closer to the unthreaded end of the sleeve.*

Be sure to slide on the unthreaded end of the sleeve first, so that it sits on the snap ring on the shock body. Remove the snap ring from the coil-over hats with a snap-ring pliers. Slide the rubber bump stop approximately 2 inches down on the shock shaft. Place the spring and hat on the shock and rotate the spring seat up the sleeve to make sure the spring pushes the hat tight against the end of the shock. Make sure the slot in the snap ring and the opening in the spring hat are not aligned, and then install the snap ring on the spring hat. (The FFR Mk4 Complete Kit assembly manual provides detailed photos of this operation.)

Install Shock on Control Arm

3 *Pass the shock body through the upper control arm with the shock body facing up, and hang the shock by temporarily running a long Philips screwdriver through its upper attachment holes. Do this to attach the .43-inch shock spacers that are supplied for the lower control arm in the FFR Mk4 Complete Kit.*

Attach Zip-Ties to Spring Hat

4 *After making sure that the spring is properly seated on the shock, run zip-ties through the holes in the spring hat and around the spring to prevent the spring from becoming unseated.*

Measure Shock Spacers

5 *The FFR .43-inch shock-to-lower-control-arm spacers are a bit oversize; they measure .438 inch on the micrometer. This means that you need to use a flat file to make the spacers the correct size to fit on either side of the lower shock end and within the lower control arm mount.*

Torque Bolts on Shock Absorbers

6 *After filing the lower .43-inch spacers to the correct size and installing the lower-control-arm-to-shock fasteners, install the supplied .675-inch top mount spacers and the top mount bolts, washers, and locknuts. Torque the upper and lower shock-to-control-arm fasteners to 40 ft-lbs with a Craftsman digital torque wrench. Torque the bolts to the specifications recommended for your manufacturer's kit. (The FFR Mk4 Complete Kit assembly manual has a front-suspension torque specs chart.)*

Front Spindles

The front spindles are very well constructed and are powdercoated black. Installing them to the upper and lower control arms is easy. What's a bit more of a challenge is installing the front hub assembly on the spindles. It's a very tight fit. The fitment of your spindles to hubs may be looser than ours. If so, you're lucky. If not, you need to evenly sand/hone the spindles, which eventually enables you to place the hub assemblies on the spindles. As with everything regarding the building of your Cobra replica, use care in sanding the spindles, so that they remain round.

Project 5: Front Spindle Installation

Assemble Front Spindles

1 Front hubs and spindles, steering arms, IFS components, a 13/16-inch socket, torque wrench, needle
nose pliers, and a rubber mallet are all used in assembling
the front spindles, hubs, and steering arms. See those
bent steering arms? We discovered that FFR mistakenly
shipped us the steering arms for an FFR 1933 hot rod.
Everyone makes mistakes. After we notified FFR that the
steering arms were for a different kit, the correct arms
arrived the next day. They included the shipping labels and
paid for the return shipping to get the 1933 steering arms
back to them.

Torque Castle Nut

2 After using the supplied fasteners and torquing the
castle nut on the ball joint, we realized we needed
to use more spacers to properly install the cotter pins. We
purchased two grade-8 spacers for each side from the
local hardware store and fit those beneath the castle nut
and above the supplied spacer. You may not need additional spacers.

With all in place, torque the castle nut to 80 to 110
ft-lbs. To prevent the spindle from rotating while torquing
the castle nut, you can wedge a rag-wrapped 2- x 4-inch
piece of wood between the chassis and the spindle. The
blue ball-joint boot goes on the bottom.

Repeat this same process with the top castle nut and
cotter pin, making sure that you install the black ball-joint
boot before fastening the castle nut, torquing it to 95 ft-
lbs, and installing the cotter pin.

Install Cotter Pin in Castle Nut

3 With everything aligned properly, hammer and
spread open the cotter pin, thus locking the castle
nut into a secure and safe position. A flashlight helps to
find the hole for the cotter pin.

Inspect Front Suspension

4 With the work completed, take a step back and
admire your work. Also inspect the front suspension
installation to make sure your work here is correct.

Torque Steering Arm

5 Upon receiving the correct steering arms from FFR, torque them to the specified 60 ft-lbs.

Torque Hub Nut

6 After evenly sliding the front hub into place, use the large 36-mm socket to torque the hub nut to 225 to 250 ft-lbs of torque. With such a high torquing force, you can secure a drum and piece of 2 x 4-inch wood underneath the spindle to keep the entire front end steady. Be sure to install the hub dust covers before moving to the next step.

Front Disc Brakes

The final component to any front suspension system has to be a good set of disc brakes. Spending the bucks on building a top-notch Cobra replica doesn't stop here. But if the disc braking system is top quality, as it is with FFR's Mk4 Complete Kit, the car most definitely stops straight, swift, and true.

By the way, FFR, in partnership with Wilwood Brakes, now offers optional larger four-piston-caliper front disc brakes.

Project 6: Front Disc Brake Installation

Inspect Components

1 The front disc-brake assembly consists of the 11-inch rotors, two-piston calipers, brake pads, fasteners, flex lines (in a large plastic Ziploc bag), torque wrench, 16-mm wrench, 12-mm socket, ratchet, and thread locker.

Install Caliper Slider Pins

2 First install the caliper slider pins on the caliper by using a 16-mm wrench, a 12-mm socket, the ratchet, and the supplied bolts. Hold the retaining nut with a 16-mm wrench and torque the bolt head at the front of the caliper.

Torque Caliper Slider Pins

3 After you have snugged up the slider pins, verify that they have been properly torqued. Make sure to torque the caliper slider pin bolts to 25 ft-lbs. Use a 16-mm wrench to firmly hold the pin while you use the other hand to torque the bolt. Anywhere in the range of 23 to 26 ft-lbs should be fine. Also install the supplied slider grease boots on the slider pins (per FFR manual photo).

Install Steel Clips

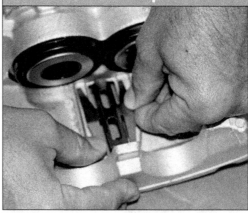

4 On the ends of the caliper hangers, place the steel clips from the hardware bag. Press them (by hand) into place on the cast hangers.

There are four clips that go on the ends of the hanger that must be installed with the long tab facing out, as shown here. The two remaining caliper clips go in the center of each caliper. Locate the long tab where the caliper pistons are and the short tab on the other side.

Install Caliper Clip

5 Viewing the center caliper clip from the outside of the caliper offers another perspective on how the clip is installed correctly.

Lubricate Caliper Slide Pins

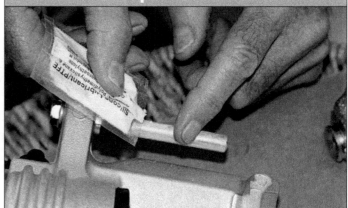

6 To ensure proper function of the front brake calipers, use the supplied silicone grease on the caliper slider pins.

Install Caliper Hangers

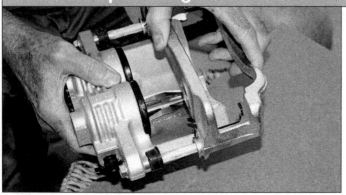

7 Use your hand to slide the caliper hanger onto the caliper.

Slide Rubber Boots over Slider Bolts

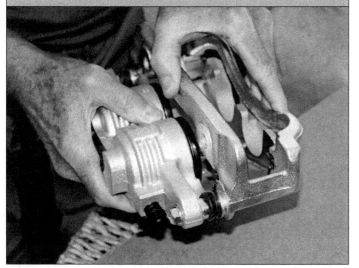

Install Brake Pads

9 *After assembling the caliper and caliper hangers, install the brake pads. Look at the backside of the brake pads to differentiate the inside pads from the outside pads. The studs on the inside pads are out near the ends of the pad. The studs on the outside pads are close to the middle.*

8 *Together, the caliper and caliper hanger look like this. Push the rubber boots over the lip on the caliper bracket to properly seal the slider bolts.*

Clean Brake Rotors

10 *Before pushing the brake rotors onto the hubs, clean them thoroughly with brake cleaner.*

Torque Caliper Bolts

11 *With the rotors on the hubs, mount the caliper on the spindle. The brake fluid bleeder must be at the top of the caliper. Torque the caliper mounting bolts to the specified 95 ft-lbs.*

REAR SUSPENSION AND DIFFERENTIAL

Factory Five Racing Mk4 kits can be built with a solid-axle, live rear suspension in a four-link configuration standard, or with an optional three-link setup. The vast majority (95 percent) of FFR Cobra replicas have been built over the years using a solid-axle rear suspension, which is less expensive than an IRS FFR Mk4.

We decided to source the new IRS from Tasca Ford in Massachusetts, but did order it from FFR. It's actually the same suspension found in a 1989–1998 Lincoln Mk8.

Here's a helpful hint if you wish to use a new IRS in your FFR Mk4. If you contact Ford Racing directly to order an IRS, they may tell you that the company doesn't make new Lincoln Mk8 IRS systems anymore. That's what they told us. We then contacted Factory Five Racing and learned that we could obtain a new IRS through the Tasca Ford connection. The alternative is to get a used IRS from an automotive salvage yard.

Our rear disc brakes are Mustang Cobra single-piston disc brakes, purchased new from Factory Five Racing. They are used with the optional IRS and also purchased as an option.

Unlike with the IRS, we had an easy time getting a hold of these brakes. These and the ones we've already installed in the front stop the lightweight FFR roadster in rapid fashion.

If you'd like even more clamping power, Wilwood recently announced optional brakes for the FFR Mk4 roadster.

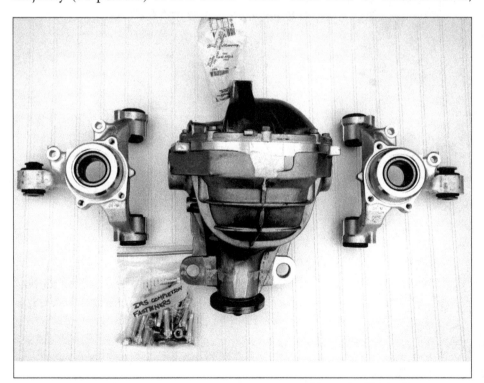

For this stage of assembly, you need the IRS hub carriers, center section, completion package, components, torque wrench, marker, snap-ring pliers, 3/8-, 3/4-, and 15/16-inch sockets, ratchet, 3.25 pints of gear oil, and 4 ounces of friction modifier.

Project 1: Independent Rear Suspension Installation

Rotate Differential into Place

1 *The correct way to install the differential is to place the unit on your hydraulic floor jack vertically. Point the nose (driveshaft flange) upward and align the halfshaft holes front to back with the chassis. Slowly jack the pumpkin into the IRS cage of the frame, while someone else holds the differential steady to keep it from falling. Our floor jack did not have a high enough lift, so we improvised with a roll of duct tape. A block of wood works better.*

With the pumpkin in the cage, correctly position it while it's resting on the floor jack. Rotate the differential so that the holes for the halfshafts run longitudinally. Tilt it forward to get the center section correctly positioned for installation.

Install Rear Bolt to Hold Differential

2 *A bolt holds the differential housing bracket on the subframe. Use a socket and ratchet to torque down the locknut. But first, just fingertighten the bolt so you can align the differential with the other fittings. Use a rear bolt through the rear cover to hold it in place. The center section weighs at least 50 or 60 pounds, so you may need to use a floor jack.*

Install Center Section Bushings and Washers

3 *Install and align all bushings and washers in preparation to install the bolts. Carefully lift the front of the IRS center section and slide in one washer and one bushing for each side of the differential's front attachment ears. Be sure to have good support for the differential so you don't pinch your fingers. Use a large Phillips-head screwdriver to line up the bolt holes. Place the bushing and washer on top of each attachment ear, line up the holes, and then remove the screwdriver to drop the bolts in the holes.*

Install Differential

4 *The center section of the independent rear suspension looks very clean. Torque the bolts on the front that travel through the bushings, and then turn your attention to the rear of the differential and torque that bolt. All four of the differential fasteners, the two through the bushings in the front and the rear fasteners, get torqued to 110 ft-lbs.*

Install Lower Control Arms

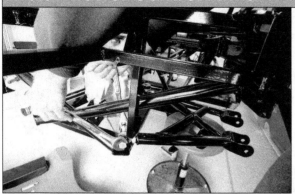

5 Use a 15/16-inch combination wrench and a ratchet and 15/16-inch socket to handtighten the rod ends with jam nuts into the lower control arms. Handtighten and then back them off four turns. Then install the lower control arms to the chassis with the shock installation mount hanging below the arm. Use three shims on the front side of the front rod end for both the left and right arms. Also install all of the supplied shims on the other rod ends on either side.

We found this extremely difficult and so may you. It's a bit easier to use a stool. Be as patiently precise as possible. When the car is finished, you need to have an alignment shop professionally install the appropriate number of shims and properly align the chassis.

With this accomplished, tighten all four bolts on each side, but don't torque yet. You are going to remove the two rear bolts, install the right number of shims, and align later. You can see it's also a good idea to prop up the lower arm with a stool or something to make your job easier.

Inspect Upper Control Arms and Rear Coil-Over Shock Assembly

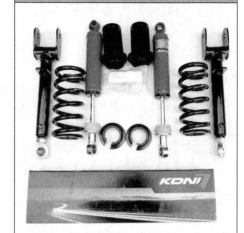

6 The upper control arms, Koni coil-over shocks, Roadster/Coupe rear shock kit, snap-ring pliers, 3/4-inch wrench, 3/4-inch socket, ratchet, and ruler are all used to finish the IRS installation.

Install Upper Control Arms and Assemble Coil-Over Shocks

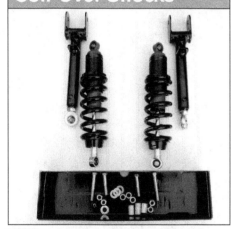

7 Place the lower shock eye in a vise and use a spring compressor to compress the spring. Then use the snap-ring pliers to install the snap-ring collar on the shocks. Very carefully follow the same correct procedure you used to assemble the front coil-over shocks.

Mount Rear Shocks on Suspension

8 Begin the installation process by mounting the coil-over to the chassis mount. Guide the bolt through the shock-mounting bracket and shock eye. Use two of the smaller-length spacers, one on either side of the shock eye. Align the lower shock eyes on the bracket of the lower control arms, guide the mount bolt through the eye, and use the large spacer. As with the front shocks, the shock body goes toward the top. Don't torque the rear shock bolts yet; wait until the suspension is aligned.

Inspect CV Axles, Upper Control Arms, Hub Carriers and Hubs

9 How cool do the CV axles, upper control arms, hub carriers, and hubs look? Even better than their looks is how well they perform when installed in an FFR roadster IRS chassis.

Install Passenger-Side CV Axle

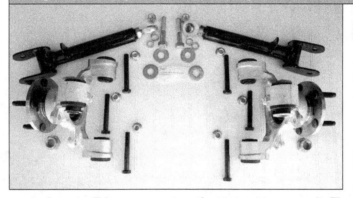

10 After you've placed towels on the arms to prevent scratching the CV axles or the lower control arms, carefully push the CV joints into the differential by hand and rest the CV axles on the lower control arms. The arms are in position if you can feel and see when they reach their appropriate position.

Install Hub on Spindle

11 Make sure that the hub is even with the spindle and press it into the spindle opening. Use your workbench vise to make sure that the hub is pushed down into the spindle evenly. Before putting the hubs through the spindle, they may require a small amount of fine and even sanding so they fit in the spindle holes. Because our CV axles were fully assembled, we didn't have to put them together the way the FFR MK4 Complete Kit assembly manual details. But you may need to.

Inspect Suspension Components

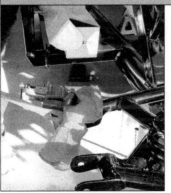

12 Installing these components may be the most challenging step in building your IRS. The rear spindles/hubs, fasteners, upper control arms, and ears for upper control arms all have come together to create one unit. The disc-brake caliper mounting holes are on the back part of the spindles when you install them.

Bend Out Control Arm Lower Attachment Ears

13 If the attachment ears on the lower control arms are too narrow to accommodate the spindle sleeves, you can wrap a shop rag around the attachment ear to protect the black powder-coat. Use a hand vise and a pry bar to pry out the ears before negotiating the spindle sleeves into their new home. Prying against the hand vise enables you to pry out the entire attachment ear in an even fashion. Slide the hub assembly and spindle on the outer CV joint.

Bend Upper Control Arm Attachment Ear

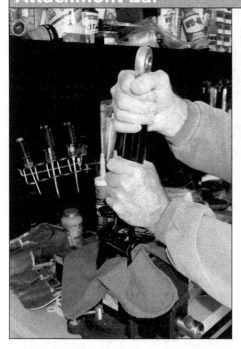

14 The attachment ear for the upper control arm to the top spindle sleeve also needs a bit of fine-tuning. Use the workbench and a trusty shop rag for protecting the powdercoat to offer some stationary and stout leverage. You now know why many mechanics have Popeye forearms.

Tighten Hub Bolt

15 Tighten the three fasteners for each rear spindle and the 36-mm hub nuts, but don't torque them yet; the independent rear suspension is aligned later.

Project 2: Rear Brake Installation

Inspect Brake Components

1 From this photo of the rear brake components—the rotors, calipers, flex brake lines, and brackets—you'd guess that the rear brake installation is a snap. The tools used to install the rear disc brakes are a 3/4-inch wrench, 3/4-inch socket, ratchet, 3/16-inch hex key, flat-head screwdriver, torque wrench, and some thread locker.

Separate Rear Caliper from Caliper Bracket

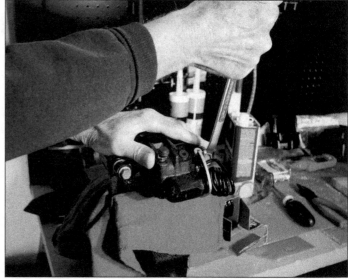

2 Using Rust-Oleum gloss black, paint the brake caliper adapter brackets and the brake flex line brackets in preparation for installing the brakes (not shown). The first actual build step is disassembly. While held in a workbench vise, remove the caliper bracket from the rear brake caliper.

Loosely Attach Brake Caliper Bracket and Torque Caliper Mount Plate

3 *Attach the rear brake caliper bracket to the dry adapter plate using just the upper bolt and spacer. The threads on this bolt and all the others that don't use locknuts get Loctite or other thread locker prior to installation. After locating the proper placement of the driver-side caliper-adapter plate (mounting bracket), torque the fasteners to 32 ft-lbs. Unless you're an experienced mechanic, you should always consult the manual.*

Install Caliper and Put in Brake Pads

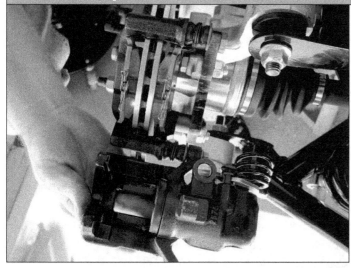

4 *Assembling the driver-side caliper and installing the brake pads can be a snap. Be sure to use Loctite thread locker on any bolt threads that don't also have a locknut, as with the caliper adapter bolts.*

Install Passenger-Side Rear Brake

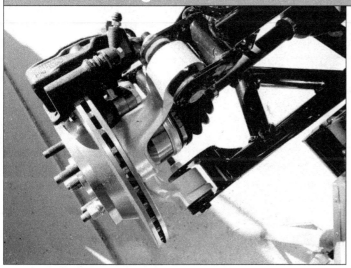

5 *Slide the rotor into place on the hub, swing down the caliper, and be sure to torque the caliper fasteners to the appropriate torque specifications, as indicated in your manufacturer's kit assembly manual. Your rear disc brakes should look something like this when you're finished with this part of the assembly, which also completes the installation of the IRS and brakes.*

PEDAL BOX, STEERING SHAFT AND STEERING RACK

Surely you've had plenty of *aha* moments in your life, when you realize something that's as true and as pure as the day you passed your driving test to get your first license. As we have throughout the build of our Factory Five Racing Mk4 Cobra, we've enjoyed countless of these profound events. The most impactful of these epiphanies is the enduring notion that we're building an automobile from a prodigious collection of parts, now located in perhaps 50 or so boxes, a chassis, and four BFGoodrich Radial TA tires. We're going to be counting on the fact that this Cobra replica is going to be safe, reliable, and fun to drive.

We don't expect it to be a miles-per-gallon champion, but it should be a well-constructed and solid road burner. And it should be as solid as if Factory Five Racing had built the car. It's a profound notion to wrap your head around. For this huge reason, it's of utmost importance that we resolved to be painstakingly careful at every phase of the roadster's build.

Firewall and Footbox

There are 62 aluminum panels in the Factory Five Racing Mk4 roadster. When we marked, drilled, and removed the overlapping pre-installed panels from the Mk4 chassis, we did grow rather weary of disassembling all these panels. This was likely due to our having to really concentrate and be diligent about accurately marking and drilling the appropriates panels, so that we could begin to put the 3-D jigsaw puzzle back together.

We were really excited to get the aluminum panels riveted in place, because we could then see the car take shape. It was also interesting to find out how well we marked the aluminum. We found this out by installing the firewall and the front of the driver's front footbox panel.

By the time you've reached this point in the build of your Cobra replica, you may begin to realize that this project is going to be finished. After all, there's a rolling chassis just waiting to receive the drivetrain.

Project 1: Footbox Panel Installation

Old Footbox Front Panel

1 *You need a drill, a 1/8-inch drill bit, a riveting gun, silicone, and a caulking gun. These tools are required to install the firewall and driver's footbox panels, and secondary body fasteners into place.*

After marking the firewall for drilling with the FFR-supplied piece of ruler-size aluminum that has the 2- and 3-inch spaced holes, drill the panel off the chassis. At this step, you're drilling the holes in the aluminum firewall panel to serve as a guide for drilling into the powdercoated square-frame tube.

Then weave the silicone around the drilled holes. Fasten the firewall panel with one of the sheet-metal screws that originally held it into position. Also use a clamp or a helper to hold the panel in its proper place, before drilling the rest of the rivet holes into the square chassis tubes. Drill the holes and then install the rivets with a rivet gun. Some of the holes may need to be enlarged with an auger.

Pedal Box Assembly

Consider the installation of the pedal box assembly. The Cobra better go when the accelerator pedal is pushed, and it better stop swift, straight, and true when you step on the brake pedal. Every system that's constructed and/or installed must be done correctly so all the systems work harmoniously and without flaw.

Project 2: Pedal Box Assembly Installation

Inspect Pedal Box Assembly

1 *Factory Five Racing supplies a well-made Wilwood pedal box assembly in the Complete Mk4 kit that is designed to use a cable clutch. You can use a mechanical clutch or install a hydraulic clutch. The pedal box assembly installation requires: pedal box hardware; supplied bare steel* brackets; pedal box assembly; 1/2- and 9/16-inch sockets; 3/8-, 11/32-, 1/2-, and 9/16-inch wrenches; 3/16-, 1/4-, and 1/2-inch drill bits; electric or air drill; 1/8-, 9/32-, 3/16-, and 5/16-inch hex keys; hammer; workbench vise; razor knife; file or grinder; and the trusty and elusive snap-ring pliers.

Front Footbox Driver-Side Panel

2 *Here is the installed front driver-side footbox panel. Install it by marking, drilling, siliconing, and riveting the panel into position. Take your time so the panels are properly aligned. Don't silicone or rivet the bottom inside wall; the engine bay inside-wall panel slips underneath this panel a bit later in the build. Please ignore the components attached to our front footbox panel. We mistakenly marked, drilled, siliconed, and riveted the front footbox panel that was pre-installed in the chassis. This replacement panel was in one of the boxes. If you're building an FFR Mk4, Factory Five has this panel pre-installed, and you won't make the same mistake we made. Also notice the brushed finish to our panel.*

We sanded every panel with 180-grit sandpaper and applied Sharkhide metal protectant to all the panels that are not covered. Sharkhide is easy to apply and protects any unpainted metal for 10 years or more. It gives the metal a satin shine, which, like the one we built sets your Cobra replica apart from all others.

Paint and Drill Hole in Brake-Switch Bracket

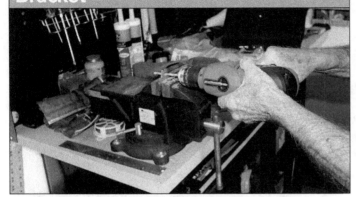

2 Rust is not your friend, so spray paint the supplied bare-metal brackets with black paint. Factory Five Racing recommends using gloss-black Rust-Oleum paint, as this is the closest match to the gloss-black powder-coated chassis.

Use inside and outside snap-ring pliers to remove the retaining clip from the brake-pedal pivot sleeve, then pull the sleeve and remove the pedal. Next drill a 3/16-inch hole in the brake switch mount. Use the workbench vice and wear safety glasses to do this operation in the safest and best way.

Install Brake Switch and Brake Pedal

4 Attach the brake switch with the provided fasteners and reinstall the brake pedal. Use your snap-ring pliers and the snap rings to safely secure the pedal arm. We were unable to reinstall all four washers but could get three washers into place. Although we tried several times to get the inside washer to stay in place while routing the pivot sleeve into position, the washer kept falling out. After installing the three washers, we confirmed that the pedal action was still smooth and without any slop. Perhaps you can install all four.

Install Brake-Switch Mount

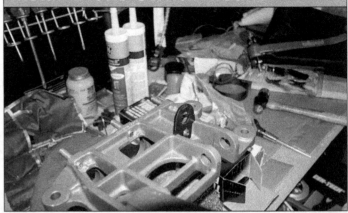

3 Install brake-switch pedal mount between the brake-pedal mount tabs closest to the brake-pedal pivot holes with the black number-8 screw and the appropriate hex key and locknut. Notice we also painted the brake-switch pedal mount gloss black after drilling the 3/16-inch hole in the mount.

Remove Snap Ring and Bore Out Clutch Quadrant

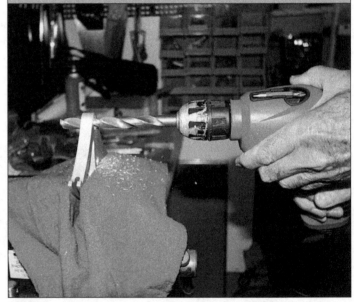

5 The FFR Mk4 assembly manual indicates that the provided longer pivot sleeve gets a retainer ring attached to it. Use this pivot sleeve to locate the clutch quadrant, if you have a mechanical clutch. If the pivot sleeve does not fit through the attachment hole in the clutch quadrant your next step is to bore out the pivot sleeve hole in the clutch quadrant by holding it in the workbench vice and boring the hole with a 1/2-inch drill bit and the electric drill.

Install Retaining Ring and Washers

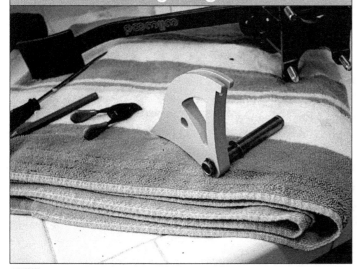

6 After precisely honing out the clutch quadrant to accommodate the longer pivot sleeve, install the pivot sleeve into the clutch quadrant and retaining ring in its proper place on the end of the pivot sleeve. Install the ring with snap-ring pliers. A supplied copper/Teflon Wilwood pedal washer is in its correct position on the other side.

Attach Clutch-Pedal Stop Mount

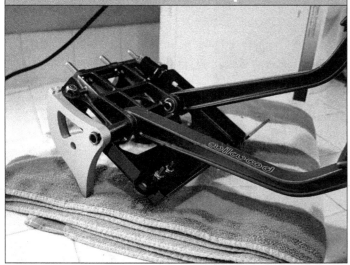

8 Using the provided 1/4-inch socket-head screws and locknuts, simply screw the clutch-pedal stop mount to the bottom of the pedal box. Torque the locknuts to the specified amount in your assembly manual. We torqued the nuts to the FFR-specified 50 ft-lbs. As the FFR assembly manual indicates, you may need to file off the stud end so the clutch-quadrant aluminum pivot sleeve clears the stud end. Notice in the previous photo that we did need to perform this operation.

Attach Wilwood Pedals to Bracket

7 Three button-head bolts with locknuts and one stud with a locknut attach the Wilwood pedals to the underside of the pedal-mounting bracket. (Notice we've painted our bracket gloss Rust-Oleum black to prevent rust.) If you're using a cable clutch, make sure that you install the stud underneath where the clutch-pedal pivot sleeve boss goes. Tapping the stud with a hammer and punch secures it so you can tighten with the supplied locknut on the other side.

We already had the clutch-pivot sleeve boss and clutch quadrant installed in this photo, but realized we had installed the stud in the wrong way. With the stud installed properly, the assembly should appear as shown.

Inspect Pedal Box Hardware

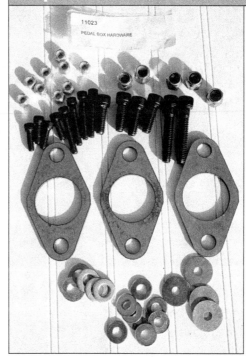

9 Installing the pedal box assembly with the supplied pedal box hardware is a relatively easy job. All of those fasteners look like overkill, but we didn't have any left over.

Drill Holes and Install Pedal Box

10 When placing the pedal box in the chassis, make sure that the brake pedal is in front of the 3/4-inch cross tube on the frame. After the pedal box is in place, mark the rear mount holes of the pedal box assembly on the 3/4-inch tubes. Then remove the pedal box assembly and drill the holes. The FFR Mk4 assembly manual does this process a bit differently than we did. Understand both procedures and then be sure you don't make a mistake.

After drilling the rear pedal-box mount holes, install the pedal box with the four 3/8 x 1-inch socket head screws through the front of the footbox wall. Install the locknuts that hold these bolts in place on the inside of the footbox. Also install the rear mount fasteners, since you've drilled the holes in the frame tubes.

Install Brake Master Cylinders

11 After threading a jam nut from the Wilwood pedals fasteners onto each of the Wilwood master-cylinder shafts, turn the threaded shaft into the threaded mount on the brake pedal and secure the master cylinder with the supplied fasteners. Repeat the threading and installing operation with the other Wilwood master cylinder into the pedal box assembly.

Tighten Pedal Box/ Master Cylinder Fasteners

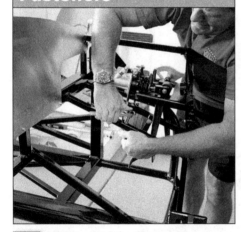

12 With all of the fasteners in place for the pedal box assembly, secure them with hand tools and torque each fastener to the torque specs in your Cobra kit's assembly manual. Perform a careful visual inspection of the entire assembly before tightening all of the nuts and bolts, to be certain that everything lines up properly and the assembly is correctly installed.

Install Screw-in Quadrant Pedal Stop

13 Next thread the jam nut onto the 3/8 x 1.25-inch screw that FFR provided in the quadrant box. Push in from the bottom of the clutch-quadrant pedal-stop mount and install the clutch-quadrant pedal-stop screw, with the locknut hand-tightened for now.

Mount Clutch-Cable Adjuster

14 Push the firewall-mounted clutch-cable adjuster through its opening in the front wall of the footbox, and then use a 9/64-inch hex key and an 11/32-inch wrench to attach the screws to the firewall. If you're not using a cable clutch, this installation is unnecessary.

Pull Rubber Mount off Clutch Cable

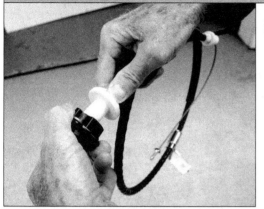

15 *Now that the clutch-cable firewall adjuster is in place, you can install the clutch cable into the clutch quadrant.*

Start by removing the rubber mount from the end of the clutch cable. Use a razor knife, file, or grinder to smooth out the cable end before the clutch cable is installed.

Install Cable into Quadrant

16 *With the plastic now smooth, you can slide the clutch cable through the adjuster and place the cable end back from the quadrant.*

Install Accelerator Pedal

17 *Separate the arms after unpacking the throttle pedal. To fit the box, you must fold the arms. The accelerator pedal sleeve needs to be removed and re-positioned, so that the arms are as shown here. When re-assembling the arms with the 1/4- x 3/4-inch screw and locknut from the pedal box hardware, leave the Allen screw hand-tightened for now so you can later adjust the fitment angle for optimal accelerator pedal action.*

For such a small component, you wouldn't think very many tools would be needed to install the part. However, there are several necessary tools required. You need: a 5/64-inch hex key; 3/8-, 7/16-, and 1/2-inch wrenches; wire cutters; a 1/4-inch drill bit; a hand drill; a Sharpie marker; and some masking tape.

To correctly mount the accelerator pedal to the mount plate in the footbox, you must align the pedal with the accelerator cable hole. This allows the cable to come out and go in straight, so the cable doesn't rub while going through the opening in its mounting point. Using the provided 1/4 x 1/4-inch screw and locknut from the pedal box hardware, install the top fastener first. The FFR Mk4 assembly manual says to install the top fastener while aligning it with the cable, marking and drilling the bottom attachment hole. Our second hole was already properly drilled.

If you are building a different manufacturer's kit, this may be a moot point. Also your FFR Mk4 may have both these holes already drilled, as ours was. Install the two fasteners and tighten them with the appropriate hand tools.

Install Accelerator Pedal from Engine Bay

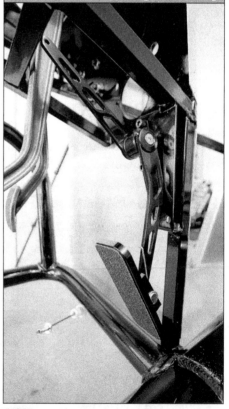

18 *If you're left-handed, as I am, the best place to install the go pedal is from inside the engine bay, especially if you need to drill the bottom attachment hole into the mounting plate.*

Cut Off Cable End and Thread Cable Through Top of Pedal

19 Cut the cylinder end off the throttle cable, using sharp wire cutters to prevent the cable from fraying. Remove the throttle cable from its sheath and thread it through the hole in the top of the accelerator pedal arm and through the retaining locknut, which is in the accelerator-cable components-assembly plastic bag (for FFR Mk4 builders).

Install Throttle Cable Sheath on Firewall Side

21 After threading the throttle cable into the throttle sheath from the inside of the pedal, tighten the cable sheath to the firewall with the supplied retaining nut. Place a piece of tape on the end of the throttle wire to prevent the wire/cable from retracting into the sheath.

Inspect Cable to Throttle Pedal

20 Everyone makes mistakes, and you're not going to install every part correctly the first time. We realized we had made a mistake when we initially routed the throttle through the wrong side of the accelerator pedal hole. The round ball stopper should be on the passenger's side of the hole as shown. Having the cable installed in this fashion allows the throttle cable to run smoothly into the sheath.

Steering Shaft and Steering Rack

The installation of the steering shaft is rather easy. You need to be careful when you're working with the set screws that are in the steering shaft adapter; they are quite small.

After we installed the steering shaft, we covered the entire assembly with Sharkhide, which protects the metal for many years. We also like the satin finish that we get from using Sharkhide.

Putting the steering rack in place is a bit more of a challenge.

Project 3: Steering Shaft and Steering Rack Installation

Inspect Steering Shaft and Installation Components

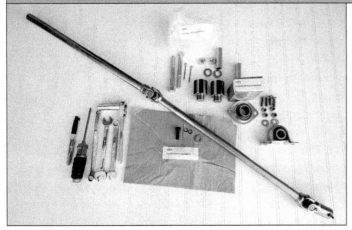

1 Unpack the steering shaft assembly and organize the tools for this installation. The steering bearings/hardware, the steering shaft, and the manual steering rack and adapter are all going into your C-car chassis, which is an exciting prospect. This kit is taking shape. After patting yourself on the back, be ready with a 5/32-, 3/16-, and 5/16-inch hex key. You also need: 1/2-inch, 9/16-inch, and 10-mm wrenches; Sharpie marker; drill; 3/16-inch drill bit; Philips screwdriver; 15-mm deep socket; and a ratchet. Then remove the splined adapter from the end of the steering shaft. The first steering shaft procedure is to remove the splined adapter from the steering shaft by using the correct-size hex key. Replace this adapter with the new one that is supplied in the steering shaft assembly components and hand-tighten the set screws with the hex key so they don't fall out.

Loosely Mount Bearing to the Footbox Front

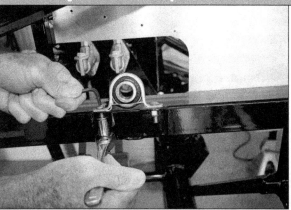

Loosely Mount Top Pillow Block on Chassis

3 Be certain that the set screw is facing toward the rear of the car. Hand-tighten the fasteners that install the top pillow block to the chassis. You need some wiggle room to properly install the steering shaft, so just barely snug on those pillow block fasteners is fine for now.

Install Steering Shaft into the Footbox

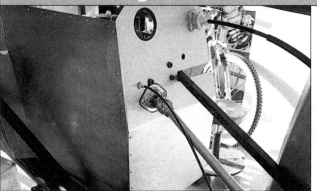

4 With both pillow blocks installed, you can do the fun part—slide the steering shaft into the footbox from the engine bay side through the low bearing. Beautiful!

2 With the set screw toward the inside of the footbox, mount the flange bearing to the footbox front, making certain that both sides of the flange are on the front side of the footbox plate.

Project 3A: Steering System Installation

Inspect Steering Rack, Fasteners and Tools

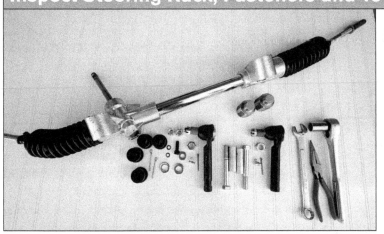

1 To install the steering rack assembly, you require the manual steering rack assembly with the steering system hardware. The inner tie-rod extensions (two standing cylinders just below steering rack) are only used with power steering racks. If you're installing a manual steering rack as we are, don't use these. You also need the two tie-rod ends, four bushings, and the following tools: needle-nose pliers, 3/4-inch wrench, 3/4-inch socket, and a ratchet.

Push Bushings and Sleeves into Mounting Bosses on Rack

2 The first order of business is to push the bushings and sleeves into the mounting bosses on the steering rack. You should be able to do this with your hands. If it's really tight, dab a little white lithium grease on the rubber before pushing it home.

Slide Steering Shaft onto Steering Rack

3 First, center the steering rack and align the steering shaft and adapter to the rack so you can easily push the rack onto the steering shaft.

Bolt Steering Rack in Place

4 It's easiest to bolt the steering rack into the frame by starting on the driver's side. Then swing the passenger's side into place and quickly fasten it. You can use a large Philips-head screwdriver to get the installation holes properly centered.

Torque Steering Rack Fasteners

5 According to the FFR Mk4 assembly manual, torque the steering rack fasteners to 110 ft-lbs. If you're building another manufacturer's kit, be sure to torque the bolts to the amount specified in your build manual.

Finish Tie-Rod Ends

6 The assembly manual specifies for the tie rod ends to be installed next. Before doing this, if your outer tie-rod ends are raw steel, paint the ends with primer and gloss-black Rust-Oleum before installing the grease fittings. To prevent rusting, allow the tie rod ends to dry before installation.

With the gloss-black Rust-Oleum all dry on the tie rods, it's time to screw-in the grease fittings with an open-end wrench.

Jam Nut and Outer Tie Rod on Inner Tie Rod

7 Upon screwing the tie-rod end and jam nut 1 to 2 inches down onto the steering-rack rod, you may realize the tie-rod end cannot mate with the steering arm. The tie rod end sticks out too far. You may need to shorten the steering-rack inner tie rods.

Cut Off Tie-Rod Ends

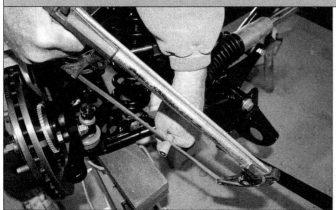

8 Cut the tie-rod threads 3/4 inch shorter. Center the steering before doing any cutting. Temporarily place the steering wheel on the steering shaft and have the three-pronged wheel with the prongs at 9 o'clock, 3 o'clock, and 6 o'clock, respectively, going clockwise. First, protect the threads of the tie rods with masking tape. Using WD-40 on the hacksaw blade makes the cutting go faster. Make sure you measure carefully—don't cut off too much of the tie-rod threads, or you may be buying a new steering rack to replace the one you just ruined. Make sure the blade is perpendicular to the steering shaft so you get a straight cut.

Torque Tie-Rod End Castle Nut on Passenger's Side

9 With the correct-length tie rod, screw the jam nut and tie-rod end 1 to 2 inches onto the tie-rod threads. Then install the tie-rod end into the steering arm from below the steering arm on both the driver's side and the passenger's side. The FFR Mk4 assembly manual specifies that thread locker is used on all threads where jam nuts and adapter screws are not used. So before you screw down the castle nuts, use blue Loctite on the threads. Torque the castle nuts to 25 ft-lbs.

Install the Cotter Pin

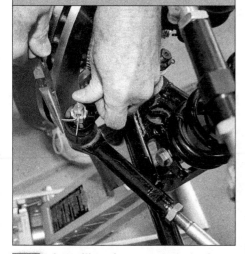

10 Installing the cotter pin is the last operation required to get the steering rack fully installed (before turning your attention to the upper steering shaft). Remember, a cotter pin goes on both sides. Use a hammer and needle-nose pliers to install the cotter pins.

Project 3B: Steering Shaft Mounting

Inspect Upper Steering Shaft and Fasteners

1 You need the upper steering shaft, the steering system hardware, and the following tools to install the upper steering shaft: 5/32-, 3/16-, and 5/16-inch hex keys; 1/2-inch wrench; and rubber mallet.

Attach Steering Shaft to Lower Shaft

2 Carefully slide the steering shaft through the upper bearing and start the smaller upper-steering shaft into the lower steering shaft. Turn the upper steering shaft so that the recessed bosses for the spring washers are facing up and place the spring washers into respective positions as shown. With the rubber mallet, gently tap the upper shaft down until the upper clip just disappears into the lower shaft. Tighten the upper and lower bearings, as well as the set screw on the upper shaft. Your steering should now be spot-on.

FUEL SYSTEM, BRAKES AND FOOTBOX

Certain aspects of your Cobra build are likely to have you scratching your head and giving you the notion that you're in way over your ability level. If you've never bent fuel or brake lines and installed them in a car's chassis, this could be one of the most daunting challenges for you.

Factory Five Racing supplies all the fuel and brake lines, as well as all of the fittings, insulated chassis hangers, and rivets for accomplishing all of the fabricating. Other kit manufacturers also supply all of the materials for doing your own chassis plumbing.

As with anything, breaking a big task into small logical steps can ensure progress through the phases of the fabrication until the brake and fuel lines are all bent, fastened to the chassis, coupled together, and fully installed. We divided this process into easy steps and were able to accomplish the fuel line and brake installation, despite the fact that this was just our second time plumbing a chassis.

The more basic and repetitive work, such as applying Sharkhide and silicone, drilling, and riveting aluminum panels into position are good for breaking up the difficult tasks.

Accomplishing the rudimentary tasks builds confidence in your ability to take on the more complex work. The satisfaction of having something else done also brings with it the very real notion that you're that much closer to having the entire car built. There really is a psychological boost that comes from seeing forward progress.

Installing the Fuel Tank

There were many occasions during our Cobra build project where we fooled ourselves one way or another. Let me explain. At first glance it seems that installing the fuel tank, for example, is very straightforward. If you look at the opening in the chassis behind the independent rear suspension, you might conclude something like, "Hey, there's plenty of space; putting the fuel tank in that opening should be a snap." That's what we expected. But I'm here to tell you that it wasn't that easy, but after a prodigious struggle, we did install that darn tank.

Project 1: Fuel Tank Installation

Inspect Fuel Tank Assembly and Required Tools

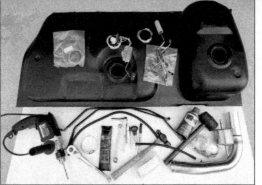

1 *If you're building an FFR Mk4 roadster, you need all of these items for installing the fuel tank. If building another manufacturer's kit, the components are very similar: OEM fuel tank components, fuel strap fasteners (not shown), secondary body fasteners assembly, fuel line components, fuel lines (not shown), 9/16- and 5/16-inch-deep sockets, ratchet, 7/16-inch wrench, hammer, marker, punch or flat-blade screwdriver, rubber mallet, 3/16- and 5/16-inch hex keys, floor jack, light lubricant, drill, 1/4-inch drill bit, and a buddy.*

Inspect Fuel Strap Fasteners and Plastic End Caps

2 *These four fuel strap fasteners with the locknuts and the washers may look all innocent and easy to work with, but they're not. Actually, these fasteners work fine. But the fuel straps are made of spring steel, hold the fuel tank in place in the back of the chassis, and were difficult to stretch around the tank to get the tank installed.*

Install Vent in Fuel Tank

4 *To aid in the installation of the filler neck, apply some lube before pushing this white plastic vent into place in the vent gasket atop the fuel tank. Spray some WD-40 or other light lubricant on the plastic vent.*

With sufficient lubricant on the plastic, push the vent into place inside the rubber vent gasket on the fuel tank. The vent should go in firmly but without too much effort.

Set the rubber O-ring gasket properly into position before installing the fuel pump pickup. The O-ring gasket is held down by the fuel pump pickup retainer ring and the fuel tank.

Install Rubber Fill Neck Gasket

3 *Before strapping the fuel tank into place in the chassis, install all of the components that go into the fuel tank. First, insert the large rubber filler neck gasket in the side of the fuel tank. By hand, place the rubber vent gasket in a small hole on the top of the fuel tank.*

Installing the Fuel Pump

The Factory Five Racing Mk4 Complete Kit includes all the components required for installing your fuel system, except the fuel pump. There's a good reason for that. If you're going to use a carburetor on your engine, you can either use the original-style mechanical fuel pump that is at the front-bottom driver-side corner of a Ford V-8 small- or big-block. Or you can use an electric fuel pump that's either externally mounted or located in the fuel tank. Your Mk4 Complete Kit includes 5/16-inch hard fuel-supply lines and 1/4-inch hard fuel-return lines. Also included are flexible rubber fuel lines in the same sizes, with quick connects for mak-

ing the connections to the engine and fuel tank from the hard lines. If you're going to use throttle-body electronic or stack-electronic fuel injection, you must use an external or internal electric fuel pump. The fuel lines supplied in any kit are sufficient for supporting an engine that has up to 300 hp. In other words, the lines are big enough in diameter to flow sufficient fuel to your carburetor or electronic fuel injection system if your engine makes less than 300 horses. If your engine produces more than 300 horses, these supplied fuel lines won't flow enough petrol. You are better off using an in-tank electric fuel-pump that can flow an abundance of fuel without overheating or burning out. Inline external

electric fuel pumps are not as efficient at pumping the fuel up to the EFI or carburetor as an in-tank pump; they tend to overheat. Since in-tank electric fuel pumps are immersed in cool fuel, they don't overheat. That's why every modern automobile has in-tank electric fuel pumps.

We initially fought this simple logic. We already had everything supplied from Factory Five Racing, so we figured we could use it. But, the hard truth was that the engine we were having built produced about 500 hp, so both the electronic fuel injection system we were employing and the electric fuel pump better be up to snuff.

In the end we did what any car enthusiast should do. We called

Aeromotive directly. Aeromotive is the premier manufacturer of electronic fuel delivery systems for auto race engines, marine applications, and high-performance show and street automobiles.

Aeromotive's director of marketing communications, Jesse Powell, gave us the hard and cold facts.

To adequately supply enough fuel for a 500-hp engine, the minimum requirements are an in-tank electric fuel pump and 3/8-inch-diameter (-6) fuel lines. Jesse prefers his customers use a 1/2-inch-diameter (-8) supply line. However, he said we'd be perfectly safe using 3/8-inch-diameter supply and return lines and one of

the company's in-tank Aeromotive fuel pumps, in addition to an Aeromotive inline fuel filter.

From a pumping standpoint, our fuel delivery problems were solved. We ordered the appropriate Aeromotive products and did some investigating regarding getting the correct-diameter hard and flexible fuel lines.

Project 2: Fuel Pump Installation

Wire Fuel Pump

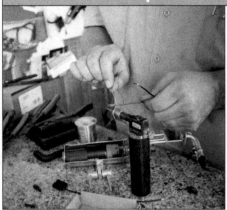

1 We decided to use an in-tank fuel pump, so we needed to have the Aeromotive electric pump wired to the NAPA fuel pickup. Dennis Clark, owner of Carlsbad Automotive Technology, wired the pump and installed it in the fuel pickup basket for us. We opted to have a professional auto electrician perform this operation, because we wanted to be certain that this was done correctly. The electric fuel pump is surrounded by fuel, so we wanted our pump to be 100 percent wired and grounded correctly.

Install Fuel Filter on Pump

2 Here's what the Aeromotive in-tank fuel pump and the NAPA fuel pickup looks like. A required modification was to have 3/8-inch threaded pipe fittings welded to the end of the supply and return lines on the fuel pickup. Warner's Mufflers in Oceanside, California, provided the precise welding. Snap the friction-fit cloth filter on the bottom of the fuel pump. This filter makes it quite a challenge to insert the in-tank pump and pickup basket assembly into the fuel tank. If the engine in your Cobra replica makes less than 300 hp, you can follow the directions in your kit's assembly manual and use the supplied components.

Install Mounting Collar

3 With the fuel pickup in place in the fuel tank, slide the mounting collar into position and tap it into place with a punch and a hammer.

Install Fuel Level Sender

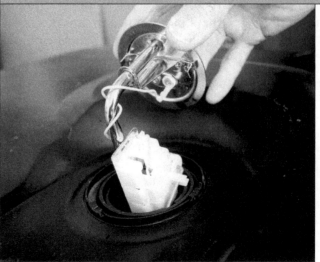

4 Installing the fuel level sending unit is similar to installing the fuel pickup, although it's easier than with the fuel pump and filter sock. Install the O-ring before placing the fuel level sender in the tank. Tap in the mounting collar (clockwise), after the sender is installed.

Install Retaining Bracket and Drill Tank Flange Hole

5 Spray some light lubricant on the fuel-filler neck tube's rubber gasket, then fit the end of the filler neck into the gasket's side of the tank.

Slide the retaining bracket onto the fuel filler tube. With a Sharpie, mark where it needs to be installed on the fuel tank. Drill out the hole with a 1/4-inch drill bit.

Attach Retainer to Tank

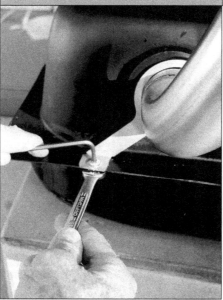

6 Use the supplied 1/4-inch bolt and locknut to attach the fuel neck filler tube retainer bracket to the tank flange, which is tightened with the appropriate-size wrenches.

Install Plastic End Caps

7 You may need to use a bit of gentle persuasion in the form of a rubber mallet when pushing on the four plastic end-caps that cushion the fuel tank flange from its tubular steel-framed location in the rear of the chassis.

Install Rear Fuel Straps

8 Attach the rear strap to the rear of the chassis with the supplied fasteners. The passenger-side strap is longer than the driver's side, because it has a longer distance to stretch around the groove in the passenger's side of the fuel tank.

In the FFR Mk4 assembly manual, the instructions advise to use a floor jack to raise the fuel tank into position. We used a floor jack, our rolling shop stool, a plastic drum, and a piece of wood for propping the tank in order to attach the straps. You need to coerce those somewhat flexible spring steel straps to the front attachment points in the chassis. (The driver's side is easier than the passenger's side.) For the passenger's side, get the strap close enough to install the front fastener and locknut. Use a wood 2 x 4 and the floor jack to jack directly under the steel strap so that it stretches as far as possible. Use vise-grip pliers to close the gap between the strap and its attachment point, which enables you to finally tighten the locknut to the bolt.

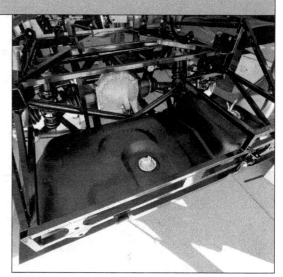

9 You may have to wrestle a bit with the fuel tank, before you are finally able to securely attach all four-strap fasteners fore and aft. As you might find in the building of your Cobra kit, some of the jobs that appear easy are actually the difficult ones. And the ones you expect to be challenging can sometimes be simple.

Adding Cockpit Aluminum

Now that our muscles have healed from the strain of installing the fuel tank, we move to the satisfying task of riveting-in some sheet aluminum in the Cobra's cockpit.

Project 3: Footbox Installation

Gather Tools and Materials

1 *With the addition of Sharkhide protectant applied to the sanded aluminum panels, these are the tools required for installing the aluminum: drill, 1/8-inch drill bit, rivet gun, silicone, number-8 self-tapping screws, caulking gun, number-8 hex nut driver, ruler, marker, brake cleaner, acetone, and rags. Work with the mounted aluminum panels, the packaged aluminum, and the secondary body fasteners provided by FFR (or other kit manufacturer).*

Install Passenger's Footbox Top

2 *Mark and drill the holes in the top flat surface only. Silicone and rivet this panel only along the bottom of the 2-inch-square frame crossmember. Use two number-8 sheet-metal screws to hold the panel temporarily along the other small chassis tube. In most cases, you space the rivet holes every 2 inches, which may mean you need to purchase additional pop rivets. Also, if you have a wide frame tube, drill two rows of rivets with 4-inch spacing and stagger the two rows 2 inches (shown here).*

Install Transmission Tunnel Cover

3 *You should have no trouble finding the A-shaped transmission tunnel piece; it has a very distinctive appearance. Drill, silicone, and rivet this panel into its transmission-tunnel home within the cockpit.*

Mount Passenger's Footbox Inside Wall

4 *Find the passenger's footbox inside wall. Mark, drill, silicone, and rivet the panel to the front-tunnel A-panel and the top of the passenger's footbox.*

Install Passenger's Footbox Wall

5 Silicone the panel and install with temporary screws before drilling through both panels and riveting them in position in the passenger's footbox. In addition, you need to apply silicone to footbox floor.

The passenger's footbox floor resides atop the flanges from the footbox walls. Silicone the wall flanges and rivet the footbox floor into place on the passenger's side.

Fasten Outer Footbox Top

6 Another unique-looking aluminum panel is the outer passenger's footbox top. Silicone the flange that's located between the outer top and the outer wall. Use number-8 sheet-metal screws to attach the two components. Then apply silicone to the remaining flanges and install the outer wall/top of the passenger's footbox with the supplied rivets. Be sure that the rear edge is flush to the chassis and free of the door hinge before you rivet the panels.

Apply Corrosion Protection

7 Rather than powdercoat all 62 aluminum panels, you may opt to use Sharkhide protectant. After sanding the exposed side of the aluminum, apply Sharkhide to the passenger's floor bottom. Since it's the next panel to be riveted, mark, drill, apply silicone, and rivet the passenger-side floor next. The FFR aluminum panels fit extremely well. You may need to trim a few edges here and there. When working with the panels, avoid cutting yourself on a sharp edge.

Apply Silicone to Chassis and Floor

8 Apply plenty of silicone to the chassis where the floor rests on the chassis. Don't rivet to the round chassis rails, but do apply silicone to all the rails. The top edge of the tunnel does not get riveted yet, though use silicone here as well.

Rivet Passenger's Floor to Chassis

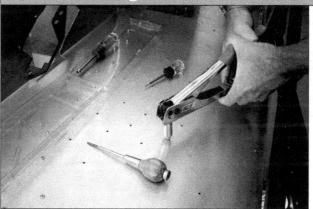

9 A pneumatic riveting gun makes this job much easier. Alternatively, your hands can get a great deal of exercise, if you use a manual gun as we did.

Install Driver's Footbox Floor

10 *The only surface that isn't drilled yet is the outer flange. Otherwise, be sure to drill, silicone, and rivet the floor to the chassis rails. This job isn't very challenging. To properly position the floor in the chassis, you need to gently flex the aluminum panel in on itself to put it in place. After it is in position, we didn't need to trim any edges. We imagine the same sort of success for you.*

Rivet Driver-Side Floor

11 *With the driver's floor in position and aligned with a few temporary screws and a punch or two, rivet the floor into place.*

Install Side Floor and Footbox

12 *A pneumatic rivet gun makes riveting this panel into position much easier and quicker. Take your time to ensure that the panel is properly aligned on the frame rails, so that the rivets firmly anchor the panel to the frame. After all, the driver's seat will be placed above this panel.*

Fasten Side Outer Walls

13 *The driver- and passenger-side (shown) outer walls are the next panels to receive the drill, silicone, and rivet work.*

Install Inner Foot Box Wall

14 *If you're building an FFR Mk4, there is a different driver-side inner footbox wall to accommodate a Ford 4.6-liter V-8 engine. Consult the Factory Five assembly manual to identify the wall to use if your powerplant of choice is the 4.6-liter Ford unit. Otherwise, install the wall as shown here. The front flange tucks behind the front wall that was previously left unriveted. Use some silicone on both sides of this flange, drill, and rivet.*

Install Rear Tunnel Cover

15 Mark, drill, apply silicone, and rivet the rear tunnel cover, also called the U-joint cover.

Install Rear Corners

16 Given their triangular shape, the cockpit rear corners are more challenging to install. First, mark and drill the corners on their bottom flange where they meet the chassis. Then silicone and rivet these well-engineered aluminum panels in their place on either side of the U-joint cover.

Install Rear Wall

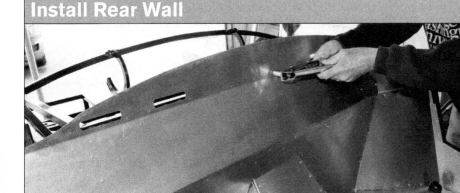

17 Mark, drill, apply silicone, and rivet the rear cockpit aluminum wall to the Mk4 chassis.

Installing Fuel Lines

You have some decisions to make before you fabricate and install your fuel lines. If you're like us and you're using a high-horsepower small- or big-block V-8 to power your Cobra replica, you need to custom fabricate larger-diameter lines.

We initially visited a few local auto parts stores to check out the fuel lines they sold, but nothing met our custom requirements. We wanted to run stainless-steel hard lines and stainless flex lines with Teflon liners for our ultimate Cobra build. After doing some investigating at several auto components specialists in our area, we found a hydraulic systems and components shop in nearby San Marcos called Rupe's.

First the experts at Rupe's hooked us up with 3/8-inch (-6) pre-bent stainless-steel fuel supply and return hard lines. After we installed the lines and bent them farther for a custom fit, we then had Rupe's fabricate the stainless Teflon-lined flex lines and all fittings to the appropriate length for the fuel tank hard lines.

We didn't purchase the flex lines for hooking up the hard lines in the engine bay to the engine's Holley Avenger electronic fuel injection until after we had shoehorned the engine and transmission in the chassis.

Project 4: Fuel Line Installation

Inspect Fuel Lines and Components

1 If your mill makes fewer than 300 hp and you're building an FFR Mk4 Complete kit, consult your FFR assembly manual. We used Rupe's stainless-steel hard and flex lines with fittings that are 3/8-inch diameter for both the supply and the return sides. We also used an Aeromotive in-tank high-performance racing fuel pump, a NAPA in-tank basket/fuel pickup that has had 3/8-inch fittings welded to the supply and return sides, an Aeromotive inline high-performance fuel filter, and NAPA insulated fuel line clips.

The tools we used include: tube bender, 3/16-inch drill bit, drill, rivet gun, Sharpie marker, tape measure, and some of the OEM fuel tank components. There's also a third fuel line in the photo that doesn't match the other two. It was used as a template to bend the Rupe's stainless-steel hard lines.

Install Inline Fuel Filter

2 There are myriad places to install the Aeromotive filter, but the most accessible is along the rear corner of the passenger-side frame rail. Being careful to mount the Aeromotive fuel filter so that it isn't going anywhere, use a large round insulated clamp, drill the frame rail, and use a 3/16-inch rivet to hold the fuel filter firmly into place.

Route Fuel Lines

3 Being careful not to have the fuel lines touching each other or rattling against the FFR frame rails, rout and attach the stainless-steel hard lines, both supply and return, next to each other with the riveted and insulated fuel-line hangers holding them to the round passenger-side frame rail. One thing we should mention is that these hydraulic-application hard lines and flex lines are rated for several thousand pounds of pressure—much more pressure than even the Aeromotive racing fuel pump can dish out. The lines and the fittings are not going to leak.

4 Rupe's custom-fabricated our stainless hard lines to our specifications, with high-pressure fittings at each end. We also asked them to bend the stainless. Notice how nicely they wrap around the front of the passenger-side foot box. To do this yourself, accurately mark where to bend the lines with a Sharpie and then use a tube bender, the same kind used to bend brake lines.

Install Flex Lines

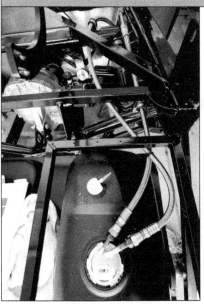

5 With the engine installed, measure the distance from the hard lines to the Holley Avenger throttle-body electronic fuel injection atop the engine and order some stainless flex lines.

Warner's Mufflers in Oceanside, California, welded-on 3/8-inch male pipe fittings to the fuel pickup at the fuel tank. The flex stainless-steel fuel lines have the Teflon liners to our measurement specs, complete with the female leak-free fittings. Be sure to securely fasten all the flex-line fittings to the hard-line fittings with the correct-sized wrenches. If you do, these hydraulic high-pressure lines don't leak!

Install Return Flex Line

6 To minimize the number of connector fittings, the return line should be longer than the supply line. Remember that the supply line has an Aeromotive fuel filter in the middle of it, which prevents you from running hard lines of equal length.

Be smart when plumbing your Cobra replica with the fuel lines. The lines must be well away from any moving components and they must be held away from each other and from the frame to prevent rubbing and rattling.

Building Brake Lines and Installing Master Cylinders

If you're constructing an FFR Mk4 Complete Kit, you're at the point in the build where you mount the master cylinder reservoir. Factory Five supplies two nice Wilwood reservoir kits complete with all the fittings and hoses for doing the job.

Our challenge is that we have a tri-pack, brushed-aluminum remote reservoir from Kugel Komponents that needs to go in our Cobra replica.

Project 5: Brake Line and Master Cylinder Installation

Use Capture Nut on L-Bracket

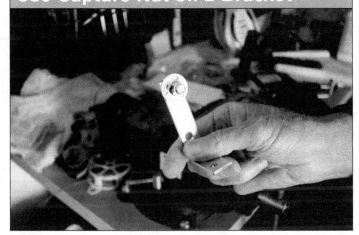

1 Use two L-brackets equipped with two capture nuts to mount the custom brake reservoir system.

Rivet Capture Nut to L-Bracket

2 After drilling three holes to mount the capture nut to the L-bracket, rivet the capture nut in place on the bracket. The L-brackets go behind the firewall in the cockpit-side of the car. You can install the custom remote reservoirs on the firewall. Clever, eh?

Mount Platform for Remote Reservoir

3 To mount the remote reservoirs on the firewall side, use tin snips to cut some aluminum from an unused panel to form a platform mount for the remote reservoirs.

Fabricate Brake Reservoir Platform

4 You can buy a block of aluminum at a steel and aluminum manufacturer that sells to the construction trade. Hollow it out and drill holes in the aluminum to install the brake reservoirs. Use a hole saw and an electric drill. Then use a small hacksaw to finish the job. With the needed area cut out, smooth the edges with a flat file. After seeing all this effort, you may opt to use the supplied Wilwood remote reservoir and install it on the front footbox wall, as FFR advises. But we would still do the custom work; we're happy with how the system turned out.

Install L-Brackets to Mount Reservoirs

5 Install the enhanced L-brackets for the reservoir mounting-block's capture nut on the cockpit side of the firewall.

Install Brake Reservoirs and Route Brake Lines

6 The custom brake reservoirs are mounted with that aluminum rectangle for a reason—the aluminum block lets you fill the canisters with brake fluid after the body is installed. Route the rubber brake-line hoses to the front and rear master cylinders using the FFR-supplied fittings. If you need a bit more rubber hose, given the different location of these reservoirs, you can purchase more hose in the same size as FFR's. FFR advocates using just one master cylinder and routing the rubber hose with a T-connector setup. With these fancy aluminum reservoirs, you have one canister for the rear brakes and a separate canister for the front brakes. You could use the canister in the middle, if you had installed a hydraulic clutch, but we opted for a cable clutch because FFR also supplied the cable clutch components.

Install Front Brake Fasteners

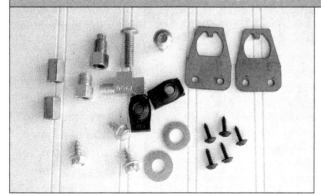

7 For the front brake lines and the front flex lines at the brake calipers, follow the instructions in the Mk4 Complete Kit manual to the letter. Here is the flex line hardware found in the brake line components. The components for another kit may look similar.

Mock-Up Flexible Brake Lines

8 Mockup the flexible brake lines to make sure they're the correct length. We held ours to the brake calipers and turned the front wheels. FFR recommends installing the brake lines on the driver's side of the chassis and hooking up the fuel lines on the passenger side. We did as they advised with the fuel lines and brake lines.

Mount Laser-Cut Brake Brackets

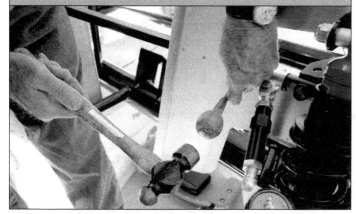

9 The laser-cut stainless-steel brake brackets go right behind the upper control arms. Center-punch the holes before drilling.

Drill and Rivet Bracket Holes

10 Drill the marked and punched holes for the brackets. The stainless brackets receive two 3/16-inch rivets to hold them fast.

Install Brake Line Adapters

11 Push the brake line adapters through the installed brackets from the outside in, and install the clips that secure them.

Attach Flex Brake Lines

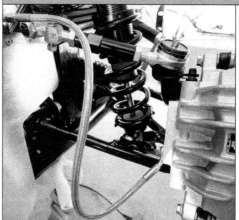

12 When attaching the flex brake lines, be sure to use a supplied crush-washer on either side of the brake caliper fitting. Then screw the other end of the line to the fitting on the chassis and hand-tighten for now. Screw in and tighten the brake-line T-fitting into the end of the driver-side brake adapter with a 1/2-inch open-end wrench.

Inspect Brake Lines

13 Use all the FFR-supplied hard brake lines. The trick is to use the lengths you have—don't cut any lines. If you cut them, you need to have an expensive line-flaring tool, and you need to be a tube-flaring expert to keep the lines from leaking.

Route First Front Brake Line

14 We used a junction fitting and one of the short brake lines; we didn't have quite enough brake line to reach the passenger-side adapter.

These brake lines bend easy, especially with a proper tube-bending tool. You can use a tube bender or the right size can or round item to get the job done. Be careful to keep your bends smooth and kink-free. When you have the line the way you want it, use the small, insulated line clips and the 3/16-inch rivets to fasten the line to the chassis. If this is the first time you've bent brake lines, you may wish to practice with your tube bender and some spare line. But the FFR-supplied lines are quite malleable, and it's hard to make a mistake.

Route Second Front Brake Line

15 Route the other front brake line from the front master cylinder to the T-connector on the passenger. Though there are several ways to route this tube, the recommended method is running the line from the 3/4-inch top tube at the footbox, where the master cylinders are located, to the T-junction on the driver's side. Drill a 7/16-inch hole just under that top frame tube to run the line through it.

Run Brake Lines

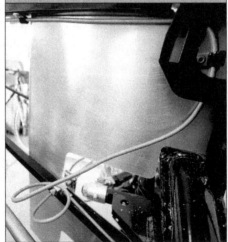

16 Be sure to use the supplied insulated brake-line clips and rivet them strategically to the 3/4-inch tube. Coil the line around a couple times and connect it to the T-junction box. To prevent leaks you're better off using this method than cutting and trying to properly flare the line.

Install Rear Brake Flex Lines

17 The rear-brake flex lines are installed similarly to the front brakes. If you have an FFR Mk4 with the independent rear suspension, be especially mindful of routing the flex lines away from any moving components (like the CV axles). Also the brake brackets are just regular unfinished steel; use gloss-black Rust-Oleum to prevent any corrosion. Use the supplied crush-washers on either side of the brake caliper bolt. Use common sense when securing the proper-length lines supplied by FFR.

Mock-Up Rear Brake Line

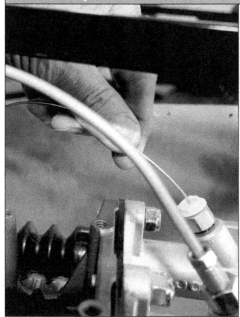

18 For a cleaner look, route the rear brake line from the rear Wilwood master cylinder inside the footbox. The challenge is that you don't want the brake line to interfere with any of the pedals. Use some wire to form a template of where you bent the actual brake line.

19 This part of the mockup wire shows where it's real tight and tricky. We managed to form our actual brake line, using this wire as the template. We tucked away the line here and used the insulated clips to mount the line well away from the pedals. If you run your line the way we did, be sure to close up the hole in the bottom of the footbox with plenty of silicone.

Route and Secure Brake Line to Frame Rail

20 Route the brake line along the driver-side frame rail and up the rear corner. Use the insulated clips to secure the lines every 12 or 18 inches. Because we have an IRS chassis, our brake lines are routed differently than an FFR Mk4 with a live-axle chassis. If you need to route your lines differently, keep the tubes away from any moving components and protected from the elements as much as possible.

Install Brake Line to T-Connector

21 As with the front brake line, the line to the T-connector gets a couple coils. We were a little short on brake lines, so we purchased an additional 50-inch line from NAPA (black line in the back). We probably had enough line, but it's more challenging to run the lines on an IRS-chassis car than on a solid-axle car.

Route Brake Line and Fill Reservoir

22 That extra brake line goes right to the passenger-side brake bracket. Remember to use the insulated clips and paint the rear brake brackets with gloss-black Rust-Oleum. For the rear brakes, use two 60-inch lines and one 50-inch line, along with the two flex lines that go to the rear calipers. Tighten all the brake lines fore and aft. Fill the brake reservoir(s) with DOT 3 brake fluid and bleed the brakes while checking thoroughly for leaks. The fluid leaks at the fittings if they're not sufficiently tight.

THE ENGINE

The original AC Bristol was just another British sports car; but once a healthy American V-8 engine was added, it became a legendary high-performance car. Equipped with the 427 side-oiler V-8 engine, the Cobra could accelerate 0–60 in less than 4 seconds. No other limited-production car could match that kind of performance in the mid 1960s. Thus engine selection largely defines the performance, personality, and overall tractability of the car.

A whole universe of engines can be fitted to a Cobra replica, and this includes the trusty original Ford Windsor and FE engines as well as the Ford Cleveland and Lima powerplants. While some purists maintain that a Cobra replica should be faithful to an original Cobra and house a Ford Windsor small-block or an FE big-block engine, the hobby has embraced all makes and models of V-8 engines. In fact, some are installing GM LS series engines into their Cobra because of the compact design, high-performance capabilities, massive aftermarket support, and ease of installation. While this may be sacrilegious for some, these combinations are becoming more popular.

Your choice of engine should hinge on a number of factors, including horsepower and torque targets (i.e., your ideal powerband), budget, and of course personal preference. Although we decided to acquire the engine parts and have a pro shop assemble our engine, many Cobra owners opt for crate engines for simplicity, convenience, and reliable performance. Many companies can deliver a turnkey engine to your residence. After all, you're assembling an entire car, and many do not want to build an entire engine from the block up.

Small-Block or Big-Block?

When it comes to powering the Cobra, you have to ask yourself, How

A universe of V-8 engines is available to power your Cobra kit car. While many fine small-block and big-block V-8s are available from other manufacturers, many Cobra owners select a traditional Ford V-8 to power their replica. I selected a Dart 351-based Windsor block that was stroked to 427 inches of displacement, and it produces 425 hp.

much is enough? What kind of handling characteristics are you seeking and how does the engine selection factor into that choice? Most Cobra replicas have a curb weight of about 2,400 pounds. Therefore the car is extremely light and has a power-to-weight ratio that few cars can match. For example, a Backdraft Racing Cobra replica with a 350-hp Ford 302 H/O small-block can propel the car to 150 mph. And that's just the tip of the iceberg, a high-performance 427-ci stroker small-block can reliably produce more than 600 hp and put the Cobra's performance into the stratosphere of supercar performance.

If you opt for a big-block you're taking on much more weight, but you can easily build an 800-hp engine. Typically, most aluminum big-blocks weigh 150 pounds more than a small-block from the same manufacturer. Adding more weight to the front of the car degrades handling characteristics, and therefore it is less agile through corners.

Whether you choose a small- or big-block engine, you need one set up for your particular application. Hence, the powerband of the engine must match the application. If your Cobra is going to be a street car, then you need an engine that produces good torque from 1,500 to 5,000 because that's the operating RPM on the street.

A small- or big-block engine with dual quad carbs, single-plane intake, large port heads, and a high-lift, long-duration cam that produces its best power from 6,000 to 7,500 rpm is not suited for the street. But an engine such as this is ideal for road racing because it spends most of its time at high RPM. Drag engines also spend much time at the top end of

the powerband. A race-type engine is such a pain to drive on the street because it doesn't idle evenly at stop lights and doesn't carburate well at lower RPM. Therefore, you often have to rev the engine and slip the clutch from intersection launches. And it doesn't pull very hard out of low-speed corners.

Ford Small-Blocks

The Ford Windsor small-blocks in 260, 289, 302, and 351 displacements as well as Clevelands in 351 and 400 displacements have been popular engines for Cobra replicas since the inception of the market. All of the small-block Fords have a deck height of 4.185 inches and easily fit into the Cobra. You can build these engines with any combination of stock components, but most owners build a small-block using premium components of forged crank, rods, and pistons, and opt for a high-performance set of aluminum heads.

Many Cobra owners opt to build a stroker combination on a stock cast-iron or aluminum block. Many of the stroker assemblies are less expensive than factory-rebuilt parts, so for many owners this is a no-brainer and they go with this option. The 302 with 3-inch stroke and the raised-deck 351 Windsors and 351 Clevelands with 3.5-inch stroke are excellent platforms for stroker combinations, as is the 400M, which is a taller-deck Cleveland.

For the 302, stroker combinations in 331, 347, and 355 displacements are popular. And for the 351 and 400 blocks, displacements of 383, 393, and 408 ci are popular stroker combinations. Scat, Eagle, Coast High Performance, and many other businesses offer high-quality stroker combinations to fit Windsor and

Cleveland blocks, so you can find a setup that works for your car and application.

Ford Big-Blocks

The Ford FE 427-ci side-oiler engine was standard equipment in the original Shelby Cobra, and many of the Cobra faithful opt to put an FE engine in their Cobra replicas. The FE (Ford Edsel) engines were built from 1958–1976 to power a wide range of Ford passenger cars, so there are a lot of blocks and engines available. Ford offered the FE in 332, 352, 360, 390, 406, 410, 427, and 428 displacements. A number of stroker combinations are available for the FE engine, including 434, 445, and 505 displacements. Survival Motorsports is a leading FE engine builder and offers a full line of engine components and services for FE engines.

The Ford 385 Series or Lima big-block engines are popular with owners who must have extreme displacement. The 370, 429 and 460 engines were offered from 1968 until 1967, and these replaced the MEL (Mercury, Edsel, and Lincoln) engines. The Lima engines were extensively installed in large passenger cars, trucks, and of course Mustangs and high-performance Torinos. The standard 429 engine featured a two-bolt main bearing cap, cast-iron cam, cast-aluminum pistons, forged-steel connection rods, hydraulic cam, and non-adjustable rocker arms.

The Cobra Jet and Super Cobra Jet became Ford's most notable big-blocks. The 370-hp Cobra Jet and 375-hp Super Cobra Jet featured four-bolt main bearing caps, 2.25-inch intake, 1.72-inch exhaust heads, and a lot of other high-performance equipment. The Cobra Jet used threaded-in rocker arms. The Super Cobra Jet was equipped with forged aluminum pistons, mechanical cam, and 780-cfm Holley carb. These engines were installed in the Mustang Mach 1, Torino Cobra, and many other cars. Many of the standard performance engines have two-bolt main bearing cap block, while the Cobra Jets feature four-bolt main bearing caps.

Of course, as with the small-block, you can stroke the Lima engines. Coast High-Performance offers stroker kits in 502/514, 521/532, and 545/557 displacements.

Crate Engines

Many used Ford small-block and big-block engines have been rebuilt and overbored beyond their limits and, therefore, are unuseable. Many owners do not want to pluck a used engine from a Mustang or other performance Ford car and perform a high-performance build up, they want a crate engine. There are many suppliers, such as Ford Racing Performance Parts, Mustangs Plus, Edelbrock, World Products, Roush Engines, Coast High Performance.

Crate engine prices run the entire gamut, and it depends upon equipment package in the engine. Mild-performance, small-block crate engines are sold for $3,000 and more while high-performance small-blocks, with forged rotating assemblies and high-performance heads and valvetrain, start at $5,000.

As with any engine, you need to select the right one for your car. The engine should have the correct equipment package for the horsepower and torque output. A 300-hp small-block crate engine can carry a stock rotating assembly, but if you're buying a small-block to make 600 hp, it needs to carry forged rotating assembly and other high-performance running gear.

Big-block crate engines are also available from many of the same suppliers, but for a big-block you are entering a new tier of performance and a much higher price. Big-blocks often start at $7,000.

Therefore, when you're doing research, you need to determine the best engine package for your car and application. Make sure your engine and transmission combination is compatible with your particular kit and whichever crossmember modifications and motor mounts are required to mount it. Call the tech line of a particular crate engine supplier and tell them you're building a specific Cobra replica, and get all the relevant information to make an informed decision.

Stroker 427 Small-Blocks

For the Mk4, you can use the entire running gear from a modern Mustang. The FFR Cobra has enough room in the engine bay to readily accept the Ford modular motor in either 4.6- or 5.0-liter Coyote iteration. However, as this book goes to press, Factory Five is developing compatible mounts and headers for the new Coyote engine to fit the Mk4. Also, the T-5, T-45 or 3650 transmission, and Ford 8.8-inch differential easily mount to the chassis.

Whether it's a genuine 1962–1967 original or a replica, the most important part of the Cobra is the powerplant. And you're right to think, "The heart and soul of any sports car is the engine." With the Cobra, it's especially true. Before Carroll Shelby and Dean Moon stuffed a Ford 260-ci V-8 mill in a 1962 AC Bristol, there was no such thing as a Shelby Cobra. The Ford small-block V-8 engine is what first transformed the beautiful little aluminum sports car from an under-powered, aging roadster to a powerful street performer and winning race car.

But there are many more power-plant options, including some classic Ford engines. The small-block Windsor family of engines, the FE-Series (390/427) and Lima or 385 Series engines, including the 428 and 460, install without great challenge.

Dart Machinery

Dart Machinery manufactures iron Ford and Chevy small-block V-8 engine blocks as Ford did for the 1960s Cobras. But it also makes them out of aluminum, as we desired. We decided to power our replica with a Dart 351 Windsor-based aluminum engine block that was bored and stroked to produce the magical 427-ci displacement. The genuine Shelby Cobra 427SC had a Ford 427-ci big-block V-8 that was cast iron and rated at 425 hp. Our engine was the same displacement, yet weighed at least 100 pounds less and produced more horsepower. That's just the sort of recipe for excitement that Carroll Shelby advocated.

Those original big-block Ford mills had heavy cast-iron cylinder heads. Dart Machinery also produces superlative Pro CNC aluminum cylinder heads. So we ordered all the goods from Dart that we could and sought the company's advice on what California-based engine builder should create our Dart 427 mill.

QMP Racing Engines

One of Dart Manufacturing's top pro-engine builders around the globe

---

is QMP Racing Engines. Dart felt that QMP Racing Engines were the best-suited pro engine shop for the job, so we first did some investigating on the QMP Web site. It didn't take long for Dad and me to give QMP's owner, Brad Lagman, a call to talk to him about the Cobra replica project and the engine we wanted QMP to build.

As an automotive author, I'm usually the one asking all the questions. But the tables were turned. Brad very thoroughly interviewed us to discover exactly what sort of engine we'd like to have in our FFR Mk4. After he knew our preferences and goals, he supplied us with a list of components that we should acquire for stuffing our Dart 351W/427 stroker aluminum V-8.

We spent the next bit of time acquiring components through Summit Racing and gathering them all in our living room. After finally collecting everything that we thought we'd need, we drove to Chatsworth, north of Oceanside, with our engine in the car. The Dart Pro CNC aluminum cylinder heads and the aluminum 351W engine block were shipped directly to QMP Racing. And then the painstak-

The QMP Racing Engines facility has the high-technology engine-building machines that equate to the checkered flag, when it comes to auto or boat racing. QMP Racing Engines has the only diamond-studded cylinder-boring machine on the West Coast, making it the perfect place to have our Dart 351/427 built.

ing craft of machining, massaging, balancing, blueprinting, and creating our Dart 427 stroker was squarely on the shoulders of the pro builders at QMP Racing.

QMP had the Dart block and cylinder heads line-bored in preparation for our arrival. When we arrived on

the scene, we dropped off all those speed shop components and took a tour of the QMP facility.

Measure Connecting Rod Clearance

2 *Using the dial bore gauge, confirm that the connecting-rod bearing clearance is correct for all eight connecting rods before proceeding.*

Project 1: Install Long Block Assembly

Hone Cylinder Block and Deburr Cam

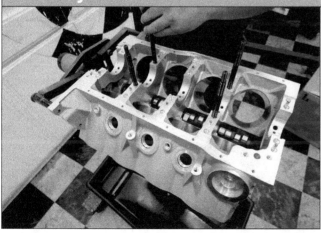

1 *With all the cylinders honed to the specified 4.1255 inches and the camshaft bearing housings freshly deburred, install the Comp Cams custom-ground camshaft and flip the engine upside down to screw-in the end-cap studs.*

Install Main Bearings

3 *Install the crankshaft bearings and the end caps after the crankshaft is in. Do this before you install the crankshaft to ensure the proper clearances are met between the crankshaft and the main crankshaft bearings. The main bearings go in first.*

Install Main Bearing Caps

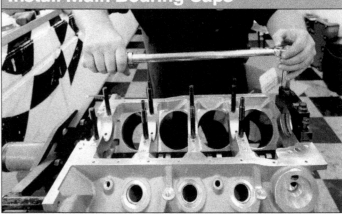

4 *Install the end cap prior to checking it for clearance. First torque the end-cap bolts to spec. Torque the biggest end-cap bolts to 100 ft-lbs of torque. Torque the medium end-cap bolts to 70 ft-lbs. Torque the smallest, outer end-cap bolts to 40 ft-lbs.*

Check Main Bearing for Clearance

5 *After installing the first main cap, use the dial bore gauge to check the main bearing for clearance.*

Splay Center Main Bearing

6 *Splay the main bearing in the center of the engine for extra strength. Notice that these end caps are four-bolt caps. Dart Manufacturing uses four-bolt mains for added strength with its mighty aluminum 351W block. A stock cast-iron Ford 351W just has two-bolt mains.*

Torque Main Cap Bolts

7 *Before checking the clearance of all five of the main bearings, torque the end-cap bolts to spec.*

Check Main Bearing Clearance

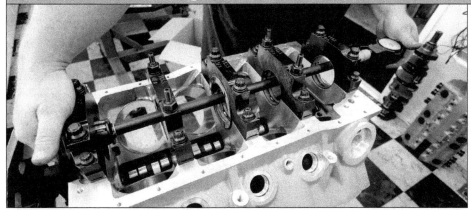

8 Check all five main bearings for clearance with the dial bore gauge. If you don't take this precaution, you might install the crankshaft and have it not turn. So avoid problems, and be precise.

Inspect Alignment Dowels

9 After confirming clearance between the crankshaft and the main bearings is within specs with the dial bore gauge, remove the main caps to fit the crankshaft. Alignment dowels enable easy installation of the main caps, a feature found on all Dart aluminum blocks.

Install Freeze Plugs in Block

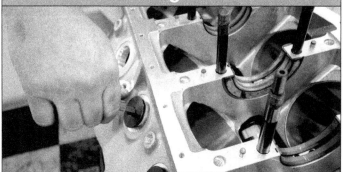

10 After applying Teflon paste to the threads of the anodized-aluminum 1/4-inch-pipe plugs, install them in the block. All Dart aluminum blocks use 10 threaded, anodized-aluminum freeze plugs. With all the freeze plugs and water drain plugs installed in the block, re-install the main bearings and put a liberal amount of engine oil on each main bearing.

Install Crankshaft

11 After all the main bearings have oil on them, move the forged crankshaft into place. As is common with Ford engines, we added a bit of Mallory metal to the crankshaft to internally balance the engine.

Lubricate Crankshaft

12 One of the most important elements in building a high-performance engine, or any powerplant, is liberal usage of motor oil. Pour some on the crankshaft prior to installing another main cap.

Torque Main Caps

13 Since the crankshaft is to spec for clearance with the main bearings, install the other side of the end caps and torque the bolts to spec. Torque the six 1/2-inch bolts in the center of the block to 100 ft-lbs. Torque the outer-center 7/16-inch bolts to 70 ft-lbs. And torque the outer bolts on the end, the smallest bolts, to 40 ft-lbs. Though possible to install the rear seal after installing the rear main cap, it is not advisable; you can ruin the rear seal. Always install the rear seal, using the supplied plastic alignment tool, before installing the rear main cap.

Torque Final Main Cap

14 Torque the final main cap bolts to proper specs before flipping the engine right side up on the engine-building rotisserie stand.

Install Timing Set Gears

15 Install the timing-set dual gear on the front end of the crankshaft before the engine is flipped right side up.

Install Dowels

16 Pound the installation dowels in place for the collar that holds those timing set gears in place on the crankshaft.

Torque Crankshaft Collar

17 After flipping the engine right side up on the engine rotisserie, carefully install the engine's timing chain on the camshaft end at the top and the crankshaft end at the bottom.

Completing the timing set installation, torque the crankshaft collar to spec.

Install Piston Ring

18 Push the piston rings into place with the piston-ring squaring tool.

Set Piston Ring Gap

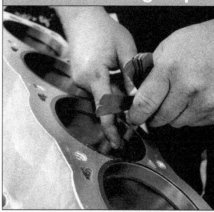

19 To determine and to verify that the piston ring gap is correct, use a feeler gauge on the just-ground piston rings. Use the piston-ring squaring tool to set the gap of the piston rings.

Install Piston Wrist Pins

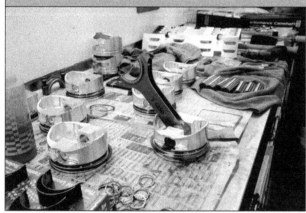

20 After the 16 piston rings are all properly gapped, assemble the first connecting rod assembly (JE Piston and Scat seen here). Install double spiral clips to either end of the wrist pin to hold the rod/piston assembly securely together. Then attach the specific piston rings to the designated rod/piston assembly that's matched to a particular cylinder. Install the connecting rod bearing, and place the oil ring on the bottom of the piston. On the big end of the connecting rod that attaches to the crankshaft, mark each rod/piston assembly for its designated cylinder. Liberally coat the assemblies with oil.

Oil Cylinders and Install Piston Number-1

21 Before installing the piston/rod assemblies, give the cylinders a good oil bath by applying oil with your fingers.

If you look closely, you see the number "1" scribed into the purple paint on the connecting rod end.

Torque Connecting Rod Bolts

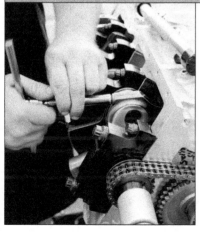

22 Before moving to piston number-2, attach the bottom of the connecting rod to the crankshaft, install the bolts, and snug the connecting rod bolts for piston/rod assembly number-1. You may need to use a piston/rod assembly persuader tool (the metal rod with rubber ends resting on the side of the Dart engine block in this photo). With help from a persuader tool, push the number-2 piston/connecting rod assembly into number-2 cylinder. Use a piston-ring/piston-squaring alignment tool. Wielding a T-wrench, attach the connecting rod end to the forged-steel crankshaft and tighten those two bolts before moving to number-3 cylinder and 4. Repeat the installation process for cylinders/pistons number-5 through -8. Use motor oil to coat the second bank of cylinders before installing piston/rod assembly number-5 with the piston-squaring cylinder. Mere seconds after this photo was taken, QMP picked up the persuader and pressed the number-5 piston/rod assembly into cylinder number-5.

Torque Bolts (Continued)

23 Finish installing the connecting rod end on piston/ rod assembly number-8 and flip the engine upside down to torque the connecting rod bolts to 60 ft-lbs in three steps: 20, 20, and 20 ft-lbs. Torque the connecting rod bolts on piston/ rod assembly number-6, and you have just two more assemblies to torque before completing this portion of the build. After torquing all the connecting rod bolts, check the side clearance of all the rods to the interior of the block. All our rods are clear by .023 to .025 inch. You now have a short block.

Determine Lobe Center of Cam

24 Use the dial indicator to dial in the lobe center of the camshaft. For us that turned out to be 114 and is spot-on for this 427 Dart stroker engine.

Install Head on Block

25 Before installing the heads, press-in a couple dowels to locate the cylinder heads (ours are Dart Pro CNC-aluminum high-performance). These dowels also help to align the Fel-Pro cylinder head gaskets. Different-length ARP studs are used to attach the Dart aluminum Pro-CNC cylinder heads. Install the passenger-side aluminum cylinder head first; except for the valvesprings for the number-1 cylinder.

Use a dial gauge to confirm clearance between the cylinder head and the piston. You only need to check one cylinder because all the clearances are the same. That's why the valvesprings are not installed on the first cylinder in this picture.

Torque Cylinder Head Bolts

26 After the other two valvesprings are installed and the cylinder head bolts are tight, torque the head bolts to 110 ft-lbs in three steps. Do this to ensure that the cylinder heads are tightened evenly.

Install Lifter, Pushrod and Roller Rocker

27 After thoroughly bathing the lifter in oil and applying assembly lube to both the cam side and the push rod end of the lifter, install the lifter, push rod, and roller rocker assembly for the number-1 cylinder.

Move down the line from valvespring to valvespring and from cylinder to cylinder until the high-performance valvetrain assembly is installed. Inspect the pushrod-to-roller rocker height. If you determine that the pushrods are too long (as we did), get the correct size.

Install Oil Pump, Oil Pickup and Windage Tray

28 *Flip the engine upside down and install the oil pump. We learned from Melling that Dart aluminum engines are so efficient at flowing oil that a stock Melling oil pump is sufficient. If you used a high-flowing racing Melling oil pump, the top of the engine would be flooded with oil.*

Mark and Trim Oil Pan

29 *If you discover that the pan needs a bit more massaging before it will fit, mark the inside lip of the pan where it needs to be trimmed.*

A pneumatic cutter makes easy work of aluminum trimming on an oil pan.

Install Timing Set Cover

30 *After confirming the oil pan modifications do the job, install the timing set cover.*

Install Oil Pan

31 *In preparation for installing the oil pan, install the gaskets. There is also a half-round gasket that fits on the timing chain cover; the timing chain is underneath.*

Use Mr. Gasket sealer over the entire Fel-Pro oil pan gasket. Notice also that our Moroso oil-pan studs are already in place. Forming the basis of a beautiful custom powerplant from top to bottom, QMP installed our custom-aluminum Moroso oil pan on the Dart aluminum block. Torque all nuts to spec.

Install Intake Manifold

32 *With all the lifters installed, attach the intake manifold gaskets and carefully apply Mr. Gasket sealer on the front and rear valley wall of the engine block. Our Weiand Stealth aluminum intake manifold is installed, with all the ARP fasteners torqued to specs.*

Install Water Pump

33 *After getting the correct-length/size Comp Cams pushrods, QMP installed them, as well as the Comp Cams roller rockers. Using two cork gaskets for the valve covers, we topped off the Dart aluminum Pro-CNC cylinder heads with Ford Racing Cobra 427 valve covers and installed the Edelbrock aluminum water pump, procured from Summit Racing.*

Install Front Accessory Pulleys

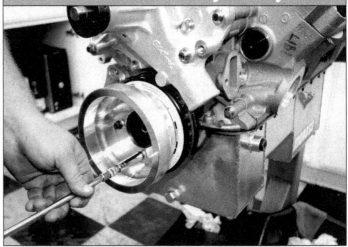

34 *Install the pulleys on the damper (shown) and on the water pump. We selected the March Performance polished-aluminum pulley system for small- and big-block Ford V-8 engines.*

Install EFI System

35 *The proverbial cherry on top of this exquisite power-plant is a Holley Avenger throttle-body elec-tronic-fuel-injection system.*

Install MSD Distributor

36 *Also at the top and even cherry red in hue, an MSD distributor is in place in this state-of-the-art Dart aluminum 427-stroker powerplant.*

Engine Dyno Day at QMP Racing Engines

We turned the various parts and pieces into a road and track burner, including the Dart 351W aluminum block, Dart aluminum Pro CNC cylinder heads, Comp Cams valvetrain assembly, JE Pistons, Scat connecting rods, Scat crankshaft, Moroso oil pan, Holley Avenger EFI, Fel-Pro gaskets, ARP fasteners, Powermaster alternator and high-torque starter, March Performance pulley system, MSD ignition box, coil and distributor. Then we felt that the best way to christen our powerplant was to have the engine-building pros at QMP Racing Engines dyno the 427 stroker.

After the engine had been together for two days, we still needed to source a few items to finish it off. Most notable were the mechanical fuel pump block-off plate, the thermostat housing, and a spacer to go on the harmonic balancer to enable the March Performance pulley system to align properly. We contacted Summit Racing and had all the components shipped directly to QMP Racing Engines.

Not long thereafter, we scheduled some quality QMP dyno time on a Friday. When Dad and I arrived on the scene at QMP in the early afternoon, Dyno Mike was ready to fire up our mill as soon as we walked in the QMP shop. The engine sounded magnificent. We don't know if the sweet cacophony is due to the fact that all those great engine components are housed in an aluminum block. The sound alone made me feel confident that we be able to take on all competitors, when we get this engine running in our FFR Mk4 Cobra roadster replica.

Mating Engine to Transmission

We acquired a Tremec T56 Magnum 6-speed manual transmission for our Dart aluminum 427 fire breather, since the T56 Magnum can handle all the horsepower and torque that our mill can throw at it. Using this transmission isn't exactly the easy way. There's a customizing premium to pay. But it's the best manual transmission, so it's in keeping with our ultimate goal.

Our Windsor-based 427-ci stroker engine, which pumps out 516 hp, has been assembled. This engine will deliver exceptional performance for our sprite Cobra roadster and it's mated to the Tremec T-56 6-speed manual transmission. Soon it will find a new home inside the Mk4 chassis.

DRIVETRAIN AND COOLING SYSTEM

Having that glorious engine built, dyno tested, attached to the transmission, and ready to go in the Mk4 chassis means that our project is close to being finished. For the longest time we had a pile of brand-new engine parts in our living room. Now those components are bathing in motor oil and have a purpose.

After we had secured a Tremec T56 Magnum 6-speed transmission to back our illustrious engine, we learned from Factory Five's tech-support team that none of their customers to date (as of this writing) had ever installed a T56 Magnum in an FFR roadster. They let us know that it wasn't a supported transmission for that very reason. So we were on our own, breaking new ground again.

We had to do some engineering exploring in short order, thanks to our desire to go off the beaten path. There were several occasions when we wished we were installing a supported transmission, like a Tremec TKO 5-speed. Still, breaking new ground is something that you might do when you create a replica. Self-expression is well regarded in the kit-car arena. After all, where is the fun if everyone built the same sort of Cobra replica?

Project 1: Drivetrain Installation

Inspect Transmission and Motor Mount Kit

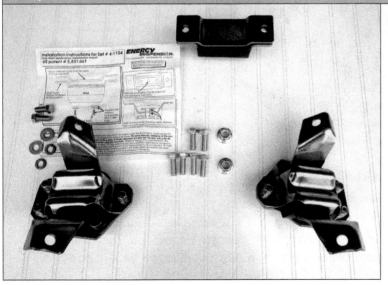

1 *Energy Suspension polyurethane transmission and engine mounts are included in the FFR Mk4 Roadster Complete Kit, along with all the required fasteners. Loosely install these mounts and snug the bolts halfway. The bolts should be held on by a couple of threads or torqued down halfway. They need some wiggle room for lining up the engine and transmission in the FFR chassis. Remove the mounting boss on the bottom of the transmission before installing the engine/transmission. We removed the mounting boss on our Tremec T56 Magnum transmission as a precaution, by shearing off the boss with a hacksaw; you could also use a rotary or air grinder.*

Install Engine Mounts

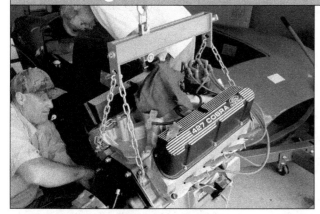

2 *Knowing that our T56 Magnum transmission had never been used in an FFR Cobra roadster replica before, we installed the engine mounts but decided to wait to install the transmission mount.*

Install Starter Motor

3 *Upon trial fitting the Powermaster XS high-torque starter, we realized the three installation holes on the starter did not align with our custom Moroso oil pan. We removed the starter installation bracket from the starter and modified the non-aligning hole with an electric grinder. After working on the non-fitting hole for a while, we managed to get the Powermaster starter installed.*

Install Engine and Transmission

4 *After wrestling with the engine/transmission, we managed to safely get the engine and Tremec T56 Magnum partially installed in the chassis.*

Install Transmission A-Frame

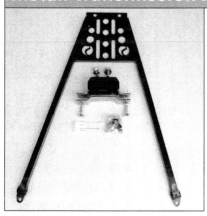

5 *We didn't put the Energy Suspension transmission mount on the Tremec T56 Magnum 6-speed yet. Leaving it off during the engine/transmission install made sense; we wanted to be sure the powertrain would fit. We modified components as necessary to make it work. If you're using a supported transmission, you can follow the directions in your manufacturer's build manual. Upon initial mock-up of the Factory Five Racing supplied transmission A-frame mount, we discovered that the beefy Tremec T56 Magnum 6-speed transmission case conflicted with the A-frame mount. Our local car customizer modified the A-frame transmission mount, so we could bolt everything together. To make the A-frame fit, much of the middle part of the frame needed to be removed.*

Torque Transmission Fasteners

6 *After test fitting the modified A-frame transmission mount, we torqued the fasteners for the Energy Suspension polyurethane mount according to the specs in the manual.*

Project 2: Driveshaft Installation

Test Fit Driveshaft

1 The driveshaft spline shaft should have 5/8 inch of play inside the transmission tailshaft. We could not fit this driveshaft in place between the tailshaft of the Tremec T56 Magnum and the IRS differential because it was too long. Based on the measurements we supplied, Oceanside Driveline shortened our driveshaft 2 inches.

Install Driveshaft

2 Install the driveshaft from underneath the car. First, put the spline shaft into the tailshaft. Then screw the four bolts by hand that hold the driveshaft's yoke to the differential U-joint. Before putting the driveshaft into place, put white lithium grease on the U-joint shaft, so it slides easily into the transmission. FFR supplies special thread locker for use on the threads of the fasteners that go into the differential's shaft. If you have an FFR Mk4, make sure you remember to use the special thread locker.

Inspect Components

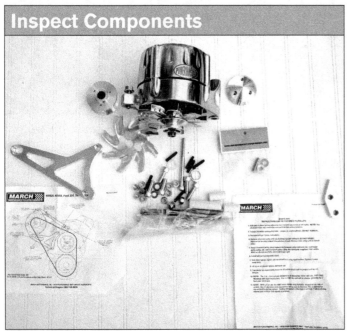

3 With the powertrain in place, turn your attention to installing the pulleys and brackets, as well as the high-performance alternator. According to our professional engine builder, QMP Racing Engines, the Ford 351W engine has more variants—in terms of different components and fasteners used—than most. When it comes to installing power accessories, like alternators, starters, pulleys, etc., the variety of different components can present quite a challenge.

Install Front Accessory Pulleys

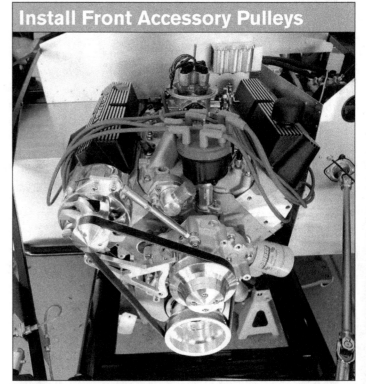

4 We aren't using a power steering pump, air conditioning, or any other power adders on our build, so we opted for a pure March Performance bracket and pulley system that performs well. After you install the system, torque all the fasteners to spec. Use thread locker, locknuts, or lock washers to keep everything fastened together.

Install Flex Fuel Lines

5 With the engine safely in place, measure the length that the flexible fuel lines should be. (We ordered ours from Rupe's). Measure from where the hard supply line stops in the engine bay to the supply side of the Holley Avenger EFI, and do the same for the return side. Pictured here are our installed supply and return fuel lines.

Project 3: Radiator Fan Installation

Inspect Components

1 To install the Afco aluminum radiator in the FFR Mk4 chassis, use a hack saw, marker, the supplied insulated clip hardware, drill with 1/4-inch drill bit, 3/16-inch hex key, 1/2- and 7/16-inch wrenches, ruler, and flat-head screwdriver. The stainless-steel radiator hose kit (not shown), roadster-cooling system, fan-mounting components, and packaged aluminum are all used.

Attach Fan-Mounting Brackets

2 There are four fan-mounting brackets for the FFR Mk4's electric fan. Push these brackets into the angled tab mounts.

Mount Fan on Radiator

3 Center the electric fan on the underside of the radiator. The radiator's pipes serve as your guide for placing the fan, so install the fan on the same side as the radiator's inlet/outlet pipes.

Mark Brackets and Tighten Fasteners

4 Mark the fan brackets to trim off the excess. You can use picks to hold the brackets into position, while marking the bracket. At this point you can also attach the fan to the radiator using the supplied fasteners.

Tighten the fasteners that hold everything together before moving to the next step.

Temporarily Attach Radiator to Chassis

5 Temporarily zip-tie the radiator into place on the chassis, with the bottom tied around the lower outlet. (As our project was underway, the radiator was mounted with the drain plug at the top of the chassis. This may be different for you if you have a later FFR roadster kit.) Measure and mark the center of the chassis and the center of the radiator. As directed in the FFR Mk4 assembly manual, offset the radiator by 1/2 inch. Also drill the top flange holes on the radiator to the two small mounting tubular crossmember on the chassis. Then use the supplied hardware to fasten the radiator to the chassis, being careful not to overtighten the bolts.

Project 4: Radiator Hose Installation

Inspect Hoses

1 These FFR-supplied aluminum flexible hoses are pretty trick. The reason they are ridged is because with so many different surfaces, it's difficult for there to be any coolant leaks. The ridges also enable the hose to be more flexible, sort of like a connected slinky. As far as those rubber hoses and clamps go, the rubber hoses are different thicknesses and diameters, which, when used in concert with each other, prevent any leaks. The smaller sections of rubber tube are used in the adapters for the smaller fittings on the radiator and intake.

Attach Top Hose to Radiator Pipe

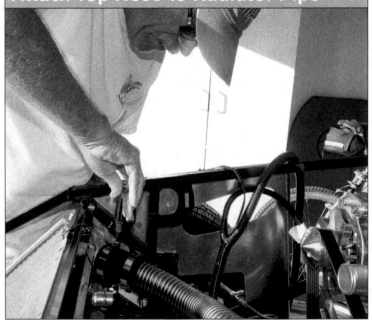

2 After mocking up, bending, and cutting the top aluminum hose to the appropriate length, attach the thin- and then thicker-diameter rubber adapters to the top radiator pipe. The different rubber adapters are used to prevent any coolant leaks between the corrugated aluminum, the rubber adapters, and the aluminum inlet and outlet pipes on the engine and the radiator. With this done, tighten the hose clamps.

Install Thermostat in Housing

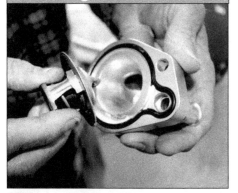

3 Install the thermostat in its aluminum housing. Notice the first-class O-ring for the GSR aluminum thermostat housing; it's a good deterrent to leaking.

Attach Top Hose

4 Attach the top aluminum hose with rubber adapters to the aluminum fill neck. It may help to have some assistance with this step.

For the fill neck to the thermostat housing, simply use the correct-diameter rubber hose. The installation feels solid, but you may swap out the hose to the thermostat housing for a different solution, if it begins to flex and sag. Be sure to monitor the hose and determine its viability. If this solution is problematic, obtain a solid aluminum pipe and the appropriate-diameter rubber hose to mate the aluminum radiator inlet pipe with the aluminum hose. Then use another rubber hose to go from the aluminum pipe to the fill neck and from the fill neck to a rubber hose that is attached to the thermostat pipe.

Install Lower Tube

5 Though the lower tube is longer, it's an easier installation because you don't need to install a fill neck in the middle of the tube. Route the tube adjacent to the 4-inch main rail and under the steering rack to the bottom pipe of the radiator. Make sure the lower tube has sufficient slack to enable fitment of the nose aluminum, which is installed when the body is on the chassis. Be certain that the lower tube doesn't hang down too low; if it does, zip-tie the hose to the frame. Snaking the hose as we've done here takes up some of the slack and enables the hose to be well above the ground. After you install the body, you are able to ascertain whether you need to zip-tie the hose to a frame tube.

Install Overflow Tank

6 The radiator's coolant overflow tank is best installed on the passenger-side F-panel (shown). Start by installing the mounting tabs loosely to enable proper adjustment for final fitment. Mark the holes for drilling and make certain that the tank can be accessed to check the fluid level after the body is on the chassis and construction is complete.

Install Overflow Hose

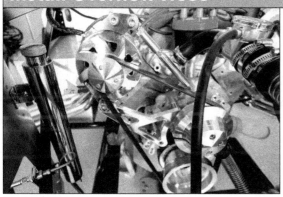

7 When installing the overflow hose, be sure to attach the hose to the tube that runs off the bottom of the tank, as opposed to the tube that extends up into the tank.

ELECTRICAL SYSTEM

In building a replica, do we need to feel as though we're masters of all the automotive trades, or maybe specialists with great expertise for just specific portions of the build? In other words, are we wimping out if we skip some build aspects where we don't feel that we're automotive gurus in certain disciplines? I suppose that depends upon your point of view.

Our objective all along was to build the best possible FFR Mk4 Cobra roadster replica, and building this industry-leading kit car is similar to building other Cobra replicas. Mind you, if we have a deficit in our abilities, we're not going to jeopardize this overarching goal out of stubbornness. We bring in the experts when we know they can do a better job than we can.

When it came time to wire our sexy roadster, we followed the FFR Mk4 Complete Kit manual to the letter because an improperly installed wiring harness can be dangerous and even result in a fire. The manual recommends reading the Factory Five/Ron Francis *Chassis Wiring Harness Installation Instructions* before tackling the car's wiring. We dutifully immersed ourselves in this manual. It's well written, provides sharp color photos, and has a thorough wiring schematic. We felt confident that, with sufficient time and a fair amount of troubleshooting, we could indeed tackle this daunting wiring task.

But did we want to do it? After careful consideration and contact with our new friend Dennis Clark, owner of Carlsbad Automotive Technology, we decided that we'd rather rely on a professional automotive electrician than on our stubborn persistence and great enthusiasm for the electrical puzzle before us.

If you have experience in automobile electrical wiring, you'll be able to accomplish a great wiring job on your Cobra replica with all the information here, your manual, and what you already know.

Beyond that, if you ever decide to put your Cobra up for sale, a high-quality wiring job is readily apparent to the trained eye. A knowledgeable potential buyer recognizes sound wiring connections, correct material use, correct termination points, wisely routed wires, and properly mounted fuse boxes.

Properly and professionally wiring your Cobra replica requires close attention to detail and correctly following the directions of the assembly manual and wiring harness installation instructions. The Ron Francis Chassis Wiring Harness Installation Instructions are reviewed, as well as the directions supplied with the Factory Five Racing instruments that we ordered as part of the Mk4 Roadster Complete Kit.

Project 1: Wiring Harness and Fuse Box Installation

Inspect Components

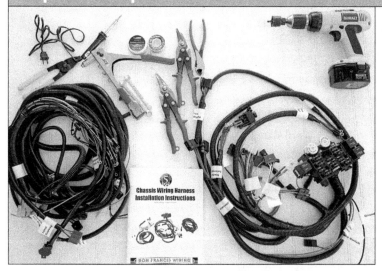

1 The Ron Francis Wiring Kit supplied in the FFR Mk4 Complete Kit is first class all the way. You get the dash harness, main harness complete with fuse box, front harness, and the rear harness. Just supply some brainpower and common sense, in addition to the following tools: wire crimp tool, rivet gun, tin snips, cordless drill, 1¼-inch hole saw, 5/16-inch drill bit, wire cutters, 5/8-inch hex key, 1/4-inch nut driver, 3/8-inch wrench, and 7/16-inch wrench. With the instruments that you order from FFR in the Complete Kit Mk4, you receive an instrument harness that is specifically for the gauges you select, in addition to the oil pressure sensor and coolant temperature sensor.

Mount Fuse Box

2 The fuse box is attached to the main harness. To begin your electrical odyssey, attach the fuse panel to the fuse panel mount using the FFR-supplied 1/4-inch screws and locknuts.

Install Fuse Box

3 Use the number-6 self-tapping screws to install the fuse box to the 2 x 2-inch frame tube and the 3/4-inch tube. Drill holes in the frame tubes with a 1/8-inch drill bit. The fuse box is positioned above the driver's left leg in the pedal box. The fuse panel hangs upside down in the top portion of the left side of the footbox, so that you can maintain access and change blown fuses.

Fabricate Shielding Shelf

4 For now, lay the main harness conduit over the steering shaft. The dash connectors and ignition switch wires need to be temporarily pulled into the cockpit area so they are kept out of the way during the installation. At this point, fabricate an aluminum platform that arches over the steering shaft and its bearing to shield the main harness from the rotating steering shaft.

Use tin snips to cut the panel out of some extra aluminum. Then bend the aluminum around your workbench vise to approximate the shape of the steering shaft bearing. Drill holes in the panel and use those panel holes to drill holes in the frame tube that the steering shaft bearing and steering shaft are attached to. We rivet the panel in place.

Install the shelf with self-tapping sheet-metal screws or rivets and run the wiper/radio harness wires toward the passenger's side along the top of the 2 x 2-inch cockpit tube.

Attach Ground Wire for Fuse Panel

5 *Thoroughly grind off all the powdercoat on the 3/4-inch tube where you install the fuse panel's ground wire. You need metal-to-metal contact between the connector and the chassis to have a consistent and reliable ground. Having a well-grounded electrical system in an automobile is crucial, but especially in a fiberglass kit car. Whenever you're attaching a ground wire, make sure to remove all the powdercoat at the spot before installing it.*

Install Brake Switch Connector

6 *Remove the plug from the brake switch wire and install the brake switch spade connectors into the brake switch. If the spade connectors are damaged by removing the plug from the brake switch wire, re-crimp these spade connectors to the appropriate wires. We did not have this difficulty, so we could simply plug the connectors into the brake switch.*

Solder Clutch Safety Switch

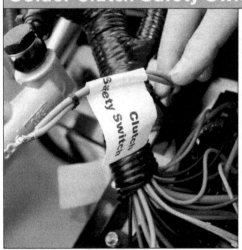

7 *When you attach the clutch safety switch, the car doesn't start if it's in gear. If you opt to not use this, connect the two wires and either terminate them with an FFR-supplied butt connector, or solder them together and insulate them with electrical tape. We chose to solder ours.*

Plug In Sending Unit Connector

8 *Find the FFR-supplied gauge-sending-unit wire harness and plug it into the sending unit connector on the main harness. The plug is a male/female setup and is brown in color.*

Enlarge Hole for Electrical Conduits

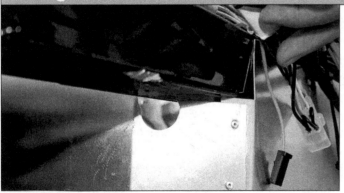

9 *Because some of the electrical conduits need to be run to the engine bay, open up the hole to the right of the driver's knee in the top corner of the pedal box. We opened our hole up with an electric drill and deburring bit. The starter/coil harness and the rear harness can be routed through this hole. Factory Five Racing also supplies some clear plastic trim to install on the rough edges to smooth these edges and prevent tears in the electrical conduit. This is a crucial step in preventing any potential wire damage. Also file the edges smooth, as we've done.*

Route Front Wiring Harness

10 There's a large hole in the top of the front driver-side footbox wall, directly under where the front brake line is run. Route the front harness through this hole. Use a hole saw and an FFR-supplied block-off plate to drill the correct-size hole. Use a 1¼-inch hole saw.

Install Conduit Hole

11 By clamping the donut to the front of the footbox, you can drill rivet holes in the aluminum conduit grommet. After these holes are all drilled, apply silicone to the backside of the doughnut before mounting it with a rivet gun and rivets.

Install Alternator Conduit and Ground

12 The Ron Francis Wiring Instruction Manual, supplied with the FFR Mk4 Roadster Complete Kit, recommends routing the alternator and gauge sender wires through the hole that we (and perhaps you) enlarged in the top-right corner of the driver's footbox. But that hole still isn't really large enough to accommodate all the conduits that are supposed to be routed there, so we opted to drill one hole in the passenger-side firewall to send the alternator wires through.

If you follow our lead, use a 1¼-inch hole saw and cordless drill to put a hole in the passenger-side firewall. Have your build partner hold a block of wood behind the aluminum panel where you're drilling. That aluminum cuts fast, and you have a better solution than stuffing a bunch of electrical conduits into one hole.

The alternator also has a ground wire, which we've grounded as shown. We used a rubber grommet, from a local auto parts store, to protect the plastic conduit that houses the alternator wires. We also soldered on a ground eyelet and shrink-wrapped the wire. FFR supplies many of these little ground eyelets in the kit.

Attach Wires to Alternator

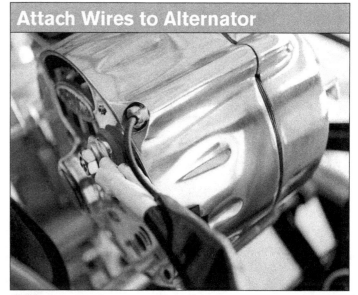

13 If you route the alternator wires in a similar manner, strap the alternator conduit (with the FFR-supplied line clamps) to the passenger-side, top engine bay tube that frames the hood and the front of the car. On our Powermaster high-performance one-wire alternator there isn't a ground terminal, so we grounded the negative wire to the alternator's case (as shown) and installed the positive power wire to the one-wire terminal.

We cut off the modern alternator plug that was on the end of this harness and soldered on an eyelet, which is compatible with our Powermaster alternator. We also soldered on a ground eyelet for the negative terminal. Installing the alternator wires like this goes a long way in creating a sanitary engine bay.

Install Fuel Inertia Cut-off Switch

14 *An easy thing to do is to install a fuel inertia cut-off switch. Locate it on the front or back of the 2- x 2-inch tube; be sure not to cover the stamped chassis numbers.* Use the supplied number-8 self-tapping screws, an electric drill, and a 1/4-inch nut driver. Also, the red switch needs to be in the upright position, as shown.

Route Rear Harness

15 *Find the rear harness in the wiring box and connect it to the connector on the main harness. The two plugs should be obvious. Run the rear harness through the enlarged footbox hole and through the transmission tunnel. Securely zip-tie the rear harness so that the conduit doesn't interfere with the driveshaft.*

Plug In Rear Harness

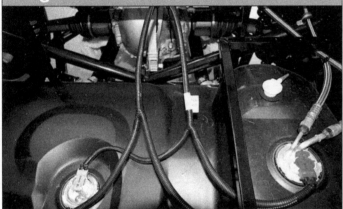

16 *Once the rear harness is successfully routed to the fuel tank, it's time to plug in the sending unit and the fuel pump. Safely and securely tie this harness to the frame tubes so it's out of the way of where the aluminum trunk floor is installed.*

Install Front Harness

17 *Remember that aluminum conduit grommet you drilled out and riveted in place in the footbox front wall? There's no time like the present to plug the front harness into the main harness. It's a black male/female plug, and both harnesses are clearly labeled. The front harness is for the headlights, the low and high horns, and the electric fan. All of these electrical components will be hooked up later, so just drape the front harness over the driver-side hood-opening rail for now.*

Route Front Harness through Footbox Wall

18 *From the front of the footbox wall, here's how the front harness looks routed through the aluminum conduit grommet.*

Install Power Distribution Block

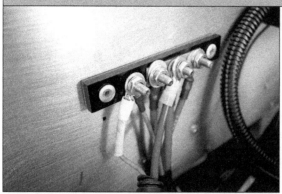

19 Our little high-torque Powermaster starter has a built-in solenoid switch. Factory Five Racing supplies an old-style Ford solenoid switch and a starter loom that has a plug on the end of the loom. To install this harness, FFR recommends you use a power distribution block (PDB) to achieve a clean installation. In this starter loom, there are three positive cables and a separate wire for the solenoid. The three positive cables are on the right and connect to each other via a copper strip. The solenoid wire is on the single connector. Other positive cables can be installed on the three positive terminals. You then can run a single positive power cable to the starter.

Wire Starter

20 The wrapped positive-conduit cable atop the starter is the battery's positive wire. The other conduit that circles below the starter is a short positive cable from the PDB. Inside the black conduit is the separate wire that we attached to the solenoid, which also runs from the lone solenoid terminal on the PDB.

Install Ground Strap

21 Before attaching the engine ground strap to the engine, thoroughly grind off the powdercoat on the chassis where the strap installs, which is located on the passenger-side engine-mount frame. On an FFR Mk4 roadster chassis, the strap is attached on the engine mount frame on the passenger's side. In fact, there is already a hole to accommodate the bolt and nut that holds the strap to the frame.

Project 2: Trunk Wall Installation

Apply Silicone to Trunk Wall

1 Before you can install the battery, there needs to be a trunk; the battery goes in the trunk. With Sharkhide protectant applied to the inside trunk wall, put silicone on the backside and rivet this wall in place. There is no battery tray included in the kit. Your battery is located on the top trunk floor, unless you prefer some other location.

Install Upper Trunk Wall

2 Apply silicone to the frame where the aluminum panels rest on the frame. This ensures that you've sufficiently sealed off the trunk from the elements and eliminate the potential for metal-on-metal squeaks or rattles. Once you have each panel held in place with a pick or two and some sheet-metal screws, rivet the panels into their new home.

Install Fuel Tank Trunk Floor

3 Rivet the top of the fuel-tank trunk floor in place. After sanding, apply Sharkhide on the front side and silicone on the bottom side.

Install Lower Trunk Floor

4 After some adroit application of Sharkhide protectant, drying time, and applying the silicone between the frame tubes and the aluminum, install the lower trunk floor.

Remove Aluminum for Fuel Tank Strap

5 The passenger-side fuel-tank strap is routed through that side's lower trunk floor. To accommodate the strap, remove a rectangle of aluminum in the panel with tin snips.

Install Lower Trunk Floor

6 Repeat the easy process of Sharkhiding, siliconing, and riveting-in the various lower-trunk floor and wall aluminum panels; do not bury the license-plate light loom.

Install License-Plate Loom

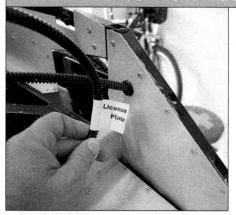

7 For the license-plate loom, drill through the passenger-side lower-trunk triangular wall and use a grommet or the clear plastic around the hole, so that the loom's conduit doesn't rip. Run the license-plate wire just under the middle of the decklid (trunk) and zip-tie it to the center tube beneath the trunk. Keep it clean.

Install Upper Trunk Floor

8 Now that the upper trunk floor has been installed, our Optima battery is placed amid all that sanded and Sharkhide-protected aluminum.

Project 3: Battery Installation

Inspect Components

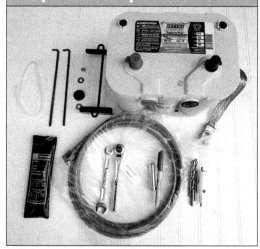

1 For our Optima battery installation, we used: the FFR-supplied battery hold-down brackets and locknuts; electric drill; a 1-inch hole saw; 3/16-, 1/4-, 5/16-inch drill bits; rivet gun, Sharpie marker, 7/16-inch deep socket; ratchet; 1/2-inch wrench; 3/16-inch hex key; the dry cell deep-cycle Optima battery; the positive battery cable; and the ground strap.

Drill Holes in Trunk Floor for Battery

2 The recommended installation location for a battery in an FFR Mk4 Cobra roadster is the upper trunk floor near the wall that separates the cockpit from the trunk. FFR provides an 8-foot battery cable, so you have plenty of length for various mounting locations, including under the trunk. We have an independent rear suspension, so we decided to go with FFR's recommendation and put our battery right where they think it's best.

Place the battery where you want it and mark where the holes need to be drilled for the two J-hook fasteners and for the battery cable and ground strap (negative battery cable). Then remove the battery. Drill the 1/4-inch J-hook holes first. Put the battery back in place and confirm these fresh holes are in the correct location for strapping down the battery. Also re-check the locations marked to drill, and install the positive and negative cables. Put the battery somewhere safe and get busy with your electric drill and 1-inch hole saw.

The J-hooks hold the Optima battery in quite well. Notice the ground strap hole is in the foreground. The dead giveaway is the fact that we have no powdercoat on the frame that's framed by the 1-inch aluminum hole we recently cut. Make sure you remove all the powdercoat/paint before you install the ground strap. If you're building an FFR Cobra, you notice that the positive battery cable is pre-made and the same applies for the negative strap. However, the positive cable is 10 feet long and likely needs to be shortened. We opted to install both cables on the side terminals for easier access, since we had to shorten the positive cable anyway.

Route Battery Cables

3 With the battery in place, route the battery cable through the hole in the floor and install the FFR-supplied rubber grommet. Attaching the ground strap is a snap. Using a lock washer and Loctite is highly recommended. Don't attach the positive cable to the terminal yet. Remember, the electrical system isn't finished.

Install Fuel-Injection ECU

4 We determined where to install our Holley Avenger EFI ECU. Before installing, we made a template so we could drill the four attachment holes in an aluminum panel.

Install Fuel-Injection ECU (Continued)

5 The FFR Mk4 Complete Kit manual recommends installing the EFI ECU on top of the passenger-side footbox in the engine bay, behind the dash on the passenger's side, or on the ceiling of the passenger-side footbox. We selected inside the transmission tunnel on the driver's side. We preferred this location for a couple reasons: the ECU is more out of the way here, and it uses up more of the harness length.

Whichever location you choose, use rubber grommets and 1-inch stainless-steel "stilts" to counterbalance any chance that the ECU might succumb to vibration. Also use lock washers, Loctite, and stainless bolts and nuts with the stilts and the rubber grommets to keep the brain intact.

Project 4: Gauge Installation

Inspect Components

1 Before we can get started on the electrical system, we need to install the gauges in the dash. However, we first need to make the dash. With an FFR Mk4 Complete Kit, the dashboard is foam-backed, vinyl-covered aluminum. Here are the gauges for the dashboard.

Enlarge Tachometer and Speedometer Holes

2 If you have the same gauges we selected with our FFR Mk4 roadster, trim the tachometer and speedometer openings to accommodate the larger-style classic instruments. Use tin snips to cut along the pre-perforated, larger-diameter opening. Your manufacturer's kit may have the same sort of arrangement. Thankfully, all the holes are pre-drilled. It's easy to cut out the larger opening if you work carefully.

Enlarge Holes with Rotary Tool

3 After cutting the opening to the larger diameter, you can use a round file or a Dremel tool with the round sander attachment to smooth the rough-cut edges.

Glue Vinyl to Dashboard

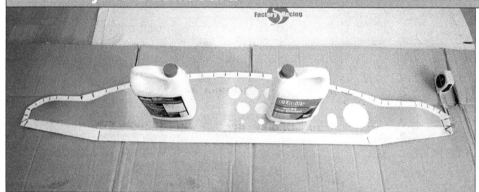

4 Glue the foam-backed black vinyl onto the front of the aluminum dashboard. Use 3M Super 77 spray-on adhesive. Also put some heavy objects on top of the aluminum to make sure the glue fastens the foam to the aluminum. To be safe, let the dash sit in this state for a couple days to thoroughly dry before performing the next operations.

You see those black lines all around the edges? Cut Vs all around, about 1/2 inch to 1 inch apart. Then apply adhesive and fold down the edges. Place heavy objects all around the border and let the glue thoroughly dry.

Install Gauges in Dashboard

5 After cutting holes in the vinyl dash pad where the gauges go and making a plus sign where the steering shaft pokes through, carefully place the gauges into slots in their designated area. The tachometer and speedometer are the same size, so you can choose where these gauges are located. The same method can be applied for fitting the smaller instruments. Either follow your manufacturer's specs or lay it out as you prefer. The instruments are pretty thin. Each instrument has a bezel screwed in on the backside of the dashboard, which firmly holds in place. The foam-backed vinyl covering the aluminum dashboard also offers a snug fit. After these gauges are secured with the provided screw-in bezels, they aren't going anywhere.

Install Dash in Cockpit

6 To mount the dashboard into the front of the cockpit, drill five evenly spaced holes into the frame hoop that holds the top of the dash in place. Use an electric drill and a 1/8-inch drill bit. FFR supplies black-finish Phillips-head screws to fasten the dash to the frame hoop.

Install Aluminum Brackets at Base of Dash

7 Two aluminum brackets are used to support the bottom edge of the dash with the 2- x 2-inch frame brace. Use 3/16-inch rivets to hold the bracket to the frame and two of the same screws that were used to hold the top of the dash to the frame hoop. Because the steering shaft provides some support for the driver's side, we spaced the brackets in the middle and on the passenger's side.

Install Dash

8 Drill holes in the dash for the three round indicator lights, the low- or high-beam headlight switch, the turn indicator switch, and the black horn button. It helps in drilling these 1/2-inch holes through the padded vinyl if you put a piece of masking tape over the area where the hole needs to be drilled. This prevents the vinyl from fraying too much. Make sure that the dashboard is securely fastened to the frame at the top and at the bottom with the two aluminum brackets, which you just fitted.

Place the switches where they look best to you, keeping in mind that they need to be accessible without interfering with the steering wheel, and they need to be within easy reach. Don't worry if the top curved part of the dash is a little jagged. The entire top edge of the dashboard will be covered by the rolled edge of the body. You will probably be able to see some of the Phillips-head screws, so it's important to have these screws on an aligned arc and equidistant from each other.

Connect Battery Ground

9 After converting the battery's negative cable to a side connection, attach the ground to the battery. Don't connect the positive terminal. You don't want to get a shocking surprise; your Cobra's electrical system doesn't want that either.

Extend and Wrap Speedometer Kit Wires

10 If you install the longer and wider Tremec T56 Magnum 6-speed manual transmission, you need to extend the speedometer kit wires. Solder on some extensions, shrink-wrap the insulation, and wrap the extended speedometer kit wires with electrical tape before plugging the wires into the transmission.

Install Gauge Dimmers and Remove Redundant Wires

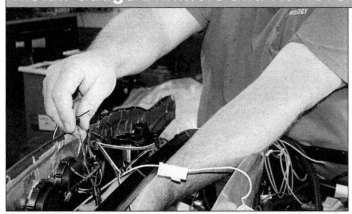

11 *With the speedometer wires set, hook up the gauge dimmers to the headlight switch behind the dashboard. Some of the wires are redundant in the dash harness because of those provided with the gauges, so you need to determine which ones are extraneous and remove them from the dash harness. We used the wiring harness with the gauges because they are calibrated for these specific instruments. Many amateur car builders might not know to use the wires supplied with the gauges as opposed to the wires in the dash harness, or which wires are redundant in the dash harness.*

Wire Fuel Gauge to Dash Harness

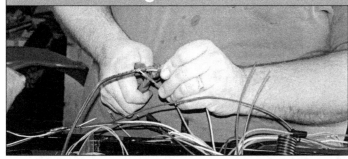

12 *Wire the fuel gauge to the dash harness, before tidying up the EFI harness.*

Wire Conduit on EFI Harness

13 *To consolidate and protect the electronic fuel injection harness, install an electrical conduit on the EFI harness.*

Tape Installed Wires Together

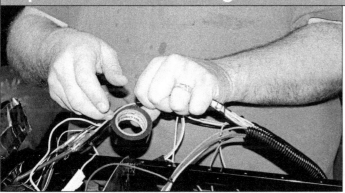

14 *Use electrical tape to separate the wires that have already been wired together from the wires that still need to be connected.*

Install Coolant Temperature Sensor

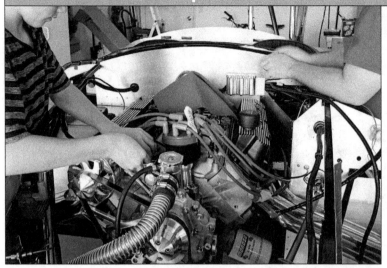

15 *Install the coolant temperature sensor in the intake manifold, which is located right next to the coolant inlet/thermostat housing. The Weiand intake manifold has a threaded hole just behind where the coolant inlet/thermostat housing is located that accommodates the coolant temperature sensor. Before installing the sensor with its adapter, apply Teflon putty to the adapter threads.*

Install Fan Switch

16 *After connecting the fan switch wire at the fan, wire and install the fan toggle switch in the dash. This is a manual switch. You can install a thermostat that automatically turns on the fan, which needs to be retrofitted. The fan comes on automatically via the thermostat in the aluminum radiator. The fan can also be manually activated if, say, you're sitting in traffic.*

Inspect MSD 6AL Ignition Box

17 *A good place to install the MSD 6AL ignition box is on top of the passenger-side footbox. We used the rubber vibration-absorbing grommets and some stainless-steel fasteners to install the box, along with lock washers, Loctite, and stainless nuts.*

MISCELLANEOUS PARTS

At this point in the construction of your Cobra replica, you've no doubt come to the same conclusion we did: there's a mind-boggling amount of details to building a kit car. If you're like us, no matter how far along you are in the project, there are many times when it seems as though the car will never be finished.

Consider the mountain of work before us in this chapter. The reality is that every little bit of work on our FFR Mk4 roadster is done painstakingly, with attention to detail and with pride. With this approach, there is no small task. They're all important, because we are the ones who are going to be driving, enjoying, and showing our FFR Mk4 Cobra roadster replica. We're sure you're taking the same sort of path with your replica's construction, whether it's a Unique Motorcars 289FIA, an E.R.A. 427SC, or a Backdraft Racing Roadster that's awaiting its drivetrain installation and final wiring hook ups.

You've likely heard the old adage, "The devil's in the details." In the construction of any replica, muscle car, or classic car, we would like to amend that statement to more positively and accurately describe the build process as, "The delight is in the details." All these build tasks are opportunities to make our Cobra stand out from the crowd. Having a glass-half-full approach to creating a Cobra replica is preferable to being mired in the seemingly endless amount of work that a build entails.

Headers

Especially when they're ceramic coated, exhaust headers make quite a visual and acoustic statement in any engine bay. The Hooker headers that come with the FFR Mk4 Roadster Complete Kit scream performance, and they're a snap to install.

Project 1: Header Installation

Install Driver-Side Headers

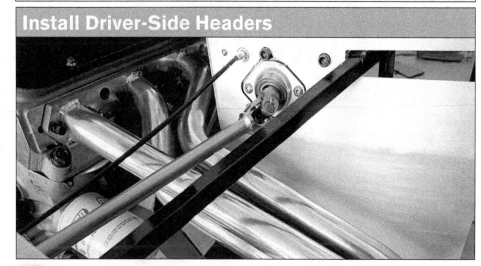

1 *Be sure to use Loctite on the supplied fasteners to help prevent an exhaust leak. The bolts do include lock washers, but we still applied Loctite to the threads. Unless you have some whiz-bang special extension for your torque wrench, you cannot use it to insure these fasteners are tight enough. Tighten them by feel, like we did.*

Torque Down Header Flange Nuts

2 *Like the exhaust headers that go in many American muscle cars, clearance is pretty tight with the firewall. You can install and tighten some of the header fasteners from above the car. The rear bolts need to be tightened from underneath the car. Do your best to make sure that all of the fasteners are equally tight, without overtightening them. This is especially important when threading bolts into aluminum cylinder heads, as is the case with us. Do not cross-thread those fasteners!*

Clutch Cable

The Factory Five Racing Mk4 Complete Kit includes many of the required components for equipping the roadster with a clutch cable, which made our decision to install a cable clutch much easier. Several prominent FFR Cobra roadster replica builders recommended using a clutch cable, rather than hydraulic, so our decision was easy.

Project 2: Clutch-Cable Installation

Install Clutch Cable

1 *Installing the clutch cable presents its own challenges. The already installed clutch quadrant and the clutch cable itself, as supplied by FFR, are excellent quality. The challenge was to adapt the 90-degree-angle bracket that's attached to the clutch cable. We could not figure out anywhere to mount the bracket that allowed us to install the clutch fork end of the clutch cable. Routing the upper end of the clutch cable is straightforward. Simply run the cable itself through the hole in the clutch-cable adjuster and affix the end to the end of the quadrant. It's a friction fit, so when you put your foot on that clutch pedal, the clutch-cable end is hard against the quadrant.*

Mount Clutch-Cable Bracket

2 *We could not find any place on the entire front part of the car to install that 90-degree clutch-cable bracket that's permanently affixed to the clutch cable. Our clever solution? We straightened out the bracket in our vice and installed the clutch-cable bracket to the Dart Pro-CNC aluminum cylinder head.*

Mount Clutch-Cable Bracket (Continued)

3 As with the top of the clutch cable and its installation with the clutch quadrant, the clutch cable is a friction fit with the clutch fork. Be sure to place the plastic housing of the clutch cable in the engine's backing plate and feed the clutch-cable end into the clutch fork. Don't worry, the installation is as easy as it appears.

Mount Clutch-Cable Bracket (Continued)

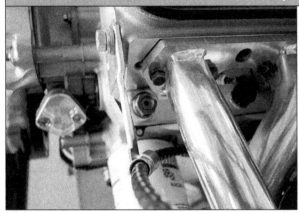

4 After testing the clutch pedal with our collective left feet, we realized that the clutch-cable bracket was a bit too flexible for our taste. The problem: When we straightened out this 90-degree bracket to let us attach the bracket to the cylinder head, we took out some of the bracket's tensile strength. We removed the clutch cable with its permanently affixed bracket and took the component to Warner's Mufflers in our hometown of Oceanside, California. At Warner's, Brett welded some metal reinforcement bars onto the back of our customized bracket. We reinstalled the clutch cable and tested the clutch pedal's actuation to confirm that we now have a properly installed clutch pedal and clutch cable.

Fill Engine and Transmission with Fluids

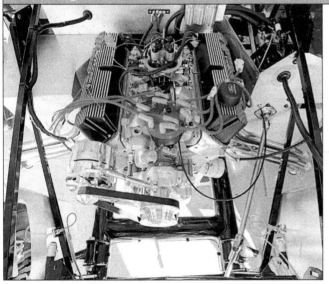

5 After the Hooker headers and the clutch cable were squared away, we could focus on filling the powertrain with fluids. The engine still has its break-in oil in the Moroso custom oil pan. So we backtrack farther and start with the Tremec T56 Magnum 6-speed manual transmission. If your engine needs oil, put it in now. Depending upon how large your oil sump is, you may need up to 9 quarts. The Tremec T56 Magnum 6-speed manual transmission we're using requires Dexron III/Mercon automatic transmission fluid. Our particular setup is a brand-new Lincoln Mk8 differential and independent rear suspension system, which utilizes SAE 75W-90 full synthetic gear oil. That's what we used. This is also a good time to pour in the coolant. We opted not to fill our cooling system just yet, because we considered making some modifications to the cooling system. You may wish to fill your system at this point.

Drivetrain Fluid

The best time to fill the drivetrain with the appropriate gear oils and fluids is when the transmission and the differential can be most easily accessed, which is before the body is put on the chassis.

Since we also installed a front shifter on the Tremec T56 Magnum 6-speed manual transmission, we removed the original shifter, installed a block-off plate, put the proper tranny fluid in, and installed the new shifter.

Project 3: Transmission Shifter Installation

Install Shifter Relocation Kit and Fill Transmission with Fluid

1 *The shifter relocation kit we procured from Modern Driveline is super easy to install. With the kit, you get a block-off plate for the rear Tremec 6-speed manual transmission and a slick, 6-speed shifter assembly that goes in the front shift location. Begin adding fluids at the manual transmission. We installed a front shifter in our 6-speed transmission, so we removed the front block-off plate and the rear shifter. Pouring in the Dexron III/Mercon automatic transmission fluid, nearly all 4 quarts of it for our Tremec T56, is easy with the rear shifter removed. If you're using a different transmission, first find out how much fluid it requires and what kind of fluid you need to use. We then filled the differential up with the synthetic gear oil, being careful to fill the differential to the proper level so it wouldn't spill out the fill hole. Using a see-through fill tube to pour the gear oil in the diff is a good way to avoid spilling the stuff.*

Install Shifter and Block-off Plate

2 *To thoroughly seal both the block-off plate opening and the front shifter location opening, apply gasket maker to the perimeter of both openings before installing the block-off plate and the shifter. To ensure a smooth shifting Tremec T56 Magnum 6-speed manual transmission, we put a dollop of white lithium grease on the internal end of the shifter. Use the same fasteners that you removed to install the shifter and the block-off plate. Before putting this together, spread some Loctite on the bolt threads and torque these fasteners to the appropriate specification.*

Roll Bar

By all appearances, it seemed that installing the roll bar would take no time at all and be simple. Since there are three installation holes that need to be drilled through frame tubes that poke up from the trunk floor and the frame, the roll bar must be fitted before the body is installed. You then need to remove the roll bar before placing the body on the chassis.

In addition, on a FFR Mk4 chassis, these attachment tubes aren't powdercoated; they're raw steel. Before doing any roll-bar fitment, you need to sand the raw steel, primer, and apply Rust-Oleum gloss-black paint to prevent rust and make those roll-bar installation pipes look nice.

Project 4: Roll Bar Installation

Paint Frame Attachment Tubes

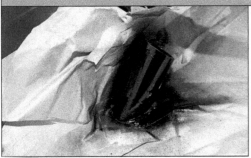

1 *If you're like us and you forgot to paint these tubes before the trunk floor went in, mask off the area around the pipes to keep overspray from getting on your shiny-aluminum trunk floor and walls.*

Install Roll Bar

2 *Just like the original 427SC Cobras, the FFR Mk4 roadster sports a roll bar that has 1½-inch-diameter tubes. Previous FFR roadsters had 2-inch-diameter tubes. We know how easy this installation looks, but it's not so. Because the roll bar has a great chrome job, the tubes don't fit in the just-painted installation pipes. Our trick to getting these tubes to fit was to use a brake cylinder hone, powered by our electric drill. We honed away at these three installation holes with a cutting-stone-tipped brake cylinder hone for 3 days! Also, once you have the right clearance to fit the tubes, install the back straight tube first and go in a full 2½ inches. If your roll bar is as feisty as ours, coax all three pipes far enough in their respective fitment sleeves with some firm whacks with a rubber mallet. There may be one or two expletives uttered during this process. This is understandable, given how difficult these pipes are to fit. Then fit the hoop in about 2 inches and raise the straight tube to connect with the hoop's rear tab.*

After properly fitting the roll bar in the round installation sleeves, use a 1/8-inch drill bit to drill a pilot hole. Place masking tape over the area to be drilled and punch a starting divot to keep the drill bit from walking. You can also use vice-grip pliers to clamp the pipes tight. This prevents the roll bar pipe from moving inside the installation sleeve. When you've gone all the way through to the other side, use your 5/16-inch drill bit to put the fastener's installation hole in the sleeve and the roll bar pipe.

Install Roll Bar (Continued)

3 *Repeat this same drilling procedure two more times with the sleeve/roll bar pipes and install the supplied fasteners. After the fasteners are holding the roll bar firmly, drill the rear roll bar tube that goes into the roll bar hoop's tab. Use some masking tape and punch a starting divot, minimizing the chance that the drill bit walks. After you properly install the roll bar, step back and admire your work. You should, because you removed the roll bar in order to install the body.*

Seating Assignments

Remember your first days of school when you made new friends and you got your seating assignment? Ideally, all your friends surrounded you. In a Cobra replica, the driver's and passenger's seats are prime real estate, so installing those seats properly for maximum comfort and great driving ergonomics is crucial to successfully building your Cobra dream machine.

Factory Five Racing gives its customers several seat choices. You can select the stock seats that are the same style as the originals, but are trimmed in vinyl, as opposed to the genuine leather seats that were in the Cobras from the 1960s. You can pay a bit more and get leather seats or you can buy some modern high-backed racing seats that have the FFR logo on them. (Other replica manufacturers likely also give you choices.)

We fit our seats and found out how easy they went in the FFR Mk4 cockpit.

Because original Cobras all had leather seats, we splurged on upgrading to leather for our ultimate FFR Mk4 Cobra roadster replica. Factory Five's Mk4 Complete Kit includes black-vinyl seats. Pay a bit more and you get these beauties that perfectly replicate the original. In the FFR Complete Kit assembly manual, you're instructed to bolt the seat frames to the cockpit floor of your roadster. We wanted adjustment for the driver, so we also ordered one set of seat tracks (instructions and fasteners are included).

Project 5: Seat Installation

Drill Mount Hole for Seat Tracks

1 *If you want some adjustment for the driver's seat in your Cobra replica, you have several options. If you're building an FFR Mk4 roadster, you can order a set of seat tracks from FFR for about $80. There are also viable alternatives from companies that make components specifically for FFR cars and for other Cobra replica manufacturers. Breeze Automotive specializes in parts for FFR, while Finish Line Accessories has components for the various Cobra replica kits. Thankfully, the FFR seat tracks come with a complete packing list, all the components required for doing the job, and a thorough set of instructions. Mind you, don't think this little installation is easy. The tools required include: jack stands, jack, Sharpie, 3/16-inch hex key, 3/16- and 5/16-inch drill bits, electric drill, 3/8-inch socket, ratchet, and a ruler.*

We were actually stumped on the very first instruction, which is to remove the studs from the seat tracks. Try as we might, we couldn't get the darn things out of the tracks. So we asked our good buddy Jim Warner, owner of Warner's Mufflers in our hometown of Oceanside, California, to remove the two studs from each seat track. After turning the seat track upside down, we marked 1/8-inch back from the side that has the square hole. As instructed, we used a 3/16-inch drill bit and then opened up the hole with a 5/16-inch drill bit. Our just-drilled 5/16-inch hole. The FFR instructions don't show an actual photo, so this is a computer graphic. The challenge of going from a 3/16-inch to a 5/16-inch hole is being able to center the drill bit after the metal material has already been removed. We took our trusty hand file and removed the material between these two holes. If you're using the same FFR-supplied seat tracks as we did, you are likely to do the same thing.

Determine Mounting Locations for Seat Tracks

2 *After finishing this first hole, mark the front bolt location of the seat track 10-13/16 inches forward of the middle of the rear rectangular hole. Drill out these two front bolt holes with the 5/16-inch drill bit and install the bolts and locknuts as shown. The FFR seat-track instruction pages recommend jacking up the driver's side of the car and placing jack stands underneath. You may as well jack up the whole car and use all four of your jack stands because we installed the passenger's side after we finished with the driver's side.*

If you're installing seat tracks in your FFR as we did, you can appreciate the detailed drawings of the cockpit of your car. After drawing a line on the floor of the driver's side that is 1 inch forward of the outer seatbelt mount and 13 inches towards the center of the cockpit floor, place the inside seat track with the adjustment-lever-track's trailing point on the edge of that line and going forward. From the start of the line that you marked on the floor, measure 4 inches and put a perpendicular line on top of the line that already exists. This is the location of the outer seat track. The front bolts that hold down the seat tracks should be 10¹³⁄₁₆ inches center to center from the rear seat track holes. We drilled the rear holes 4 inches in on the line for the outer seat track and 13 inches total from the start of the line (or 9 inches in from the outer-seat track hole). These 3/16-inch holes are drilled into the 4-inch round frame tube, so you can use the supplied self-tapping bolts to screw the backs of these seat tracks into the frame tube.

Install Rear Bolts for Both Seat Tracks

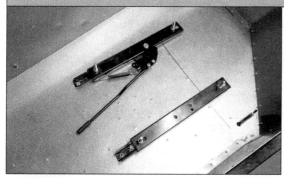

3 Push the seat track tops all the way to the rear position and drill the front seat-track bolt holes 10-13/16 inches center to center in front of the rear holes. Measure it out and drill, remembering these tracks must be parallel with each other or the seat won't move. After drilling the holes, you can install the seat tracks as we have done. If you drilled into the black metal floor or frame, you can use a self-tapping bolt. If you went through aluminum, use a stainless-steel bolt, washer, and a locknut.

Drill Driver-Side Seat Frame

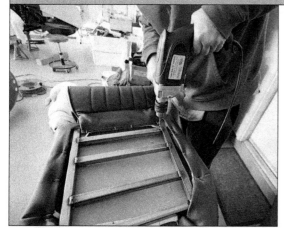

4 Here is one of many crucially important steps in properly installing the driver-side seat track and seat. After measuring the distance between all four bolt studs in the seat tracks numerous times, we drilled the seat frame of the driver's seat to accommodate those mounting bolts. We used the empty Hooker headers' box as a platform to drill upon, being extremely careful not to drill through any Cobra leather. We refuse to divulge exactly what our measurements were for doing this process because we want you to carefully measure your specific installation yourselves. This hopefully means that you measure many times and only need to drill the holes in the seat frame once. We did not make any miscalculations, though we did clean up our drilled holes with a round hand file, before installing the driver-side seat.

Install Driver-Side Seat

6 If you've installed your driver-side seat correctly, here's how the install should look with the seat bottom held out of the way. After the adjustable driver's seat is installed, it's easy to install the passenger's side. Simply place the passenger's seat where you want it to be, drill four holes through the seat frame and the floor below, and install the fasteners. If you go into the frame, you can use the supplied self-tapping bolts. If you go into aluminum only, you'll need to use stainless-steel bolts, washers, and locknuts. Hint: We decided to have the seats aligned perfectly, so we drew a line on the passenger-side floor exactly as we did for the driver's side. We then installed the passenger's seat in that stationary position.

5 After drilling the four holes properly, install the seat on the seat tracks' four mounting studs and tighten the locknuts. After you have the driver-side seat in place, climb in and test out the travel of your seat. If your seat doesn't move, you don't have the two seat tracks installed parallel to each other. If you cannot find a comfortable driving position, start over. Fortunately, we had a good fit.

Inspect Installed Seats

7 *If you installed modern racing seats in your Cobra replica, perhaps you shouldn't look at this photo. The driver-side seat is about 1-inch higher off the floor than the passenger's side, due to being on the adjustable seat tracks, but you can't see any difference from this vantage point. What you can see is how great the original-style leather seats look in a Cobra replica.*

Emergency Brake

Try as we might, we could not get the FFR-supplied emergency-brake (E-brake) system to work properly, after we fully installed the system. Remember, we're using a Tremec T56 Magnum 6-speed manual transmission that has never been installed in a Factory Five Racing Mk4 roadster chassis. The case of this transmission is wider and longer than any FFR-supported Tremec transmission.

When we finally installed the supplied E-brake system, the bracket that holds the E-brake on the passenger's side of the transmission tunnel interfered with the E-brake T-connector cable when setting the E-brake. There simply was no way that we could modify the existing emergency-brake system so that it worked effectively.

Rather than try to re-engineer these E-brake components, we ordered a Lokar universally adjustable chrome E-brake system and emergency brake cables. To our delight, the Lokar system is easy to install and offers great adjustability.

If you're building an FFR Mk4 (and don't have a Tremec T56 Magnum 6-speed), and you wish to install Factory Five's emergency brake system, follow the FFR Mk4 Complete Kit manual. If you wish to install Lokar's system, follow these steps.

Project 6: Emergency-Brake Installation

Inspect Components

Drill Emergency-Brake Handle Holes

2 *Though Lokar's universal E-brake handle is designed to install in the floor, we knew we could install the handle on the top of the transmission tunnel. We learned this from doing some investigative work on the two Cobra replica Web forums, www.FFCars.com and www.ClubCobra.*

1 *We ordered the Lokar chrome universal emergency-brake handle and universal emergency brake cables, which were everything we needed to equip our FFR Mk4 Cobra roadster replica with a superior E-brake system. Everything about these components is high quality and the instructions were through and easy to understand.*

com. We confirmed this was an excellent location for the Lokar E-brake handle with Thomas Mauldin, owner of Texas Venom. Thomas is our good friend and fellow FFR replica enthusiast. He's building his own FFR Mk4 roadster and has created many great FFR Type 65 Coupe replicas and FFR Mk1, Mk2, Mk3, and Mk4 Cobra roadster replicas for customers over the years. We figured out the optimal place to install the Lokar handle and drilled the top of the transmission tunnel frame. Hint: Put some masking tape on the slippery powdercoated frame and then punch drill bit starter holes through the masking tape. Drilling through the Lokar E-brake handle's mounting bracket holes also helped keep the drill bit where it needs to be.

Install Adjustable Emergency-Brake Cables

3 *Following Lokar's directions, install the adjustable E-brake cables holder, which is held in place with the supplied cotter pin as shown.*

Install and Route Emergency-Brake Cables

4 *One of the most challenging aspects of installing the E-brake system is carefully routing the passenger- and driver-side E-brake cables to the Lokar cable holder. Keep the cables away from any of the moving suspension components, whether you have an IRS system or a solid-axle Cobra replica. After you successfully route the cables towards the Lokar handle, put the two cables through the FFR frame eyelets as shown in the right of this photo. Then put the cable ends through the Lokar E-brake cables holder holes, being sure to have the cable sheaths removed from the cable ends. The cable ends are held tight with set-screws that are tightened with a hex key. Make certain that these set-screws are nice and tight. Notice that we also used some blue thread locker on the adjustment bolt, so that we can be certain that all is nice and tight. And then install the handle.*

Sidepipes

If you wish to run the engine in your Cobra chassis before installing the body, you need to install the sidepipes. In fact, the best way to identify any rattles in the chassis is by driving your roadster without the body. You may need to trailer the chassis to a remote parking lot or some other deserted location. Be sure it's safe to drive around and see how well everything works. Making adjustments to the chassis is much easier without the body installed, but be sure you won't get into trouble by tooling around in just your Cobra chassis.

If your engine is equipped with electronic fuel injection, start the engine with the sidepipes installed and the oxygen sensor in place in one of the sidepipes. Otherwise, you could damage your electronic fuel injection's electronic control unit (ECU). You're also better off installing the sidepipes and fitting the sidepipes' brackets. Depending on what drivetrain you're using, you may need to customize your sidepipe hangers, similar to what we've done.

Project 7: Sidepipe Installation

Install Sidepipes

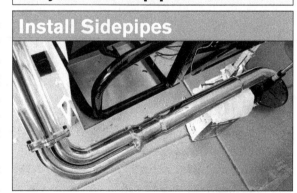

1 *The first step in installing the stainless-steel sidepipes is to find the fasteners and the gaskets. Snug the four supplied bolts/nuts tight enough to hold the sidepipes well and find a box or a spare jack stand to prop up the sidepipe.*

Install Sidepipe Brackets

2 *Factory Five Racing also supplies two first-rate stainless-steel sidepipe brackets, which very safely and securely installs the sidepipes. The button head fasteners, replete with locknuts are also stainless steel. Snug the two button-head bolts with the locknuts against the installation mount on the side of the sidepipes. You install these so you can see where to drill the two other installation holes into the chassis tube that is located at the back of the footbox floor on both the driver's and passenger's side. First use a small drill bit to drill a pilot hole. Then drill a hole large enough to accommodate the long bolts that run from the back of the footbox beneath the floor and into the undercarriage. If memory serves, we used a 1/4-inch drill bit; but don't quote us on that. Match up the diameter of the FFR supplied bolts with the appropriate-size drill bit. Drill the holes from underneath the car. You can make your job easier by using the appropriate-sized uni-bit drill bit from a hardware store. Unfortunately, we weren't able to find one in the two stores that we visited. So we suffered through with the drill bits that we had in our toolbox.*

Install Passenger-Side Bracket for Sidepipe

3 *Warner's Mufflers again came to our rescue by welding a stainless-steel mounting tab to our driver-side sidepipe bracket. To properly install the driver-side bracket, we needed this additional mounting tab.*

We also needed to modify the passenger-side sidepipe hanger. We drilled through the stainless-steel bracket itself, so we borrowed our next-door neighbor Mike Wilson's drill press. Drilling through the hard stainless steel is a royal pain. We fried a couple cobalt drill bits before we finally had the additional hole bored. We also purchased a couple extra rubber exhaust hangers, one of which we cut in half for the passenger's side. We were just fitting these sidepipes temporarily; so when you do, snug the locknuts to about 90-percent of their required tightness. If you're going to drive your car around as a go-cart to see if there are any rattles that need to be remedied or any adjustments that you need to make, be sure every nut and bolt is nice and tight.

Weather Strip

The weather strip needs to be in place so that the body sits correctly on the chassis. This is crucial, because the first and second steps in the bodywork and paint prep process are: proper alignment of the body on the chassis/frame and getting the doors, hood, and trunk to align perfectly with the body.

There is a FFR decal on the nose of the body. It states that the hood, trunk, and doors are cut a bit oversize and that they need to be trimmed to make a 3/16-inch gap all around the openings. This gap will be perfect, because various painting materials build up to narrow it.

Project 8: Weather Strip Installation

Install Weather Strip on Trunk Hoop

1 *If you're building an FFR Mk4 roadster too, the weather strip and shears are all you need for this part of the build. The rectangular-shaped weather strip (PN-10857) has an adhesive backing. This weather strip frames the engine bay and is also used on top of the frame hoop that arches over the trunk. The other weather strip we installed goes on top of some of the aluminum panels in a friction fit.*

Stick the rectangular weather strip along the trunk hoop by peeling back the wax paper on the back of the weather strip, and cut off the other end at the end of the frame hoop. Before sticking this little strip on, make sure that all your frame rails and the aluminum panels are clean and free of any dust or dirt.

Install Weather Strip on Engine Bay Frame

2 Now that you know how to install the adhesive-backed weather strip like a pro, put the weather strip on the frame tubes that run the length of the engine bay. For the driver-side tube, stop the weather strip before the top of the pedal box. Install the weather strip on the passenger-side tube as well. We ran ours up to this point. For both sides, they run down to the point where the frame angles down and terminate before the frame angles down.

Install Weather Strip atop Firewall

3 Measure how much friction-fit weather strip needs to be installed on top of the aluminum firewall panel. Cut the length you need and push the weather strip onto the firewall aluminum panel. You may need to pry the weather strip material apart with a flat-blade screwdriver to get the material pliable enough to beginning installing it on the aluminum panel.

Pry Weather Strip Apart

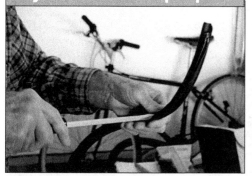

4 To make your friction-fit weather strip that much easier to apply, first pry the groove apart a little bit with a large flat-blade screwdriver.

Install Weather Strip on Trunk

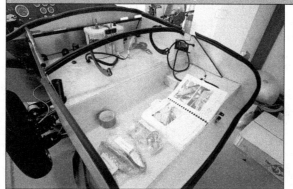

5 Patiently push down on the friction fit weather strip atop the trunk aluminum walls to get a good even fit on this material. Factory Five Racing provides a liberal amount of weather strip in the Mk4 Complete Kit. Even after installing it, you should have some left over. This proves to be a good thing because you likely need to replace some of the weather strip after installing and removing the roadster body two or three times for bodywork and painting.

Install Quickjack Bolts and Sleeves

6 After you and your friends have put the body back on the chassis, install the four Quickjack bolts and sleeves. These four fasteners let you properly locate and align the body on the chassis. One huge word of caution here: Though the picture shows the bolts running from the inside of the body to the outside of the body with the locknuts on the outside, this is incorrect. The FFR Mk4 Complete manual shows this as the way to install the rear bolts. Run the bolts from the outside in. In other words, have the heads of the bolts on the outside and the threads and locknuts on the inside. If you do it in this fashion, you shouldn't have to drop the fuel tank. When you've tightened these four fasteners, you can load your Cobra replica on/in your trailer and head to your designated body and paint experts. Otherwise, you can start fitting the doors to begin the bodywork process.

BODY FITMENT AND PAINT

I've driven Cobra replicas that wore primer only. I've ridden in a brushed-aluminum with polished-aluminum Le Mans-striped Kirkham Cobra replica. I've driven a silver FFR and 289 Unique Motorcars Cobra, a yellow Factory Five Racing Mk3, an FFR still clad in Gel Coat, a black-over-red Backdraft Racing Roadster, and so on. Despite the rainbow of hues, or lack thereof, my single favorite Cobra color dates to the mid 1960s. That's when Ford sprayed some Cobras and some Ford Mustangs in the heavenly hue of Caspian Blue.

Dad and I contemplated for several months what color(s) our roadster should be. For the longest time, he lobbied to have our FFR Mk4 Cobra roadster replica in a racy shade of red. Cobras do look wonderful in red, but knowing the history of those racing Cobras of the early through the mid 1960s, I did not want our roadster to be red. The Cobra's biggest rival has always been Ferrari. When these two foes battled, the Ferraris were red, and the Cobras were always white over blue.

During my tenure as editor of *Kit Car* magazine, I may have photographed more white-over-blue Cobra replicas than any other man in history. But our car just couldn't be white over blue any more than it could be Ferrari red or any shade of red.

We agreed upon a midnight blue color. As silly as it sounds now, we were actually going to have a one-color Cobra replica. We came to realize that we wouldn't quite be honoring the Snake. The majority of original Cobras wore Le Mans

A total of 62 aluminum panels are installed in an FFR Mk4. The panels fit together quite well and form an extremely strong and rigid chassis, once the panels are riveted into place. Installing the panels takes considerable planning, patience, measurement, and work.

racing stripes. A few months elapsed as we were toiling away at our FFR Mk4 in our home shop. Then we finally decided to also have the team stripes on the driver-side fender. Not too long thereafter, we gave two thumbs up to those delightful Le Mans over-the-top stripes in a sort of titanium color.

We wanted House of Kolor paint on our FFR Mk4 roadster, which was a no-brainer. The tough part of our decision was trying to find a reliable, professional, and reasonable body and paint shop to bring our House of Kolor Cobra to life.

We know now that the best way to find a top-notch shop would have been to contact House of Kolor and ask for painter recommendations that use its products in the area, and then go talk to them. Whether you're using House of Kolor products or some other manufacturer's painting finishes, contact an expert at the company and seek professional painter references in your area, either via the paint company's Web site or on the old-fashioned telephone.

Make sure that you follow up on any body/paint referrals you get from your paint supplier. And when you negotiate a body and paint project with potential shops, get detailed written estimates. You are also well served by talking to customers of the shops that you're investigating to see how pleased they are with the outcome on their body and paint projects.

Another way to get body/paint referrals is by talking to members of your favorite car clubs and car-buff buddies. The point is: complete your homework on this all-important aspect of your Cobra project.

Project 1: Fitment Procedure

Install Passenger's Door

1 *Pro-painter and bodywork maestro Ray commenced fitting the doors. We located the door fasteners and hung the doors for Ray. Starting at the top, Ray adjusted the fasteners attached to the hinges in their slots to align the panel surfaces with the body. He proceeded to work with the passenger-side door hinge to get the door to hang right and to get the gap as even as possible before adding any sort of filler (if needed).*

Drill Hole to Rivet Body to Chassis

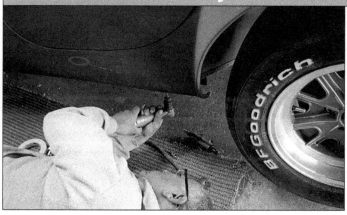

2 *After the top of the door panel is in alignment with the body, the bottom of the body can be moved in and out a bit to assist in achieving the best fit between the bottom edge of the door and body. After Ray found the desired alignment, he used a couple of long 3/16-inch rivets to attach the bottom lip of the body with the chassis. Of course, he first needed to drill a couple 3/16-inch holes in the body lip/chassis to rivet the two together, shown here on the driver's side of the car.*

Project 2: Door Latch and Hardware Installation

Install Door Latches

2 *Use the right amount of shims (washers) to bolt the striker onto the chassis. This is done to bring the base of the striker head flush with the door latch pad when the door is closed. Because* the next step is to latch the door latch onto the striker and close the door, this is already shown in this photo.

After latching the door latch onto the striker and adjusting the striker to fit the latch to the driver-side-door cutout, Ray was almost ready to mark where the holes need to be drilled into the door latch pad to install the door latch. If needed, you can use the FFR-supplied door latch spacers to assist with the alignment of the door latch to the striker. To prevent binding between the door latch and striker, use some lithium or silicone grease on the moving parts.

1 *To get the doors to fit inside the door jams properly with an even 3/16-inch gap all the way around, the* door latches needed to be installed. Find the door components and the door latch assemblies. Use a 1/2-inch wrench, a 1/8-inch drill bit, a Phillips-head screwdriver, a Sharpie, and lithium or silicone grease. First remove the original mounting bracket from the door latch striker. Only the striker and the washers are used. The mounting bracket and the nut aren't used, so you can save them for your next project.

Install Door Latches (Continued)

3 *With the doors marked, use a 1/8-inch drill bit to bore the bolt holes to install the driver-side door latch. The holes all drilled, install the driver-side door latch. Repeat this same process for the passenger side.*

Install Pipe Spacer

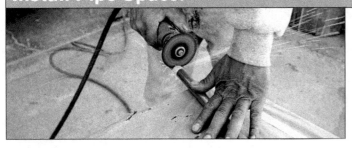

4 *Rather than use several shims to properly space out the driver- and passenger-side strikers to align with the door latch, Ray cut off the correct width and diameter of stainless-steel pipe to serve as spacer sleeves. After cutting, he installed the driver-side spacer.*

Install Trunk Lid

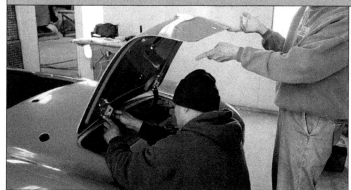

5 Find the fasteners that hold the decklid (trunk lid) on the FFR Mk4's hidden hinges and install the lid. Just snug these bolts and locknuts for now. Leave the fasteners loose enough so that you can adjust how the lid fits the gap in the back of the body. To hold the lid's surfaces level with the back of the body, you can temporarily use some of the rubber bumpers that are supplied for proper fitment of the hood.

6 The fit of the decklid, prior to any bodywork taking place on the back of the car, is superb. Both Jorge Guerrero and Ray Rosales remarked at how great the quality of the FFR fiberglass is and how well the doors, trunk, and hood fit the gaps without needing any bodywork. In fact, this photo was taken before using any rubber bumpers to hold the trunk lid even with the back of the body.

Construct Template for Patch Panel

7 There are numerous occasions when you must take a MacGyver or improvisational approach to getting work done. We needed to plug the stock hole on the passenger's side of the interior where the stock emergency brake is typically installed, so Dad used my note pad as a straight edge to draw an outline on a spare piece of cardboard that served as the template for the aluminum patch panel we cut out to plug the hole in our cockpit.

Make Template and Fit Aluminum Panel

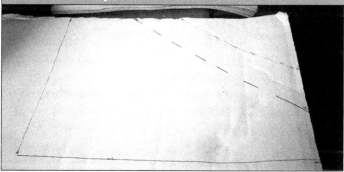

9 We cut out the cardboard template and put it against the opening in the aluminum. This confirmed where we needed to bend the aluminum panel. Tracing this shape on the spare aluminum panel came next. We then cut out the aluminum patch panel using the very same tin snips. We marked the bend in the aluminum by transferring where the bend should be from the template. We bent the aluminum over a workbench, marked the holes, and then drilled rivet holes in the patch panel.

8 From looking at our very simple template, you're probably wondering why we even needed to bother with a template. Those dotted lines show where the aluminum needs to be bent, which should give you a clue as to why we need the template.

Install Aluminum Patch Panel

10 After applying the silicone on the back of the patch panel where it attaches to the transmission tunnel wall and floor, we riveted the panel into place in the interior. The panel is hidden by HushMat sound and heat insulation and the FFR-supplied black carpet, so there's no need to make the panel perfect. It just needs to be air- and water-tight, which is where the careful application of silicone becomes important. You can also see the custom Lokar emergency brake, which works far better than the supplied E-brake system and looks great.

Drill Holes for License Plate

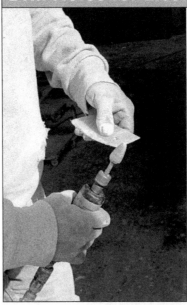

11 Ray used a scrap piece of plastic to make a mounting template for the trunk's license plate light. Notice that he already has drilled the installation holes in the template, which enabled him to locate where the holes need to be drilled in the decklid to properly mount the license plate light. He trimmed the edges of the template with an air deburr tool.

Mark License Plate Light Holes

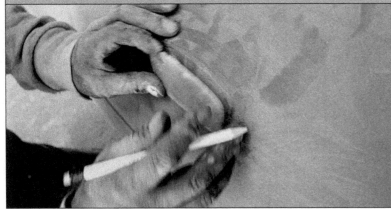

12 With the template properly shaped and drilled, Ray held it against the trunk lid, so that he could mark where the license plate light installation holes need to be drilled.

Drill License Plate Holes

13 If you're going to do your own body and paintwork, use a respirator or at least masks to help prevent poisoning your insides with fiberglass. A cordless drill with the appropriate-sized drill bit is sufficient for quickly boring holes in the fiberglass. Just correctly locate where the holes need to be, or you'll be repairing the mistake and re-drilling.

Install License Plate Light

14 *After drilling the installation holes, temporarily install the license plate light to check that the bracket is properly centered and is level. Take the light back off and securely store it with the fasteners for installation after the body has been painted and the trunk lid has been hung.*

Fit Trunk Latch Components

15 *To temporarily install the trunk latch, find the latch and components in the three-lock set in your FFR-supplied boxes of parts. You need to use a 3/8-inch socket, the ratchet, a flat-head screwdriver, and a Phillips-head screwdriver to complete the installation.*

Install Trunk Latch Handle

16 *Prop the trunk lid up with a 2x4 and install the trunk handle/ latch mechanism with the Phillips-head screwdriver and a 3/8-inch wrench, or socket and ratchet.*

Install Trunk Latch Pin

17 *We had to modify our trunk latch pin that installs at the base of the trunk to beef it up a bit. Typically, the latch pin screw goes through the fiberglass rear wall of the trunk. On the inside of the trunk a stainless-steel sleeve fits around the screw. The threaded end of the screw, for which the locknut fastened on the backside, is fit through the pre-drilled aluminum panel. An added reinforcement L-bracket was riveted behind the aluminum wall, which nicely beefs up how the latch grabs onto the pin. (Also see step 18.) Test how well the key works in the handle. But these trunk latch components don't get to stay on the car. Remove them and secure them for quick retrieval after the body and trunk are ready to re-assemble (after the painting and curing process).*

Install Hood Hinges and Fasteners

18 To install the hood hinges, you need a rivet gun and 3/16-inch rivets, 3/16-, 7/64- and 5/8-inch drill bits, an electric drill, Sharpie, measuring tape, 3/16-inch hex key, and a 1/2-inch wrench.

Find the hood hinges and the fasteners. The steel hood hinge mounts need to be primered and painted. Ray sprayed Rust-Oleum red-oxide primer and gloss-black Rust-Oleum paint on the steel platforms and let them dry before he and Jorge proceeded to perform this rather elaborate hood and hinge installation.

Mount Hinge Arms

19 The simplest part of mounting and aligning the hood is to press those copper-colored sleeves into the aluminum hinge arms. We didn't paint our hinge arms, but protected them with Sharkhide protectant to prevent oxidation. You may choose this route, or you could paint them with Rust-Oleum.

Install Hood Hinge Pivot Mounts

20 Rivets are used to install the hood hinge pivot mounts on the underside of the front of the hood. FFR pre-drills these rivet holes, though they may need a bit of cleaning up with a 3/16-inch drill bit and cordless drill. Just a few rivets are required since this is a first fitting. Preferably, you want to remove the pivot mounts when the car goes to paint. If you're building an FFR Mk4 like ours, one of the first things you likely noticed was the FFR sticker on the nose of the body. It states that all of the body panels are made oversized, so that they can be trimmed to fit and make a 3/16-inch gap all the way around. As we've mentioned previously, the fiberglass on the FFR Mk4 body and body panels is first rate. We didn't have to trim the door panels or trunk lid on our car to get the gap to the optimal 3/16-inch space. To foreshadow a little, the hood is slightly trimmed on the passenger's side and a miniscule amount on the driver's side, but Jorge didn't trim the hood until after he had perfectly fitted the hood to the hood hinges.

Install Passenger-Side Hinge

21 From this perspective, you can see exactly how the hood hinge assembly goes together. It's really a well-thought-out design, so you can properly align the hood with the hood hole. Notice that Jorge intentionally has the bolts and nut loose, so he can easily change how the hood fits in its opening by moving it side to side or fore and aft. In order to make fitment adjustments, use a 1x2 to prop the hood open. Also temporarily install the hydraulic hood's prop arms on either side of the hood, which is fully detailed in the FFR Mk4 Complete Kit manual. Jorge hadn't installed this here because he wanted to get the fitment of the hood perfect before doing any trimming on the hood.

Project 3: Eliminate Mold Line and Trim Body Panels

Apply Mar-Glass to Mold Seams

1 To smooth the mold seams, You can use a 3M bodywork product called Mar-Glass. Mar-Glass is a short-strand reinforced filler and is very much like fiberglass. It's harder than Bondo. Apply it over the mold seams and let the Mar-Glass dry for about 15 to 20 minutes before sanding the seams and the Mar-Glass with 40-grit sandpaper.

Sand Away Mold Seams

2 Sand away the mold seams until they disappear and the adjoined body panels appear as one.

Set Hood Gap

3 With the hood now fitting as it should, use an air grinder to sand off just a smidgen of the hood on the driver's side.

Mark Hood for Trimming

4 If your passenger's side of the hood requires more trimming, use some painter's tape to mark a straight cut-off/grind-off line just prior to wielding the air grinder.

Trim Passenger's Side of Hood

5 If you look closely, you see that almost half of the passenger's side of the hood has been trimmed down to the tape. If you are doing this job yourself, easy does it is a great way to go when using the air grinder. Don't cut off too much of the fiberglass. Though fiberglass is easy to work with, it's more challenging to build up a straight edge than it is to cutoff that same edge. Right after trimming the passenger's side, the back of the hood received the same treatment.

Determine Location for Driver-Side Hood Handle

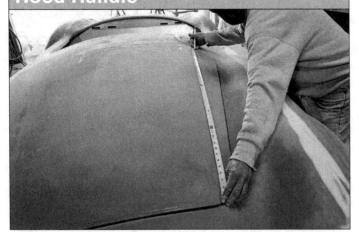

6 Take measurements to determine where to locate the driver-side hood handle. The FFR Mk4 Complete Kit manual offers a more elaborate explanation on how to locate the handles, if you are doing this part of the work yourself on your Mk4.

Drill Hole for Driver-Side Hood Handle

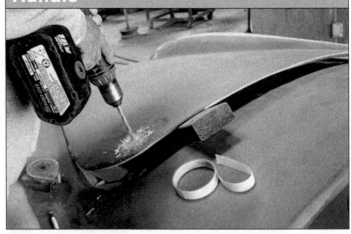

7 With the driver-side hood-handle-hole location determined it is time to do some drilling. Use a smaller drill bit than the required 5/8-inch-diameter hole first. So that you don't mistakenly drill into something that you don't intend to, prop the hood up with a short 2x4 before drilling.

Enlarge Driver-Side Hood Handle Hole

8 If you have an air compressor and some air tools, you too can easily open up the hood-handle holes to the 5/8-inch-diameter requirement. Simply use the deburring tool on the end of your air drill.

Install Hood Handle Paddle

9 After boring out the hood-handle holes to 5/8-inch, drill the two 1/8-inch bolt holes for attaching the hood handle to the top side of the hood. Then install the paddle with the 2.5-mm hex key and the hex-head bolt. After confirming the lock worked on the driver-side hood handle, repeat the same process to install the passenger-side hood handle.

Mark and Drill Holes for Fuel Filler Cap

10 You can use the Le Mans fuel-filler cap's rubber gasket as a template for marking and drilling the installation holes in the rear passenger-side fender.

Apply Mar-Glass to Side of Hood Sides

11 *Though the hood now fits the gap well, with a 3/16-inch space all the way around, the sides of the hood needed a bit of beefing up to mate with the hood. Apply some Mar-Glass right next to either side of the hood, which is to be sanded smooth with 40-grit sandpaper and covered with a skim coat of Bondo.*

Trim Hood and Hood Sides

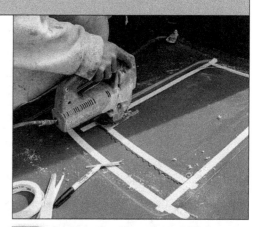

12 *It may take two people to get the hood sides squared away, in anticipation of removing the hood to cut out an opening for the Cobra's hood scoop.*

Project 4: Hood Scoop Installation

Cut Out Hood Scoop Hole

1 *After the hood fits its opening, remove the hood from the hood hinges and secure away the hood handles. Remove the hood to mark and cut a hole in the hood that accommodates the functional fresh-air hood scoop. Turn the hood upside down. Trace the cutout for the scoop on the liner, 1½ inches in from the side and rear edges and 4 inches back from the front edge of the scoop recess. Use a large enough hole in the liner and fiberglass to enable cutting out the hood scoop hole with a jigsaw.*

2 *Cutting the fiberglass with a jigsaw should be quite simple. Make the cut as straight as you can and be sure to wear a mask or a respirator.*

Smooth Hole for Hood Scoop

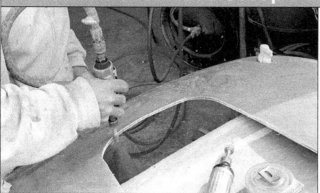

3 *After cutting out the hole in the hood for the hood scoop, clean the cut edges both with a deburring tool attached to the air drill and also 40-grit sandpaper on a hand block sander.*

Apply Mar-Glass to Cut Edge

4 To finish off the cut edge, apply Mar-Glass, waited the appropriate time for it to dry, and sanded it smooth.

Make Cut Line for Hood Scoop

5 Even though the hood scoop looks as though it's ready to install, the flange needs to be trimmed so that it's 3/4-inch wide on the sides and on the back. You can show off your pinstriping prowess by using a finger to draw the 3/4-inch cut line. After this cut line is drawn, mark rivet holes every 3 inches along the flange.

Drill Rivet Holes

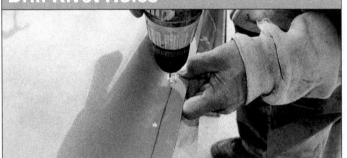

6 Use 3/16-inch rivets to install the hood scoop. Drill out the rivet holes with a 3/16-inch drill bit before trimming the hood scoop.

Sand Bottom of Hood Scoop Flange

7 After drilling the rivet holes in the top of the hood scoop, sand smooth the underside of the scoop's flange.

Trim Hood Scoop Flange

8 With the hood scoop turned right side up, make quick work of the trimming with the air tool and its cutoff-wheel accessory. Then sand the cut edge smooth and apply Mar-Glass and sanded it smooth.

Drill Rivet Holes in Hood

9 To drill the rivet holes in the hood that attach the hood scoop to the hood, firmly hold the hood scoop in place while you drill through the rivet holes in the scoop. Use the hood scoop as a drilling template to precisely locate where the rivet holes should be in the hood. The challenge with drilling the hood this way is to firmly hold the hood scoop in position.

Project 5: Primer Application

Sand Body of Car

1 Before the body and panels gets its first sanding primer coat, give it a thorough sanding of all the body panels with 400-grit sandpaper. Obviously, this photo was taken prior to cutting the hood for the scoop.

Apply Sanding Primer

2 Apply two coats of sanding primer get all the body panels. Each primer coat is thoroughly sanded with 400-grit sandpaper. In these sanding coats, imperfections in the fiberglass appear in the form of tiny pinholes and larger bubbles. Also, any imperfections in the body/paint prep can be remedied. Everyone was impressed with the top-notch quality of the Factory Five Racing fiberglass. Hardly any pinholes were found and nary an air-bubble void.

Apply Seal Primer

3 After the two coats of sanding primer, the car is thoroughly coated with sealer/primer in the same general color as the car. Given the company's reputation for providing the finest automotive paints, we selected House of Kolor paint for our FFR Mk4 Cobra roadster replica. The HOK sealer/primer used on our road burner is KD3005 Kustom DTS Foundation Surfacer/Sealer Blue, which should is a clue of the actual hue of our roadster. The HOK sealer primer is mixed with four parts primer, one part HOK KD3000 Series DTS Hardener, and one part House of Kolor RU301 LV Warm Weather Reducer.

Project 6: Complete Footbox

Modify Pedal Box Roof

1 While you spray the House of Kolor sealer/primer on all the body panels, modify the driver-side aluminum pedal box roof to meld with the remote brake reservoir block. You may have riveted enough aluminum panels to know how this roof was installed. What you don't know is that we applied HushMat sound and heat insulation panels on the ceiling of this roof panel prior to the sanding, applying Sharkhide, applying silicone, and riveting it into place.

Install Insulation on Pedal Box Ceiling

2 *The HushMat insulation panels are easy to install. Cut the panels to size, peel off the backing paper, and stick onto the aluminum panels.*

Project 7: Painting Procedure

Wipe On Post Sanding Cleaner

1 *Before spraying any paint over the House of Kolor sealer/foundation primer, the primer received a thorough cleaning/degreasing with House of Kolor KC20 Post Sanding Cleaner. The top coats of paint need to be applied over the HOK sealer primer within 4 to 6 hours max of the sealer primer's application. If the top coats of paint are applied after the 6-hour window, the sealer primer must be sanded with a 600-grit wet sanding to ensure proper adherence.*

With the body and all other panels wet sanded with 600-grit sandpaper and the paint booth dust-free and ready for the painter, thoroughly apply the House of Kolor KC20 Post Sanding Cleaner to all surfaces to be painted.

Use Compressed Air to Blow Off Dust

2 *Carefully blow off any remaining dust or dirt on the surface of all the body panels three times, waiting several minutes between each session. This approach is very effective. After letting the air settle for a couple minutes, run your hand lightly over the body. You can feel some dust. When you blow off the body a second time, there is less, but still noticeable. Once the air settles the third time, you feel no dust. Now you're ready to lay down the House of Kolor Shimrin 2 (S-2 for short) Stratto Blue paint.*

Select and Mix Paint

3 The new House of Kolor Shimrin 2 paints are VOC compliant in all 50 states. Right now, there are 400 different colors available in the Shimrin 2 hues. Later this year, there will be 1,500 colors. The Shimrin S-2 custom auto paint system eliminates the need to pick a stock OEM color and gives car enthusiasts and auto painters the ability to create their own custom-paint colors that can be kept top secret. In our case, we're going with a very dark midnight-blue hue, based upon the fantastic House of Kolor Shimrin S-2 Stratto Blue as the car's main body color. We reveal the other colors after Ray lays down the paint. But for now, he mixed four parts of the Stratto Blue with one part of the House of Kolor RU301 LV Warm Weather Reducer. Spraying this paint over the same color primer means that we used less paint, achieved better coverage, and produced a deeper and richer finish.

Apply Base Coat of Paint

4 To make sure that the air hose is kept away from the body, drape it on your back as you sprayed the first coat of HOK Stratto Blue with his high volume low pressure (HVLP) paint gun. Only spraying at 20 pounds of pressure, still gets awesome coverage and no overspray. That blue tape on this fender is protecting some driver's team stripes that have already been applied. For now, you just have to guess what color is beneath the masking tape.

Apply Base Coat of Paint (Continued)

5 It's just a few minutes later and Ray is already laying down a second topcoat of our top-secret shade of House of Kolor Stratto Blue. These colors really pop in natural light—day or night. House of Kolor has been providing premium custom finishes since 1956. With the several coats of Stratto Blue now on the Mk4 roadster body and body panels, Ray next shot the Klear. He used USCO1 House of Kolor Kosmic Urethane Show Klear.

Mix Clear Coat for Application

6 There are three parts Klear, one part HOK RU-300 VOC-exempt Reducer, and one part Kustom Catalyst Urethane System HOK KU152 Catalyst mixed together to perfectly shoot the House of Kolor clear on the Cobra.

Apply Clear Coat

7   To culminate the shooting for the day, Ray sprayed several coats of clear at 10-minute intervals.

Tape for LeMans Stripes

8   *Painter's tape is applied on the front of the roadster all the way to the back of the car to outline the car's stripes. In Cobra parlance, this* duo of over-the-top stripes is known as Le Mans stripes. They're named after that world famous endurance racecar contest known as the 24 Hours of Le Mans, held in Rheims, France. Typically, Le Mans stripes are each 6½ inches wide and are separated by 2 inches. We decided to have our Le Mans stripes a little larger. Ours is 7 inches wide, but still separated by 2 inches of top-secret Stratto Blue.

Apply LeMans Strips

9   *Though the color appears to be a shade of brown in the paint booth, it is actually a secret mix of House of Kolor Shimrin S-2 Galaxy Gray with* some HOK Kosmatic Sparkling Pearl metal flake. We didn't want to have yet another Wimbledon White over Caspian Blue Cobra replica, although there's nothing wrong with that famous paint scheme.

Apply Clear Coat Again

10   Now that the stripes are all in place, several coats of House of Kolor Klear are applied on all the painted surfaces. We're still not going to reveal those driver's team stripes yet.

Buff Paint to Finish

11   After allowing the House of Kolor paint and Klear coats to cure for a couple days in the paint booth, we color sand and then buff the paint job. Use rubbing compound, ultrafine machine polish, and spray wax for the buffing process shown here. This complete process takes a few days to complete.

INTERIOR AND WINDSHIELD

The interior largely determines your driving experience. After all, it's what you're in touch with when you drive the car. The seats, carpet, gauges, steering wheel, console, and all the related parts project the personality of the car. While most kit car manufacturers supply a complete interior kit, there's nothing to stop you from choosing an interior that's different than the one supplied by the manufacturer.

In many cases, the Cobra kit car manufacturers provide an interior that appears similar to the original to provide that vintage English roadster/Cobra driving experience. And there's nothing wrong with that. But if you want to outfit your Cobra differently than the manufacturer supplied interior, there's a whole universe of options. You can select different carpets, racing or performance type seats (need to have low backs, so they don't extend over the body lines), modern steering wheels, electronics, gauges, and so forth.

For space considerations here, we cannot go into every single combination an owner could select. However, many owners stick with the manu-facturer-supplied interior and often that's a wise choice because mounting the seats, dash, and other components follows the manufacturer's instructions.

Windshield

To avoid being redundant, we won't again describe how the doors, trunk-lid, and hood go on the car.

Project 1: Windshield Installation

Install Windshield Stanchions

1 *Using the supplied FFR fasteners, the first step in the windshield's installation is to install the windscreen's uprights or stanchions. You need the supplied short Phillips-head screws to attach the uprights.*

Once you've attached the uprights, you and an assistant need to place the stanchions through the stanchion holes on either side of the body. Be careful in sliding the stanchions through the openings, especially if your car has already been painted. The optimum time to fit the windshield is right after you put the body back on the chassis and aligned the body on the chassis with Quickjack bolts. When you've successfully placed the stanchions into the openings, the uprights likely bottom out on the chassis tubes. Mark the stanchions to be cut. Cut off the stanchions at a 45-degree angle to get the proper pitch of the windshield to the body. Because the frame has already been drilled to install the stanchions to the frame, carefully trace the installation holes onto the stanchions before removing the windshield.

Suffice it to say that we managed to install all the painted panels and get them to fit their respective openings with the right amount of gap all the way around.

What we must talk about, however, is installing the windshield. This crucial step was supposed to take place before the body had been painted. Fortunately for us, putting the windshield in place was not difficult. It's best to pre-fit the windshield before your Cobra replica has been painted. But, if you don't, you still should be able to get the glass in without incident.

Shorten Windshield Stanchions

2 *After removing the stanchions or windshield side-bars, cut off both stanchions. You can perform this within minutes of pulling the die grinder's trigger. Using a hacksaw takes at least twice as long.*

File Cut and Drill Stanchion

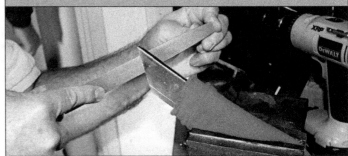

3 *Make a clean cut on both stanchions because then it requires just a little touch up with the flat file to make the stanchions install-ready, with the exception of drilling attachment holes. With a 1/2-inch bit, drill the attachment holes that you traced when the stanchions were temporarily in place.*

Tighten Stanchion Bolts & Nuts

4 *Re-attach the uprights onto the windscreen frame using the aforementioned short Phillips-head screws. Then, use a 3/4-inch wrench, 3/4-inch socket, and ratchet to tighten the fasteners that hold the sidebars to the frame. With the holes successfully drilled, get your companion to help you slide the windshield uprights into their home in the body.*

Floor Liner and Carpet

We decided early in the planning stages of our project to equip the car's interior with sound and heat insulation. The reasons for doing this were pretty obvious. Cobras usually run big and hot V-8 engines that make a great deal of noise and create a fair amount of heat. The powerplants are set far back in the chassis to achieve a perfect 50/50 front/rear weight distribution, which enables superlative handling capabilities at high speeds. It also means that the hot, noisy drivetrain is almost in your lap. Indeed, you're almost surrounded by heat and noise in a Cobra. There is a sidepipe on one flank and an engine/transmission on your other side.

Dynamat, Fatmat, B-quiet, and others make quality sound deadening mats. Dynamat is a popular aftermarket option and common for restoration builds and many project cars. We decided to equip our roadster with HushMat Ultra, the fastest growing thermal insulation and sound deadening material available for the automotive industry. Every automobile manufacturer in the United States, Mexico, and Canada uses HushMat, so the state-of-the-art foil constrained layer-damping technology was installed in our sports car.

Project 2: Floorpan Finishing Procedure

Trim and Rivet Sill Panel into Place

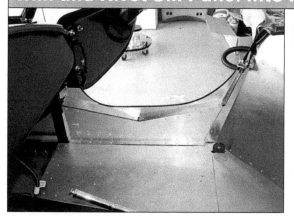

1 Before you install the insulation in the interior, rivet two more aluminum sill panels into place. Test fit the panels, as they are a unique shape and may need to be trimmed. Our passenger-side sill plate did not need any modification, so we applied silicone to the frame, placed the sill plate into position, and drilled the rivet holes while the silicone was doing its job sticking. The sill plate bridges the small gap between the interior's framing and the fiberglass body, so it's very important that the panel is a good fit. Trim the surfaces that need modification with a pair of tin snips. You may need to trim along a curved radius. Once you cut off the required amount of the aluminum, use a flat file to smooth the cut edges. Apply silicone to the sill frame underneath the driver-side door opening, place the panel in place, drill it in place, put a couple strategic sheetmetal screws to hold it while riveting the panel, and finalize the riveting process for the aluminum sill plate panel.

Apply Silicone to Seal Against Elements

2 Before installing the HushMat sound and heat insulation in the cockpit, use a silicone gun to seal any cracks in the aluminum panel floors and walls to protect the interior from the elements. We had a couple cracks in the footbox far corners, which we sealed with silicone and a crack where we filled the hole where the original emergency brake handle is supposed to go. We installed a Lokar custom E-brake system, so we closed the opening with an aluminum panel.

Install Floor Liner

3 HushMat is extremely easy to install. Take one of the 1x2-foot panels, peel off the paper that is attached to the sticky layer beneath the constraining foil and adhere the sticky side onto the aluminum floor or walls. Use brake cleaner or Acetone to clean all aluminum surfaces before installing the HushMat, so it firmly adheres to the surface.

To make your life easier, use kneepads or kneel on a furniture pad. Cover the passenger sidewall and work your way down into the passenger side, toward covering the lower floor inside the footbox and the entire footbox interior. You have to get into some fairly awkward positions while installing these high-tech insulation panels, but the end result will be worth it. For the longest time we resisted permanently covering the transmission tunnel because we wanted to maintain top-side access to the Holley Avenger EFI computer installed along the driver's side wall of the tunnel. But there's not really any advantage to having a lift off tunnel top since we do have easy access to the Holley EFI computer from underneath the tunnel

Trace Cutouts in Trans Tunnel

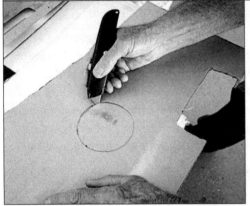

4 Put the transmission tunnel top on top of the underside of the HushMat Ultra panel. Trace the two cutouts in the panel, one for the Lokar emergency brake handle and one for the shifter lever and boot.

Cut Out Trans Tunnel Top Panel

5 Use some old shop scissors or a utility knife to cut out the trans tunnel top panel and apply the Hush-Mat Ultra.

Use Razorblade to Cut Out Shifter Hole

6 Wielding a razorblade to cut out the shifter opening is the right way to go. Trace the correctly sized cut out with a Sharpie and make sure not to over cut because you cannot add material back on. Peel off the HushMat Ultra's backing paper.

Apply HushMat Panel to Trans Tunnel Top

7 Applying HushMat Ultra is very simple. After sticking it on each panel, smooth it out with your hands. You can also use a kitchen rolling pin or slide a rubber mallet across the HushMat to firmly install it. Once completed, the covered trans tunnel lid is now ready to be riveted atop the trans tunnel.

Inspect and Clean Floor Liner

8 With the exception of the tops of the sill plates, the cockpit is covered, and sound and heat/cold insulated with HushMat Ultra. Before gluing in the carpet, make sure the HushMat foil top is clean and free of any HushMat remnants or dirt. Vacuum the interior, and then proceed to adhere the carpet.

Mask Off Body Where Needed

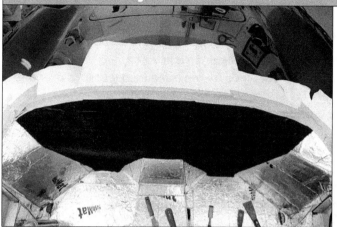

9 As with the HushMat Ultra insulation material, the first aluminum surface to receive carpet is the rear wall of the cockpit. Factory Five Racing–supplied carpet sections all come pre-cut from the FFR factory. Use 3M Super 77 Multi-purpose Adhesive to glue the carpet to the HushMat foil layer. (This is the same adhesive that FFR recommends for gluing the padded vinyl dash panel to the aluminum dash.) You should be able to fairly easily control the spray of the 3M Super 77. To be safe, mask off any paint and body surfaces where you don't want glue. Use painter's masking tape and painter's masking paper to protect these areas. We used an old hot rod poster that had seen better days.

Our FFR rear wall carpet came pre-slit to accommodate the Simpson Racing harnesses that routes through the rear wall and attaches in the front part of the trunk. If your carpet also has these four pre-cut slits for the shoulder harnesses, here is a helpful hint: Use four thick pieces of cardboard, temporarily placed in the cutouts. When you initially glue the carpet to the rear wall, push these four cardboard pieces in the carpet slits and into the four harness openings within the rear cockpit wall.

Another helpful hint is to use a putty knife to gently push the carpet up under the edge of the body, being careful not to scratch the body paint with the putty knife. Of course, be sure to protect the bodywork with paint and the hot rod poster paper. This first carpet panel to glue in is the most challenging panel to adhere, as it's a large panel that is hung vertically. You'll be fighting gravity and a large surface area, so having a friend to help put the panel in place is highly recommended.

Project 3: Interior Carpet Installation

Install Carpet on Rear Interior Wall Corners

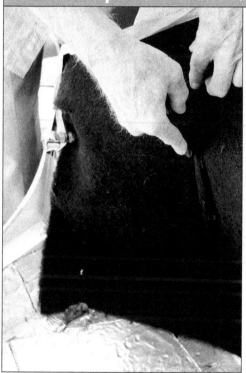

1 The FFR Mk4 Complete Kit build manual instructs you to unpack and lay flat your carpet sections for several weeks prior to gluing in the carpet. This is done to make sure that any folds and creases in the carpet sections from being shipped in a box all disappear before installation.

When you glue the carpet to the aluminum (or HushMat insulation), push the carpet evenly onto the surface. Also, coat the aluminum/insulation surface with an even spray of Super 77 and where possible, do the same with the back of the carpet. If you spray adhesive on the back of the carpet, be careful not to get too close to the edge of the carpet. You need to be able to hold an unglued portion of the carpet to then stick onto the aluminum/insulated surface. If you get the glue on your fingers, the sticky stuff winds up on top of the carpet.

Shown here is the rear cockpit wall passenger corner piece. The passenger-side rear corner wall slice and the driver's rear corner piece are the second and third sections to be glued into place.

Cut Shifter Hole in Carpet

2 *Because you haven't installed your trans tunnel top yet, cut out the openings in the carpet for the Hurst shift lever and the Lokar custom emergency brake handle. The FFR carpet piece for the trans tunnel drapes over and covers the entire tunnel, both top and sides. Hence, before you cut, make sure that the trans tunnel top is perfectly centered in the middle of the carpet piece. Lay the carpet upside down and the trans tunnel top upside down on top of it and center it. Confirm it is dead center by measuring and re-measuring the carpet and top. Cut out the openings with a razor knife. Even though boots cover both openings, you should still trim as carefully as possible.*

Rivet Transmission Top

3 *Rivet the transmission tunnel top panel into place, after protecting the Lokar emergency brake handle with masking tape. Glue the carpet on the top of the transmission tunnel and on the sides.*

Trim Passenger-Side Carpet Tunnel Section

4 *Cut the FFR carpet sections generously so you have enough for complete coverage. You may need to trim here and there to make the carpet a near-perfect fit. Then glue down the top carpet section of the trans tunnel first, trim it where needed on the sides and then glue the sides onto the tunnel walls.*

Install V-Section of Carpet

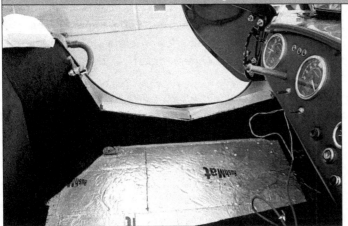

5 *Install the V-sections under the doors. The section that wraps around the front frame tube is tricky. Fit the notch around the tubes on the passenger-side V-section. Be sure to test fit each section before applying glue to the HushMat and the backside of the carpet.*

Install Carpet on Footbox Walls and Floor

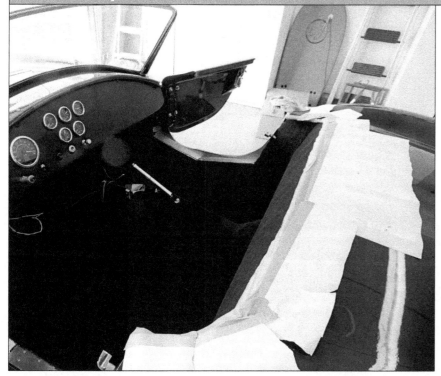

6 Use a furniture pad on the floor of your garage. You need to kneel and wrestle this carpet section behind the footbox frame tubes and then pull the panel across to the inner footbox wall, which is the wall section behind the pedal. When you've finally pulled this carpet into position, hold sections away from the walls and spray the Super 77 on the walls and on the back of the carpet. Smooth down this section as well as possible with your hands.

After the outer and inner footbox walls and the section under the dash are glued in, glue down the passenger-side floor and then the driver-side floor. The passenger floor goes up to the footbox area, with a small triangular section that glues atop the round frame tube. It's a little easier to install than the driver's side, so we recommend you glue it down first.

Install Carpet on Doors

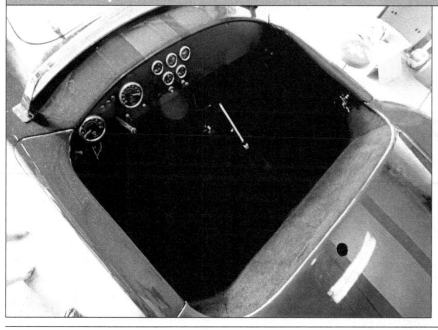

7 The last sections to glue down are the pieces that go under the doors. These two little multi-section pieces of carpet are also a real challenge to glue into place. To get the installation done right, spend a good deal of time test fitting these pieces. Figure out the best way to cover the aluminum, and apply the glue to the section and put them in the proper positions. FFR supplies the C-trim piece that runs from the bottom of the door hinge to the bottom of the door latch. Cut this trim piece to the appropriate size and press the C-trim on top of the body/aluminum/carpet edge.

Seats

The mounting holes for the seats were drilled earlier in the assembly process, but now it's time to install the seats permanently. For a couple reasons, re-installing the seats is a somewhat difficult proposition. The FFR build manual recommends that you put a wire or something in the holes that you drilled in the floor to bolt down the seats. Since we installed HushMat insulation, we covered those holes long ago. But we did manage to find them.

Project 4: Seat and Restraint System Installation

Install Passenger Seat

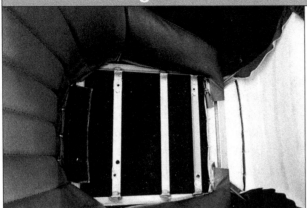

1 Remember that we needed to drill two holes in the passenger-side floor to bolt down the passenger seat, when we first installed the seats while the body was still removed from the chassis? Now you drill the other two seat installation holes in the round frame rail that runs adjacent to the trans tunnel wall. After putting the roadster up on jack stands, roll under the car on a mechanic's creeper and find the two black holes that contrast nicely with the Sharkhide protected aluminum floor. Poke the holes open with a pick, right through the HushMat material and the carpet. Align the passenger seat frame with the two picks that were sticking up from the floor and put the seat in place.

Take another pick from topside and hunt around for the other two holes that you previously drilled in the frame tube.

After initially installing the passenger seat, by attaching the four fasteners, we discovered that the edge of the seat rubbed against both the door striker and the door, so we made the proper adjustments. We removed the seat and drilled four more holes into the seat frame that would line up with our four holes that we had already drilled in the cockpit floor. Hence, we didn't need to drill any additional holes in the cockpit floor, but we had to drill four more holes in the passenger-side seat frame.

When we installed the driver's side seat, we ran into a similar challenge. You'll remember that we installed the driver's side seat with an optional FFR procured seat track system. Dad was able to find all three holes that were in the aluminum floor and frame/plate. Regrettably, we learned that the installed seat hit in the same places on the driver's seat, the striker and the top edge of the door. We re-drilled the four holes in the seat frame and once again solved the problem.

Drill for Lap Harnesses

2 These Simpson five-point safety harnesses are included with the FFR Mk4 Complete Kit. You need a 3/4-inch wrench, 3/4-inch socket, and ratchet, so you can install the harnesses. In the FFR build manual, the directions show these safety harnesses being installed prior to the body being on the chassis. Thus, the carpet has already been glued in place on the rear cockpit wall, the seats are temporarily in place and the Simpson harnesses are installed. Had we done it this way, it might have been easier to install the harnesses, since we wouldn't have to reach into the trunk with the trunk lid hitting our back. We might have had to re-do the safety harness installation, just as we had to re-drill the seat frames. Perhaps, doing it our way is the preferred method.

After removing the seats, place a clean shop rag or a towel on the carpeted cockpit floor to minimize the mess. Use an electric drill and a 1/2-inch bit to drill a hole in the lower rear corner of the transmission tunnel that is directly behind the hole in the lap safety harness attachment ear. There is already a hole in this attachment, so you just need to feed the 1/2-inch drill bit through the hole to drill through the carpet/HushMat/aluminum. When you've drilled this hole, get on your creeper and install the washer and nut on the inner trans tunnel side. Have your buddy install the harness and the 3/4-inch harness bolt in the cockpit.

Install Lap Harnesses and Seats

3 *For proper installation of the Simpson shoulder harnesses, attach the Simpson lap harnesses and then re-install the seats.*

Adjust Shoulder Harness Straps

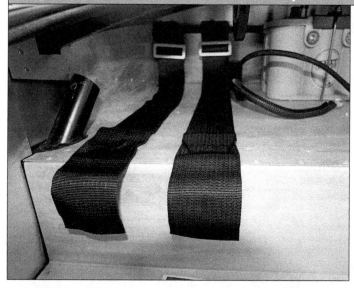

4 *To correctly install the Simpson Shoulder harnesses, remove the attachment ear and the sliding adjustment buckle from the harness. Feed the harness strap through the slit in the back wall of the cockpit. The shoulder harnesses are left and right, so feed the left-oriented strap in the left opening and the right-oriented strap in the right opening. (The metal clasps that attach with the lap harness should come to the center; that's how you know whether the strap is for the left or the right shoulder.) Once you've fed the straps through the opening, lay them out in the trunk so that the strap length is roughly even. Re-attach the sliding adjustment buckles and the attachment ears. Check the strap alignment on the seat back. If the Simpson straps are even in length on the seat back and in your trunk, you have properly adjusted them.*

Install Driver-Side Straps

5 *When you are satisfied that you've properly adjusted the shoulder straps, feed the straps back through the sliding buckle and tuck away any excess strap. Then, use a 3/4-inch open-end wrench on the nut side and washer side of the fastener and a 3/4-inch socket and ratchet connected to the bolt head and washer side of the fastener. Firmly tighten these fasteners.*

Install Driver-Side Harnesses

6 *Here is how a properly installed Simpson racing safety harness should be installed. Notice that the passenger side could use some adjustment to be the same length. After shooting this photograph, we adjusted the passenger side.*

Custom Steering Bezel and Steering Wheel

On many customized vehicles, the steering wheel crowns the dashboard. It is the single coolest element in a first-class interior. The original Moto-Lita wood-rimmed and aluminum tri-spoked steering wheel came standard in the AC Bristol roadster, the 260, 289, and 427SC Shelby AC Cobra roadster, and many other sports and race cars of the 1950s and 1960s. It has a high-performance, yet timeless classic appeal. For this reason alone, we knew right away that we wanted that sort of steering wheel adorning the dashboard and immortalizing the cockpit of our roadster replica.

Several companies, including Andy's Autosport and Tony D. Branda, offer reproduction Shelby Cobra steering wheels for that authentic look. But there's nothing to prevent you from a selecting a modern steering wheel from a respected manufacturer, such as Momo, Grant, or NRG. Thankfully for us, this three-spoked wheel comes standard as part of the FFR Mk4 Complete Kit. When the time finally arrived to install this stylish piece, we were as excited as can be.

Project 5: Steering Wheel Installation

Inspect Custom Steering Wheel Bezel

1 *Custom touches are always appreciated, even in high-speed sporting and racing machines like our FFR Mk4 Cobra roadster replica. One of the few items that Factory Five does not supply as part of the Mk4 Complete Kit is a steering wheel bezel to cover the opening in the dashboard-padded vinyl where the steering shaft pokes through.*

We had an unused alternator pulley wheel from a PowerMaster high-performance chrome alternator. It just happened to have about the same diameter as our steering shaft. We took the pulley wheel to our local machine shop and asked the shop to slice the wheel in half laterally. We then had three installation holes drilled in the bezel with a drill press. Then three holes were countersunk to accommodate the button-head Allen stainless-steel 3/4 by 6/32-inch fasteners and 6/32-inch stainless washers and 6/32-inch lock nuts. We carefully drilled the three holes in the dash using a tiny bit and successfully installed the stylish alternator pulley/steering wheel bezel in the dashboard.

Install Steering Wheel

2 Use a Phillips-head screwdriver, 5/16-inch Allen key, and 10-mm wrench to install the steering wheel. Find the steering wheel and hardware in the FFR box or your kit manufacturer's box. Spray a little WD-40 on a shop rag to spread it around the steering shaft at the top where the steering wheel goes into place. Slide the steering wheel boss into position and place the steering wheel against the boss. The six installation holes around the steering wheel boss and the circumference of the steering wheel are not symmetrical, so the wheel only installs in one position. Also, the steering shaft, the boss, and the steering wheel are all keyed, so these components also only install one way. When you've put the wheel in place, attach the wheel to the boss with the supplied Allen-head screws and locknuts. Use thread locker on the bolt that goes in the center of the steering wheel and tighten the bolt.

Install Factory Five Steering Wheel Emblem

3 The next step in the steering wheel's installation is to fit the Factory Five Racing emblem on the steering wheel's center section. This center section has an O-ring on the back edge of the piston portion that pushes into the center of the steering wheel and forms a friction-fit seal between the wheel opening and the center of the steering wheel.

We've opted not to install the emblem yet, as we need to drive the car for several miles, before we take it to the alignment shop. The shop initially aligned the entire chassis, while the body was being prepared for paint at the body and paint shop. In case the alignment shop needs to remove the steering wheel for any reason, we don't want them to mar the wheel or the center section/FFR emblem by prying it out with a screwdriver.

Miscellaneous Bits & Baubles

Some people call these dress-up items. They include the mirrors, shift lever, shift boot cover and bezel, and check straps.

Install Hurst Shift Lever & FFR Boot/Bezel

Ever since we relocated the shift point on our Tremec T56 6-speed manual transmission to the mid-shift point, we had an impossible time trying to find a short throw shifter. We wound up getting a Hurst Shifter with a black 6-speed shift knob that was 7 inches long. That length lever would look and work great in a 1960s-era muscle car, but it's a full 2 inches too long for our Factory Five Mk4. We decided to lop off 2 inches at the bottom of the shift lever with the die grinder. We also drilled two attachment holes in the bottom of the shift lever. We then drilled four installation holes using our cordless drill and a 1/8-inch bit.

Here's another helpful tip for finding the drilled holes in the black carpet. Squirt a little blue thread locker where you drilled the four holes. You'll see the blue thread locker, so you can screw in the fasteners with a Phillips-head screwdriver. The bonus is that the threads of the screws get a coating of thread locker as they go through the holes in the carpet.

FINAL FITMENT

Our Mk4 is more than ready to take us wherever we want to go, whether it's a Cobra car club cruise, a track day at Mazda Raceway at Laguna Seca, a street rod and muscle car show, or a blast up to California's Central Coast for Monterey Car Week. That's precisely the allure of a replica. We can drive it anywhere. If we had restored a 1968 Mustang fastback, built a 1934 Ford roadster hot rod, or renewed a 1954 Jaguar XK120 roadster, we'd be too afraid to drive it for fear that it might get scratched or stolen.

There are a few more things to finish. They're vital components to be sure, such as roll bar, fuel cap and filler hose, head- and taillights, turn signals, and several more aluminum panels for both form and function.

We also want to install the Quick-jacks that go on the front and the rear of the car, after they are powder-coated. Once that's done, they bolt right on. We may also install a lockable glove box in the dashboard, but that can wait.

Our build talents have grown considerably since the start of this project. And these skills will not diminish because we'll continue to improve our FFR Mk4 roadster as time and funds permit. We'll also build and/ or restore other projects. The three of us are automotive enthusiasts, with more than just a passion for driving fast and going to shows. Somewhere in our Smith lineage there must have been blacksmiths.

Project 1: Roll Bar Installation

Install Roll Bar

1 To help the fit, rub Tri-Flow Teflon lubricant on the ends that go into the frame pipes. Lay a towel under the three roll bar holes to protect the roll bar hoop. Then carefully guide the straight pipe all the way into the angled pipe.

Next, place the hoop into its two-pipe receptacles. If your hoop is like ours, it's a snug fit. To coax ours in, we folded up another towel to cushion several well-intentioned blows on the top of the hoop using a large rubber mallet. You can see how far you need to go by looking at the frame pipe under the fender. Measure the distance you need to go by the hole in the chrome roll bar compared to the hole in the upright frame pipe. Once you get the hoop low enough, place a pick or a small screwdriver through the holes to align the holes, remove the pick, and install the FFR supplied hardware.

To tighten the hardware use a 1/2-inch wrench for the locknut and a 3/16-inch hex key for the bolt face. With the hoop installed, screw up the straight pipe to meet the hoop. You may need a little coaxing from a pick or a small screwdriver to get the attachment holes to line up. Be persistent, and you'll have an installed roll bar that looks as good as ours.

Project 2: Fuel Cap and Fuel Filler Hose Installation

Install Fuel Fill Hose, Gas Cap and Parts

1 *If you like instant gratification, you'll enjoy installing the pop-open quick-fill Le Mans racing fuel cap, fuel filler hose, and ground strap. These fuel system components are easy to put in place, and they look amazing. Use the Le Mans fuel cap rubber gasket, and drill the six fastener holes used for installing the cap if you didn't do it before the body was painted. Put a couple layers of masking tape on the top of the body to prevent any errors when drilling.*

Install Fuel Filler Hose

2 *Though the FFR Complete Kit build manual recommends installing the fuel filler hose on the fuel filler pipe that comes out of the fuel tank, you may opt to install the 5-inch shortened fuel filler hose on the Le Mans fuel cap pipe and then drop the fuel cap, cap gasket, and fuel hose assembly down through the hole in the fender. That's right; carefully cut 5 inches off the end of the supplied fuel filler hose before attaching the shortened hose on the pipe that comes from the bottom of the fuel cap.*

Align Cap Installation Holes

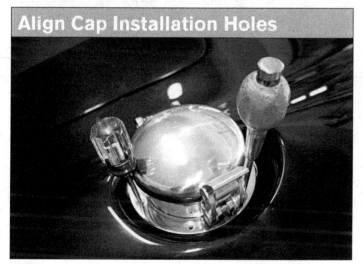

3 *Use a couple picks through the fuel cap holes, through the fuel cap gasket, and through the holes in the recessed fuel cap area in the passenger-side fender. It helps line up these holes for the Phillips-head screws.*

Install Phillips-Head Screws

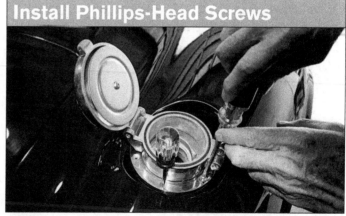

4 *Open the cap to obtain direct access to the screw holes in the base of the cap. Leave a couple picks in the holes while you screw in the Phillips-head screws (the longer machine screw, washer, and locknut are used to install the ground strap). Use the hole in the cap's base that is located on the right side of the pop-up cap's upright.*

Fasten Fuel Hose & Ground Strap

5 Slide/coax the fuel hose down onto the fuel filler pipe. Tighten the lower hose clamp that is on the fuel hose over the fuel filler pipe. Attach the ground strap to the underside of the fuel cap by using the longer Phillips-head machine screw, washer, and locknut. Drill a 3/16-inch hole in the frame upright on top of the aluminum wall and install the supplied metal screw to affix the other end of the ground strap. Make sure you also use the other supplied washer to form a solid ground.

Project 3: Headlight Installation

Inspect Headlight Components

1 Installing the headlights is challenging because there are small parts and fasteners that need to be properly attached. Take your time to do it right. You need the headlight components, the headlight mounting assembly, and a Phillips-head screwdriver.

Push Grommet Into Bucket

2 Push the electrical-wire grommet into the side of the headlight bucket. We had success by getting the groove in place on one side and then coercing the rest of the grommet into the bucket by coaxing the rest of the grommet's groove around its plastic rim hole.

Screw in Adjuster Screws and Install Light Plug Harness

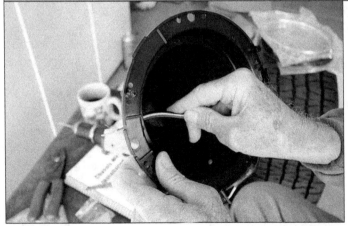

3 Screw the adjuster screws about halfway into the headlight bucket. Insert the light plug harness wires through the wire grommet that you just installed.

Install Mounting Flange

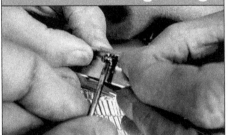

4 Install a mounting flange (ring) around the headlight. Three small screws go into three small tabs. Affix these three tiny screws with a Phillips-head screwdriver, making sure that the headlight is right side up.

Inspect Mounting Flange

5 *If you've properly installed your headlight's mounting flange, it looks like this. The writing on the headlight should be right side up.*

Install Headlight Gasket

6 *Place the headlight gasket on the backside of the headlight bucket. The adjuster housings should poke through the two larger holes in the gasket.*

Install Headlight Bucket

7 *Carefully drill four 1/8-inch attachment holes to mount the headlight bucket. Then, use the supplied Phillips-head screws to install the headlight bucket in the front fender.*

8 *With the two upper screws set wider apart than the two lower screws properly installed, the headlight bucket looks like this. The headlight adjuster screws are at the 9 o'clock and 12 o'clock position on the driver's side and passenger's side.*

Plug Light into Connector

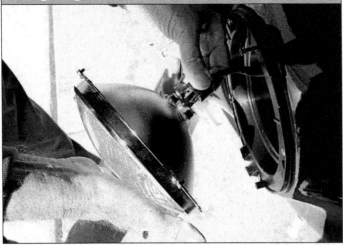

9 Plug the headlight bulb into the connector before installing the bulb into the headlight bucket.

Mount Flange

10 The slot (or groove) in the two-adjuster screws holds the slotted part of the mounting flange. Screwing these two adjuster screws in or out enables the beam of the headlight to be adjusted up, down, right, or left.

Install Chrome Ring

11 To finish the headlights installation, push the spring clip onto the boss near the bottom of the bucket on the right side. Hook the chrome trim ring over the bucket on the top and screw it into the bottom right, just left of the spring clip, using the supplied countersunk screw.

Project 4: Turn Signal Installation

File Mounting Holes

1 In contrast to the headlights, the turn signals are very simple to install. There are washers, locknuts, and two threaded studs on the back of each light. The FFR Mk4 Complete Kit has the openings in the body to accommodate the lights, so all you need to do is lightly file the two mounting holes already drilled into the body with a small round file.

Tighten Locknuts

2 Use a 5/16-inch-deep socket and ratchet to tighten the two locknuts North and South on the turn signals. We left the wiring details to Dennis Clark of Carlsbad Automotive Technology. The front harness contains all the wires necessary. The white, red, and black wires in the harness are wired to the headlights, and the remaining wires in the loom are soldered and insulated to the turn signal wires.

Project 5: Taillight Installation

Install Taillights

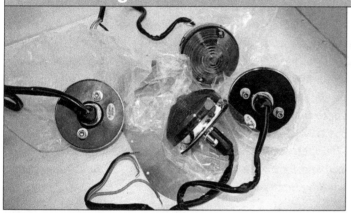

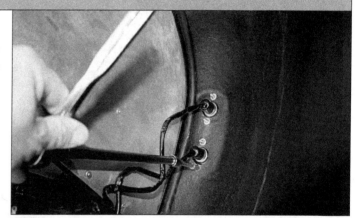

1 The four taillight assemblies are installed in a similar manner as the turn signals. There are two threaded mounting studs with washers and locknuts. Widen the mounting holes with a small round file before placing the taillights in the back of the rear fenders.

2 With the rear wheel/tire removed, sit inside the rear fender and use a 5/16-inch-deep socket, long extensions, and ratchet to tighten the two locknuts on the back of each taillight. Be sure to place a washer on each threaded stud before screwing on the locknut.

Inspect Installed Taillights

3 Our FFR Mk4 Cobra roadster replica's caboose now looks every bit as sexy as its nose with the taillights installed. We left the wiring details to Dennis Clark of Carlsbad Automotive Technology.

Project 6: License-Plate Light Installation

Inspect License-Plate Light Assembly

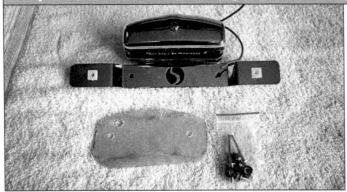

1 *You'll remember that the two attachment holes for the rear license-plate light were pre-drilled during bodywork. Another hole was drilled to route the unit's electrical wires. That plastic template was used to show where the holes should be drilled in the trunk lid.*

Install License-Plate Light Frame

2 *Before drilling to mount the license-plate frame, which is attached to the license-plate light, mount the license plate in its two attachment holes and route the wires through one hole. Stick on two layers of masking tape. These two layers of tape serve as protection for drilling into the painted trunk lid. Use a marker to indicate on the tape where to drill the rivet holes. Remove the license-plate light. Use a 3/16-inch drill bit to carefully drill the holes for the 3/16-inch rivets. Reinstall the license-plate light with the supplied hardware and attach the license-plate frame using two 3/16-inch rivets and a rivet gun.*

Project 7: Side Vent Installation

Apply Sharkhide

Install Driver-Side Vent

1 *There are certain iconic items that must be on all Cobras, real or replica. One of these crucial components is the side vents that are used to extract warm air from the engine bay. They install on the sides of the body, not far behind the exhaust headers. First, treat them to a careful covering of Sharkhide protectant.*

2 *Place a fairly generous amount of silicone on the top edge above the louvers and also on the bottom edge. Temporarily use duct tape on the top edge and on the bottom edge until the silicone has time to set. Stick each side vent on the inside of the front fender at the opening within the body. Be sure the vents face rearward so they funnel the hot air out of the engine bay.*

Project 8: Miscellaneous Panel Installation

Install Final Aluminum Panels

1 Several more critical aluminum panels need to be SharkHide protected, drilled, silicone, and riveted into place. One is the nosepiece that fits in front of the radiator and supports the bottom of the radiator. There are two side triangle panels that attach via rivets next to the radiator within the nose. There are also a couple patch panels above the fuel tank, which have already been covered front and back with SharkHide protectant.

Project 9: Splashguard Installation

Install Driver-Side Front Splashguard

1 Press on the bulb weatherstrip along the outer edge of the alumi-num curvy panel that runs underneath the body. Carefully test-fit the panel and decide whether you need to trim the aluminum. (Our driver-side guard fit perfectly, with the exception of the upper left-hand corner of the panel. We needed to trim a little piece out to make room for the front harness loom.) Use a small clamp at the bottom to temporarily affix the splashguard to the front of the F-panel flange.

The FFR-supplied aluminum rivet hole marker tool has holes drilled every 3 inches on one side and every 2 inches on the other side. It's your choice as to which you use (we opted for 3-inch intervals on the driver's side and 2-inch intervals on the passenger's side). Mark, punch, and drill the holes using a 1/8-inch drill bit and electric drill. To hold the panel sufficiently in place while drilling, install several of the small sheet-metal screws (shown).

Install Driver-Side Front Splashguard (Continued)

2 After cutting a notch in the upper left-hand corner of the driver-side splashguard, this panel should install and seal exceptionally well. This notch allows the front harness to travel unencumbered to the front lights and turn signals.

Install Driver-Side Front Splashguard (Continued)

3 When you've successfully drilled the splashguard, remove the temporary screws and rivet the panel in its place with 1/8-inch rivets. Remember to use silicone on the back edge of the panel where it rests atop the F-panel's rear flange. The bottom right tab (on top of the front fender) must be drilled with a 3/16-inch bit from the bottom so that a 3/16-inch rivet can be installed from the bottom of the body through the aluminum tab.

You may wish to drill a 1/8-inch pilot hole before drilling the final hole as an additional paint/fiberglass protection step. When drilling this hole through the body panel, put two layers of masking tape on the body to protect the paint job. Go slow and easy with the drill as you penetrate the fiberglass.

Install Driver-Side Rear Splashguard (Continued)

5 The passenger-side rear splashguard required no trimming or modification but the driver-side rear splashguard requires a great deal of trimming and customizing. Here's how the panel appears with its bulb weatherstrip in place on the curved edge prior to modification.

To install the driver-side rear splashguard, you may have to bend down the front flange of the fuel tank. This can be accomplished with a pair of pliers and some brute force. Trim the lower edge of the panel on the left side with tin snips. (We also put a slice of bulb weatherstrip on this trimmed edge, in an effort to tightly seal this modified splashguard all around.) Getting the panel to fit just right may mean you have to trim the radius on the bottom on the right side. Silicone where the panel attaches to the frame and use 1/8-inch rivets to securely install the driver-side rear splashguard.

Install Passenger-Side Rear Splashguard

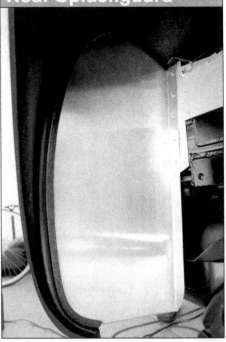

4 As with the front splashguards, push on the bulb weatherstrip around the edges. The long, vertical, flat edge is riveted to the frame upright at either 2- or 3-inch intervals with 1/8-inch rivets. Therefore, first mark and drill the holes with a 1/8-inch drill bit. On the driver's side, we didn't have to trim the panel at all; verify that you don't have to trim here either.

On the front fender splashguards, you needed to drill through the bottom of the body into the splashguard tab. In the rear, however, just use a 1/8-inch drill bit. You can either use a 1/8-inch rivet or a small machine screw with a locknut. Remember to put silicone between the frame and the splashguard's vertical edge where it's riveted to the frame.

The flat, bottom-edge surface of the panel has its thickness pointing rearward. You also need to be careful not to pinch the fuel cap's ground cable with the splashguard. Our ground cable tucked nicely out of the way of the panel. Make sure yours does, too.

Project 10: Front Apron Installation

Install Front Apron

1 *The front apron is a supporting panel, which adds support for the bottom of the radiator. The FFR Mk4 Complete Kit build manual indicates that this panel can either be installed with rivets or with machine screws and locknuts.*

We decided to use buttonhead Allen fasteners with neoprene washers on the top side of the nose's fiberglass body with larger fender-style neoprene washers on the bottom and stainless-steel washers underneath the neoprene washers held tight with a 3/8-inch locknut. Neoprene washers are used against the fiberglass to protect the paint job.

The hardware used on the bottom of the radiator is all stainless steel. The advantages of using machine screws and locknuts are twofold: First, the radiator can be easily removed, if necessary. Second, if you use a bunch of rivets, you might wind up cracking the fiberglass with the passage of time.

Install Passenger-Side Front Triangle Panel

2 *There are two remaining panels to install, the ones that go on either side of the radiator within the nose of the roadster. Install the bulb weatherstrip and test fit the panel. Mark on the backside of the panel where the 3/4-inch frame rail goes. Once you have these two lines traced on the backside of the panel, remove it from the nose. Mark, punch, and drill these holes in the panel with a 1/8-inch drill bit and your trusty electric or cordless drill.*

Place the panel, put a protective towel over the radiator, and drill the holes in the aluminum panel through the 3/4-inch frame tube. Take the panel out one last time and apply some silicone. Rivet the panel to the frame and repeat this same process on the driver's side.

No trimming was required on our passenger's side, but the driver-side triangle required a fair amount of modification.

Chassis Alignment

After final assembly, you need to take the car to a professional alignment shop to get the chassis aligned. Factory Five's Complete Kit build manual recommends that everyone do that, when the car is fully assembled.

Roger Daniel's Alignment & Brake shop in Santee, California, aligned the chassis while the body and body panels were being painted.

So, our car should be ready to go for a little jaunt on the boulevards. The alignment shop said that we should bring the roadster back for some fine-tuning after we've put some shakedown miles on it.

THE TEST DRIVE

The test drive is packed with excitement and some trepidation. You get to actually drive and enjoy the car you've been diligently building over the past several months, but at the same time, you need to be keenly aware of what the car is doing. You need to identify any problems, particularly serious engine, transmission, and suspension problems that need to be resolved for your safety and the car's health. At the same time, you need to become acclimated to driving your new car.

Ease your Cobra out of the garage and make sure that the clutch is engaging and disengaging properly. With our fire-breathing 427-ci stroker mill making a glorious noise even at idle, we glanced at the gauges in the dash and acknowledged that all was well so far. We coasted out of the garage and tested the brakes on the driveway. Thanks to the electronic fuel injection, the Mk4 started up easily. It stops sure, short, and straight.

When you're on your first drive, it's a good idea to stay within a few miles of your home and perhaps rumble around your neighborhood for the first 15 minutes. If you

To finish our car, we selected one of the finest automotive paints in the business, House of Kolor. Our hues of choice were Galaxy Gray with some special-effect metalflake mixed in for the Le Mans stripes, Re-entry Red team stripes, and Strattos Blue. Since a ton of Cobras have white Le Mans stripes, we opted to go understated, with a carbon fiber–like mix of the Galaxy Gray. The Re-entry Red stripes signify the Internet automotive magazine that my business partner, Ben Moment, and I have created. Many original Cobras were painted a midnight blue, or more specifically, a Ford paint hue called Caspian Blue. Our shade of House of Kolor Stratto Blue is a modern interpretation of that Caspian Blue Ford hue from 1965 and 1966. When you build your Cobra replica, create the car of your dreams. We prefer the look of the original size 15-inch Halibrand style knock-off wheels, so that's what we ordered from Factory Five Racing. You may like the look of 17-inch rolling stock better. If so, you have more selection when it comes to choosing high-performance radial tires for street or track.

On the QMP Racing Engines engine dynamometer, our 427 Dart Manufacturing aluminum block V-8 engine topped with Dart pro-CNC aluminum cylinder heads made 516.7 hp and 492 ft-lbs of torque. Original Cobras had aluminum bodywork and cast-iron engines. Ours has fiberglass and aluminum bodywork and an all-aluminum engine. Hence, our Factory Five Racing Mk4 Cobra roadster replica should have a significantly lower curb weight. What's more, the engine produces almost 100 more hp than the 427 cast-iron lumps of yore.

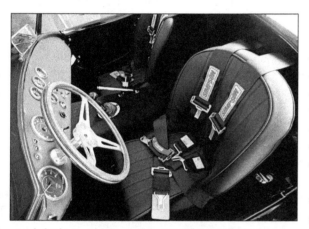

With four exceptions, our cockpit comes standard in the Factory Five Racing Mk4 Roadster Complete Kit. The leather seats are custom as is the steering wheel bezel, which we modified from an aluminum alternator pulley wheel. The gearshift lever was obtained from Modern Driveline. It's a Hurst 7-inch straight lever that we shortened by 2 inches, so we wouldn't run into the dashboard with it. As mentioned previously, the Lokar chrome emergency brake handle and system is also a much-needed modification.

The Mk4 Complete Kit includes the four round taillights, like the originals had. Well, we should say that most of the original 427SC Cobras came equipped with the round taillights. Some of them came with one large rectangular light on each side. An old automotive enthusiast rumor was that the 427SCs that had the rectangular taillights were equipped with the less powerful 428-ci V-8 engines. Whether that rumor is true or not, we prefer the look of the four round taillights.

encounter problems, you're not far away and can be easily rescued. You need to get accustomed to your roadster. Most Cobras have a curb weight of around 2,500 pounds, with powerplants that produce from 300 to 700 hp. This power-to-weight ratio makes these Cobras super cars, so take your time and be careful. You don't want to mangle your new roadster on your first drive.

As you drive, listen to the engine carefully. Shift through the first three gears and make sure that the transmission is properly selecting the gear and staying in gear. Listen to the rear end; make sure there is no clunking. Feel how the suspension is operating in the corners and over road bumps. It should drive in a straight line, providing smooth yet firm dampening, track predictably through corners, and brake securely.

Check the speedometer, tachometer, fuel gauge, amp meter, and in particular the temperature gauge. Make sure the engine temperature is within the normal operating range. If it's too hot or cold, you may have a thermostat issue, there might not be enough coolant in the cooling system, or the engine may be losing coolant. Make sure the climate controls, as well as the heater and air conditioning (if equipped), are functioning properly.

After running the car for 15 minutes, pull into a filling station, perform a visual inspection, and check all fluid levels—engine, transmission, power steering, and so forth. Look for anything that appears unusual or out of place. Look under the hood and under the car for leaks. If there are no leaks, proceed to the next phase of the shakedown test.

If you can find a large, wide-open parking lot, such as one at a mall or industrial park, use it with discretion to ascertain the running condition of the car. Away from other cars, check the steering again by cranking the wheel from lock to lock. Accelerate to 40 mph and brake aggressively but do not lock the brakes. You want to bed-in the brake pads, yet not glaze them over, and at the same time verify operation. If everything is in good working order, you can proceed to the freeway.

On the freeway, accelerate hard (but not insanely fast) through the gears, once again listening to the engine, transmission, and differential. At this speed, you need to be sure that the chassis feels solid, the car is tracking straight, and the suspension is performing correctly. There should be no vibration through the steering; no clunking, thumping, or other abnormal sounds from the suspension when encountering expansion cracks, potholes, or road ripples.

If you do encounter steering issues or suspension noise, these may be attributed to an unbalanced tire, a flawed or out-of-round wheel, a faulty ball joint, or other suspension issue. If you quickly identify and remedy the problem, that's great. But if you need help sorting out the suspension, take the Cobra to a tire service center or alignment shop. A short test drive by a professional will be a great help. As mentioned previously, we're glad that we had the alignment experts give our chassis a professional and thorough going over before we attempted our first drive.

When all systems are fully functional, it's time to conquer your favorite road, road course, or quarter-mile.

Our Maiden Voyage

On our maiden voyage, the Mk4 performed like a champ. The QMP Racing Engines Dart aluminum 427-ci stroker mill with the Dart Pro CNC aluminum cylinder heads seems to have endless torque and horsepower. There's no way we could test the limits of this powerplant on the highways and twisty country roads of America. She'll need to be exercised on a closed sports car racing circuit someday soon. But for now, the engine produces a lusty idle. It's loud enough to set-off three car alarms going 15 mph up and down our dual cul-de-sac street once.

To our knowledge, we've constructed the only FFR Mk4 roadster that has a Tremec T56 Magnum 6-speed manual transmission. We're very pleased to say that this bulletproof trans shifts easily and precisely. Having that 6-speed Hurst shifter by our side and the gearbox attached to it, we feel as though we're piloting a much more current sort of race car than a replica of the world's fastest production sports car of the 1960s.

The manual rack-and-pinion steering on our FFR requires a little muscle at slow speeds, but the steering is precise and gives great feedback. Likewise with the actuation of the cable clutch pedal; a strong left calf muscle is needed to engage/disengage that third pedal, as is the application of the brake pedal for the other calf.

I suppose there's something special about piloting any sort of race car, which is what the original Shelby Cobra 260, 289, and 427SC were. The feeling that I get every single time I drive our Cobra is one of swelling pride and accomplishment. Dad and I have constructed a beast of a car that handles better and is faster than 95 percent of the cars on the road! From a fiberglass body on the chassis, 62 aluminum panels, 22 boxes of parts, another 25 to 30 boxes of engine and transmission components, a pile of money, endless enthusiasm, and perseverance, we crafted a Factory Five Racing Mk4 Cobra roadster replica that offers stunning and reliable performance and is absolutely beautiful to gaze upon or pamper with yet another coat of auto wax.

It seems we do have the Blacksmith gene after all. Perhaps you do, too. You simply need to have a yearning desire to create something with your hands, your brain, your bank account, your spouse's approval, your unending persistence, and a commitment to excellence. Of course, it also helps that you have this particular book to assist you in your creative endeavor.

Are you ready to take your journey? You're sure to have mostly triumphs and maybe a few mishaps in your Cobra replica building adventure. When you create the sports car of your dreams, you'll be doing something that most haven't done before.

A GUIDE TO COBRA KIT CAR MANUFACTURERS

The Cobra established itself as an automotive icon, and when production of the original came to a halt, the revered roadster was destined to return as a replica. For more than 30 years, a variety of manufacturers have offered Cobra replicas as kit cars or in the form of a rolling chassis. When selecting a Cobra replica, determine your intended use, budget, mechanical skills, and application. Once you have determined these factors, you need to do your homework on the kits that fit these parameters.

The following guide provides exceptional insight and information to the Cobra replicas on the market, but it is by no means the end point, so talk to Cobra owners, manufacturers, and perform the appropriate Internet searches to acquire the information to make an educated buying decision.

Factory Five Racing

Founded in 1995, Factory Five Racing wasn't the first Cobra replica manufacturer but it is the largest. To date, the company has manufactured and sold well over 7,000 Cobra repli-

cas. FFR also creates the Type 65 Daytona Coupe kit, the GTM supercar that utilizes Corvette drivetrain and suspension components, the 33 Hot Rod, and Project 818, a mid-engine sports car that weighs 1,800 pounds.

Challenge Car

The Challenge car is a heavily modified Factory Five Racing Mk3 roadster kit designed for wheel-to-wheel professional and amateur racing. The big differences between the competition-focused Challenge kit and the street roadster kit are found on Factory Five's website.

The Challenge kit is sold in only one form, the base kit. But this base kit contains many more parts than the base roadster kit. You can still use some Mustang parts, but not as many as with the roadster kit.

Base Kit

In Chapter 1, I provided detailed coverage of the components in the Mk4 Complete Kit. Factory Five also offers a Mk4 Base Kit at $12,990, so you can assemble a Cobra roadster with less financial investment by using the additional components from a 1987–2004 donor Mustang.

Factory Five Racing offers the Cobra Mk4 in Complete Kit for $19,900 and a Base Kit for $12,990. The owner needs to source the engine, drivetrain, and some related parts for the Complete Kit while the Base Kit requires the use of a Mustang donor car.

The Base Kit contains the same high-quality Factory Five components as the Complete Kit, but it simply does not include many of the suspension, brake steering, and other parts that are sourced from the donor car.

Due to the complexity of different Mustang parts from 1987 to 2004, Factory Five Racing provides two simple packages that address these parts differences. Nearly all the kit parts that are included are interchangeable.

Major components sourced from the 1987-2004 Ford Mustang are: engine and transmission assembly; driveshaft; 8.8-inch rear end assembly with quad-shocks, springs, and control arms; front and rear brake assemblies with master cylinder; and front-wheel spindles and lower control arm.

Minor components from the 1987-2004 Ford Mustang are: radiator and cooling fan shroud, Mustang steering rack (with factory ignition for 1987–1995 cars), EFI computer and wire harness (or use aftermarket), fuel tank, fuel filter, emergency-brake handle, and pedal box. Other items you need are paint and wheels.

People who use Mustang parts from 1996 to 2004 get a few extra parts and don't need some others. The ignition switch is transplanted, which includes the key, switch, and electrical connectors to use with 1996–2004 parts. The brake hydroboost mount assembly is used by those with 1996–2004 hydroboost brakes and includes tool. They also use the 1996–2004 radiator mounting assembly, 4.6L oil pan and

Hot Hues Blue is the paint color of Alan Slide's sweet Unique Motorcars 427SC, shown at the 15th annual Unique Motorcars Homecoming Celebration, held in May 2008.

All Unique kits include a reconditioned Jaguar independent rear suspension (IRS). Rather than using a donor-chassis approach, Unique offers its customers different finish levels for its kits.

Unique Motorcars Minimum Order Kit

The Minimum Order Kit ($10,495) includes the following:

- 427 or 289 hand-laminated fiberglass body
- Doors hinged and latched
- Hood and deck lid installed
- All inner panels installed

Box Steel Frame
- Jig-built to accept custom front suspension, Jaguar independent rear suspension, with engine and transmission mounts on frame
- All necessary welding completed
- Some engine and transmission options (extra cost)
- Suspension not included

Original-type Windshield Frame and Glass
- Original specifications
- Extruded, brass plated, assembled, and installed

- Original-type surround plates installed

Original-Type Lights
- Two headlamps with trim rings
- Two front turn-signal lamps
- Four round taillights for 427
- Two rectangular taillights for 289
- License-plate light
- All lights pre-installed

20-Gallon Aluminum Gas Tank
- Installed in trunk floor
- Fuel sending unit installed

Misc. Parts and Installations
- Original door latches installed
- Side louvers installed
- Fiberglass dash panel (not upholstered) installed

transmission mount assembly (the later-model oil pans are too low, so an aftermarket needs to be used). Finally, these assemblies are also used: the fuel filler tube, radiator hose, A/C eliminator bracket, and air filter mount.

Unique Motorcars

Jean and sons Maurice and Alan Weaver run Unique Motor-

cars, a Cobra roadster and 1936 Ford Cabriolet replica business. Unique Motorcars, established in 1977, has been building 427 SC roadster replicas since 1979 and the 289FIA competition cars since 1991. To diversify the company's product line, Unique introduced a 1936 Ford Cabriolet kit in 2006 that's every bit as nice as the Cobra replicas.

E.R.A. Replicas

E.R.A. Replicas has been producing 289FIA, 427, and E.R.A. GT (Ford GT40 coupe and spyder) replicas for almost as long as Unique Motorcars. The company's component kits are very well engineered, designed, and constructed. In fact, E.R.A. Replicas is known in replica circles as being very authentic reproductions of the

Unique Motorcars Pallet Kit

The Pallet Kit includes the choice of 427 or 289 body ($10,495) plus the following parts and assemblies and any added (itemized) costs, which are subject to change without notice:

Wilwood Engineering Parts
- Brake and clutch pedals with 3/4-inch Wildwood master cylinders installed: $650
- Accelerator pedal and mechanical linkage installed: $235
- Original-style hood and trunk latches installed: $440
- Custom aluminum radiator installed: $500
- Original-style steering wheel with hub installed: $375

- Original-style steering column installed: $395
- Steering intermediate shaft and steering joints installed: $280
- Custom headers: $515
- Original-style side pipes (un-plated) installed: $510
- Functional roll bar installed
- Choice of chrome or black, forward or rear brace: $675
- Hood and trunk props installed: $125
- Standard rolling chassis (includes custom coil-over front and Jaguar-type independent rear suspensions, black-powdercoated brake lines, fuel line, and battery cable) installed: $8,705

Unique Motorcars Deluxe Pallet Kit

The Deluxe Pallet Kit includes the choice of 427 or 289 body and the following parts and assemblies and any added (itemized) costs, which are subject to change without notice:

- Pallet kit: $23,400
- Interior (leather seats, vinyl door panels, hinge covers, and carpet for cockpit and trunk) in standard black (colors extra): $1,800
- Complete standard dash assembly installed

- Vinyl dash cover, Stewart Warner Deluxe Gauges or AutoMeter Smith-style, switches and indicator lights; add $150 for 289 dash and add $150 for Competition Dash: $705 total
- Custom wiring harness (includes flashers, fuses, and horn relay): $450
- Dual electric radiator fan: $335
- Wiper assembly installed: $410
- Le Mans Quick Fill Fuel Cap installed: $245

E.R.A. replicas pay accurate homage to the race cars they emulate. The 289FIA (left) kit and the Ford GT40 Spyder (right) replica are extremely close to the originals. Of the first three Cobra replica companies in the business, Unique Motorcars, E.R.A. Replicas, and Contemporary, only Unique and E.R.A. are still preeminent Cobra kit manufacturers. Contemporary's molds, tools, and dies were sold to Factory Five Racing. FFR is now the largest Cobra replica manufacturer in the world.

original British-American Shelby Cobras.

Unlike my experience with FFR and Unique, I have not had the opportunity to test drive an E.R.A. car. But all of the E.R.A. Cobra replicas that I have seen show superior fit and finish and are exceedingly true to the original Shelby Cobra in terms of body shape and components that go into the vehicles. Neophytes in the Cobra arena are often fooled by the appearance of E.R.A. cars and believe them to be genuine Shelby Cobras, which no doubt makes the roadsters' owners proud.

If you prefer the look of the 289 Slabside street Cobra, E.R.A. has announced that a Slabside Kit will be available soon.

Everett-Morrison Motorcars

In 1983, Buford Everett (B-E) purchased an original mold of a Cobra body and the tooling for the Cheetah Chevrolet race car's chassis from Dean Morrison, in Chicago, Illinois. Everett married the Cobra body with the Cheetah's chassis and had a Cobra replica.

Over the initial five years of development, Everett's replica went from having a solid rear axle to using a Corvette's independent rear suspension (IRS), like an original Cheetah, and

then to implementing a Jaguar XKE IRS. In the 1990s, the roadster chassis went from a 90-inch wheelbase, like an original Cobra and Cheetah, to 93 inches and finally to 96 inches. During this time, the company began to use a coil-over independent front suspension (IFS), as opposed to a single shock and kingpins.

E-M began an extensive re-design of the Cobra in 2002, which included a stainless-steel tubular and ladder frame chassis and doing away with the chopper-gun fiberglass body creation in favor of the hand-laid cross-strand fiberglass construction process. The result of all this hard work was the introduction of the all-new Generation-IV Cobra replica in 2003.

In 2007, E-M's founders brought in new management and sold E-M to the current CEO, Julie Fenimore, who is a licensed professional engineer. In addition to all the enhancements made to the Generation-IV Cobra,

E-M upgraded its customer service and marketing functions, which enhances the customer experience.

The Generation IV's wheelbase, now 93 inches, offers 3 inches more cockpit legroom than an original Cobra. But the external dimensions and look of the E-M Cobra still appear as a genuine Cobra does—a sort of optical illusion, so to speak.

There are three forms of E-M Generation-IV Kit: Phase 1, Phase 2, and Accessory & Driveline Package. When all three packages are ordered together, everything needed to achieve a drivable Cobra is yours, with the exception of wheels, tires, engine, and paint. Optional components are also available. And Everett-Morrison can build a turnkey replica if you prefer.

An important note: The E-M Gen-IV roadster is a replica of a 427SC, so the chassis is set up for a Ford FE engine. The FE-series engines

Shell Valley showed off a stunning 427 roadster at the Kit Car Nationals in 2007. Proving there's real value in painstaking attention to every detail, the car's merlot paintwork sets this Shell Valley 427 roadster apart from most other Cobra replicas.

are Ford big-block V-8s—the 390, 406, 427, and 428.

For detailed information, including pricing on the all-new Everett-Morrison Generation-IV roadster, visit E-M's Web site, and/or contact Everett-Morrison Motorcars.

Shell Valley Classic Wheels, Inc.

Shell Valley Motors and Shell Valley Fiberglass were founded in 1971. Rich Anderson purchased the company in 1997 and then acquired a Cobra replica competi-

tor, Midstates Classic Cars & Parts, from Bob Kallio in 1999. Anderson brought the company into the new millennium stronger than ever. In 2007 he introduced the Generation-II Cobra, which offered a melding of the best features from

E.R.A. Replicas Standard 289FIA Kit

This kit costs $19,900 and comes with the following parts and assemblies:

Body, Fit to Chassis
- Aluminum inner panels, splash shields, and trunk, all installed
- Aluminum side-vent louvers installed
- Aluminum firewall, wheel-houses, floors, rear bulkhead panels with removable access panel, all installed
- Doors, hood and trunk lid, hinged, fit, and installed and latched with reproductions of the original hardware and stainless-steel fasteners
- Footboxes (fiberglass as original) with insulation installed
- Hood and trunk stay with brackets, all installed
- Built-in hood scoop or smooth hood
- All holes for lights, bumpers, mirrors, top and tonneau snaps, emblems, etc., drilled or cut out
- Removable aluminum transmission tunnel installed
- Separate left and right fiberglass footboxes with thermal insulation installed
- Windshield installed
- Integrated steel front and rear cowl surrounds acting to fully support the body shell and doors
- Driveshaft safety strap

Braking System (all installed)
- Floor-mounted brake and clutch pedal assemblies mounted directly on the main chassis rail with needle bearing pivots and pivoting pedal faces
- Dual Tilton master cylinders with balance bar enclosed in box below floor
- Steel brake lines, front and rear junctions with insulated clamps

- Flex lines to the front calipers and rear suspension
- Brake fluid reservoirs and brackets with filler lines
- Dual brake-light switches with warning light
- Reservoir fill lines supplied and installed on the kit
- All lines (brake, clutch, and fuel) secured to chassis with buffered clamps

Chassis
- All mounting points for engine and transmission, steering and suspension, body, brake system, radiator, and fuel tank
- Integrated door hinging and latching
- Functional roll bar with forward brace

Clutch System
- Pedal and all linkage, master cylinder, mounted on chassis, with filler tube
- Slave cylinder, bracket, flex line, and all fittings

Cooling System
- Radiator and oversized aluminum core with bleeder mounted in chassis with top and bottom pins into rubber insulators
- Electric fan, thermostat controlled with manual override switch and relay
- Aluminum shrouding
- Aluminum connector tube from water pump to radiator

Dashboard and Instruments
- Reproduction street or competition-style dashboard; he competition dash is in bare aluminum, the street dash is covered in all-weather vinyl
- Stewart Warner instruments including 3-inch tachometer and speedometer, plus 2-inch oil

E.R.A. Replicas Standard 289FIA Kit *CONTINUED*

pressure, oil temperature, water temperature, ammeter, and fuel-level gauges with appropriate senders
- High-beam, turn-signal, and brake-system warning indicator lights
- Fresh-air vent, pull cables, and knobs
- All dash switches appropriate for competition or street trim

Electrical System
- Special modular wiring harness, color coded, tagged, and soldered
- All original-style dash switches, appropriate to dash style
- Fuse blocks, horn and fan relays (pre-wired), and flasher
- All grommets, clips, securing hardware, etc.
- Headlights, parking lights, taillights, and license-plate lights, all installed
- Dual horns with relay
- Windshield wiper motor bracket with adapter tubes, and wiper relay
- Battery mounting system (in rear quarter)

Fresh Air System Installed
- Fresh-air inlet ducts
- Left and right control valves
- All hoses, clamps, etc.

Fuel System Installed
- Aluminum tank, 19-gallon, fully baffled
- Filler, Monza-type aluminum, with all fittings to tank
- Steel fuel line from tank to engine
- Complete carburetor throttle linkage

Standard Race Interior
- Seats, quality Naugahyde on fiberglass buckets (vinyl or leather street seats optional)
- Door hinge covers
- Dash support tubes
- Left-foot dead-pedal

Steering and Suspension
- Front upper and lower control arms with ball joints, bushings, and hardware
- Custom-fabricated steering knuckles
- Steering tie rods with ends
- Rear trailing arms with rod ends
- Lower steering column with U-joints

Trim and Attachments
- Interior and exterior rearview mirrors (see options for street-style)
- Grommets for instruments, cables, etc.
- Top and tonneau snaps, with holes in body drilled
- Side louvers in aluminum installed
- Ferrules for top bows and side curtains
- Jack pads with all hardware

The Street Trim Option
- Defroster vents on dash
- Weather stripping for doors, hood, and trunk
- Carpeting, door panels
- Street seats (427-style)
- Aluminum step moldings
- Front and rear chrome over-riders
- Sun visors and wind wings
- Top frame socket built into the chassis
- Assembly manual with illustrated step-by-step instructions with numbers and sources for all necessary other parts

Major Components Not Included in Standard Kit
- Engine: Ford 289/351
- Transmission: Mustang 5-speed, Ford Toploader, Richmond Gear, or Tremac 5-speed recommended
- Jaguar XKE or XJ sedan-style rear suspension unit, or ERA replacement (Jag requires custom ERA subframe)
- Flaming River steering gear (FR1502-3X3) or equivalent
- Upper steering column and steering wheel
- GM front rotors and calipers (bolt-on wheels only)
- Front coil-over dampers
- Wheels and tires
- Handbrake handle and cable
- Exhaust system

E.R.A. Replicas 427SC Standard Assembly

This kit costs $21,900 and comes with the following parts and assemblies:

Body Mounted on Chassis
- All inner panels, splash shields, and trunk, screwed in place
- Aluminum side-vent louvers installed
- Aluminum engine compartment firewall, floors, rear bulkhead panels with removable access panel, all installed
- Doors, hood, and trunk lid, hinged, fit, installed and latched with reproductions of the original hardware
- Hood and trunk stay with brackets installed
- Hood scoop, rivet-on standard (bonded-on optional)
- All holes for lights, bumpers, mirrors, top and tonneau snaps, emblems, etc., drilled or cut out; lights and jack pads installed
- Removable transmission tunnel (aluminum) installed
- Separate left and right fiberglass footboxes, screwed in place; roll of thermal insulation
- Windshield in triple-chrome-plated brass frame installed; optional wind wings and sun visors
- Powdercoated steel jack pads and all mounting hardware installed
- Steel front and rear cowl surrounds built into the chassis, fully supporting the body shell and doors
- Driveshaft safety strap, plated

Braking System (all installed)
- Floor-mounted brake and clutch pedal assemblies mounted directly on the main chassis rail with needle bearing pivots and pivoting pedal faces
- Dual Tilton master cylinders with balance bar enclosed in box below floor
- Steel brake lines (front and rear) and junctions, with insulators
- Flex lines to the front calipers and rear suspension
- Brake fluid reservoir bracket with filler lines
- Dual brake light switches with warning light

Clutch System
- Pedal and all linkage, master cylinder, mounted on chassis, with filler tube

- Slave cylinder, bracket, flex line, and all fittings

Cooling System
- Radiator, aluminum 2½-inch core, w/bleeder, mounted in the chassis with rubber insulators and full shrouding
- Electric fan, thermostat controlled with manual override switch and relay
- Aluminum lower connector tube

Dashboard
A reproduction of the original Street or SC style, with the following installed:

- Stewart Warner instruments including tachometer, mechanical speedometer, oil pressure, oil temperature, water-temperature gauges, ammeter, and fuel-level gauges with appropriate sender; Smith gauges are optional
- High-beam, turn-signal, and ignition warning indicator lights
- All toggle and rotary switches
- Fresh-air vent pull cables and knobs
- Glove box with fully finished and latched door

Electrical System
- Special modular wiring harness, color coded, tagged, and soldered
- Fuse blocks with fuses
- Horn and fan relays
- Flasher and taillight relay, mounted on bracket (at right)
- All grommets, clips, securing hardware, etc.
- Headlights, parking lights, taillights, and license-plate lights, all installed
- Dual horns with relay
- Windshield wiper motor bracket with adapter tubes
- Battery mounting tray with hold-down
- Fresh air system installed, including:
    Fresh-air inlet ducts with grills
    Left and right control valves
    All hoses, clamps, etc.

E.R.A. Replicas 427SC Standard Assembly *CONTINUED*

Fuel System Installed

- Custom aluminum tank, 19-gallon, fully baffled with one-way doors
- Filler: Monza-type aluminum, with all fittings and hoses to tank
- Fuel level sender installed
- Steel fuel line from tank to engine
- Complete carburetor throttle linkage, from pedal to carburetor, including the rod-end pivots and link ends

Interior

- Seats: quality black vinyl on steel frames (leather and other colors optional)
- Carpets: 24 pieces from black-nylon cut pile, bound, with heel pads and snaps; felt liner for the trunk lid; trunk carpeting is optional.
- Door pockets, emergency-brake handle boot
- Shift-lever boot and chrome trim ring
- Door hinge covers and aluminum step moldings
- Dash support tubes
- Trunk-lid felt liner
- Left-foot dead-pedal

Steering and Suspension

- Front upper and lower control arms with ball joints, bushings, and hardware
- Front fabricated steering knuckles
- Steering tie rods with ends
- Rear trailing arms with bushings and rod ends
- Lower steering column with U-joints

Trim and Attachments

- Fender and interior rearview mirrors, original design
- Top and tonneau snaps; the holes in the body are factory-drilled
- Aluminum windshield frame end-bezel
- Ferrules for top bows and side curtains
- Weather stripping for doors, hood, and trunk
- Defroster vents on dash
- All grommets for instruments, cables, etc.
- Assembly manual with illustrated step-by-step instructions, with numbers and sources for all necessary other parts

Major Components Not in the Basic Kit

- Engine: Ford 427 or 428 recommended; others possible
- Transmission: Ford Toploader, Richmond Gear or Tremec 5-speed
- Rear suspension unit based on Jaguar XJ sedan, or custom outboard-braked design
- Flaming River steering gear (FR1502-3X3) or equivalent
- Upper steering column and steering wheel
- GM front rotors and calipers (bolt-on wheels only)
- Front coil-over dampers
- Wheels and tires
- Handbrake handle and cable
- Exhaust system (side pipes or undercar)

the Shell Valley Cobra and the Mid-states Classics roadster.

Along with the 427SC Cobra replica, Shell Valley manufactures a 1951 Jaguar C-Type kit, a 1963 Cheetah replica, a 1928 Ford Model A Roadster replica, and a 1964 Daytona Coupe Series-II replica and offers fiberglass Jeep replacement bodies.

Shell Valley Classic Wheels, Inc. provides both a Basic Kit, with pricing starting at $9,995, and a Complete Kit for a 427 Cobra replica.

For more information on these kits and components, visit the company's Web site.

Lone Star Classics

Lone Star Classics offers several component kit cars, in addition to the company's LS427 Roadster (Cobra replica). The LS32 Highboy is a replica of the 1932 Ford roadster. Lone Star's Route 66 Roadster is a 1953 Corvette replica kit. Rounding out Lone Star's corral of kits are the LS300, a Mercedes Gullwing replica, and the Growler, which looks similar to the recent Plymouth Prowler convertible.

The list of components included in Lone Star's LS427 Roadster package for a complete kit is extensive.

For all the details of what's included, visit the Lone Star Classics Web site.

B&B Manufacturing

B&B Manufacturing has more than 20 years' experience manufacturing component kit cars. For an enhanced customer experience, B&B Manufacturing recently launched a new Web site and now offers a Roadster Build-Sheet process. This approach enables customers to spec out what B&B calls "the "66 Roadster" precisely the way they wish to build their dream machine within their budgetary constraints.

Customers can specify either a Stage-I 1966 Roadster Kit, a Stage-II 1966 Roadster Kit, a Stage-III 1966 Roadster Kit, or a Turn Key Minus 1966 Roadster Kit.

The other component kits that B&B Manufacturing provides include a "34 Coupe" (Ford 1934 3-window coupe replica), a HCS Coupe or Street Coupe (Cobra Daytona Coupe replica

Randy Thigpen bought his LS427 already built and then customized the roadster to his taste. He made subtle changes, such as a Cobra oval air cleaner underhood and an NOS bottle for a big boost in horsepower, and these improvements put his personal stamp on his Lone Star 427 roadster.

in race trim or street trim) and a GT-45 Coupe (Ford GT40 coupe replica).

For all the details, specifications, and pricing visit B&B Manufacturing's Web site.

Hurricane Motorsports

Hurricane Motorsports makes an authentic-looking replica kit called the "427 Roadster." Cobra enthusiasts who have built the Hurricane

component kit rave about this car. The company did cease production for a time in 2007 and was sold to new owners. In 2009, Hurricane Motorsports started producing the 427 Roadster once again.

For more information on the Hurricane Motorsports 427 Roadster kit, visit the Web site. Hurricane also supports a web forum for its owners and fans. More information is available from forum members as well.

The Turnkeys

Several manufacturers offer Cobra replicas in what is known as turnkey or "turnkey-minus" form. These replicas are all built, painted, wired, have completed interiors, and only require careful installation of an engine and transmission and final fitment of the necessary wiring. These replica Cobras are for enthusiasts who aren't inclined to build a car of their own, or perhaps don't wish to take the time to construct a Cobra. They'd rather buy the turnkey, have the engine and transmission installed by a professional, and then drive it as soon as possible.

Superformance, LLC

For the past 15 years Superformance has distributed complete rolling-chassis (turnkey replicas) and continuation vehicles in the United States. Hi-Tech Automotive is one of the largest specialty car production facilities in the world. Both located in South Africa, the two companies have enjoyed a long-standing and successful builder/distributor relationship, distributing more than 4,000 rolling-chassis turnkeys worldwide.

Carroll Shelby endorses and licenses the Daytona Coupe, GT40, and Cobra replicas that Superfor-

mance/Hi-Tech builds and distributes. He states that the Superformance machines aren't true Shelbys, but that they are "well-built and as close to correct as possible." The Shelby Cobra Daytona Coupe is sold through Shelby Distribution USA.

Superformance/Hi-Tech Automotive creates several coupes, in addition to the Cobra replicas. The Ford GT40 replica, Cobra Daytona Coupe, Perana Z-one (a Zagato-bodied supercar), and Corvette Grand Sport Coupe replica (under license with General Motors) are all road-worthy coupes with an abundance of street or track credibility.

For more information, including pricing, visit the Superformance Web site, where there is detailed information on all the rolling chassis vehicles, as well as a list of dealers.

The MKII

Superformance's latest Cobra replica offering is the MKII. It comes in two variants: the MKII FIA and the MKII USRRC. Both of these cars are careful emulations of the 289-powered FIA and USRRC race cars that achieved so many victories, fame, and fortune for Shelby American and privateers in the 1960s. Superformance has an exclusive agreement with Carroll Shelby for the MKII FIA, making it the latest Shelby-licensed product in the Superformance corral of road burners.

The MKIII

Superformance/Hi-Tech Automotive has provided the Cobra 427SC replica for more than 15 years. Called the MKIII, it comes in three versions: the MKIII, the MKIII Roadster, and the MKIII-R Edition.

Visit the Shelby American Web site to learn about the Shelby American versions of the MKIII.

Backdraft Racing

The Backdraft Racing Mark I Roadster has been a sensation and instant hit since development first started in December 2000 and shown as a finished turnkey by October 2001. Since 2003 the cars have been built in a 53,000-square-foot manufacturing facility in South Africa. The Backdraft Racing Cobra replicas are produced in left- and right-hand drive versions, and are available for worldwide distribution. There are four dealerships in the United States and three more dealers internationally.

For more information on any of the Backdraft kits, or to find a dealer, visit the company's Web site.

The RT3

The Backdraft Roadster is a refined, high-quality sports car that has been developed over many years. This turnkey car offers comfort, quality of construction, a comfortable ride, and exhilarating performance, all in an economically priced package.

The RT3B

The B in this model designation stands for Black Label, which indicates that the RT3B is fitted with styling components influenced by and used by the world's best supercars.

The TD

If you guessed that the TD stands for touchdown, you're not entirely wrong. Rather, Backdraft Racing uses the TD designation to stand for the company's Track Day terrorizer. Features such as a full roll cage that still accommodates a passenger, more suspension adjustments for fine tuning at the racetrack, a full aero package, and weight reduction make a veritable ultra-competitive race car for track-day action. If track time is what you're seeking, the BDR TD may be just your ticket to commanding your local race car circuit.

Kirkham Motorsports

One day in 1995 the Kirkham Motorsports legacy began with the following words scribbled on a piece of paper and sent via fax to Poland, "Can you guys build an aluminum-bodied car?" Less than a day later brothers David and Thomas Kirkham received the faxed reply that they had hoped for, "No problem."

What started the idea for the Kirkham brothers was the fact that a relative had purchased and imported a Polish MIG fighter jet at the same time that they were restoring an original Shelby Cobra CSX3104. Seeing the fighter jet up close and personal, the brothers realized many similarities between the aluminum jet and their aluminum roadster. They found

James Yale's BDR RT3 gets transformed into a BDR TD when he wishes to take it to the track. He installs a front air dam/diffuser, pads the twin roll bars, installs a Kirkey racing driver's seat, installs racing wheels and tires, and then transports his car to the race course.

the manufacturer's name on the MIG and decided to send the fateful fax.

With a toy model Cobra, an English-Polish dictionary, and a large enough dream to make even Steven Spielberg blush, David Kirkham flew to Warsaw one week after receiving the "No problem" fax. He met with MIG fabricators and toured the idle factories that had produced Cold War aircraft and fighter jets for more than 60 years. Wouldn't any car enthusiast in the same situation as David be thinking the same thing, "If those craftsmen can build supersonic aluminum fighter jets, couldn't they can create some aluminum-bodied roadsters that replicate the Cobra?"

He left Poland with build contracts in hand and, with his brother, launched a component-car company that is held in high regard by every automotive enthusiast who knows kit cars. More than 15 years later, Kirkham Motorsports is going strong.

The Kirkham's Web site has detailed information on all six turnkey Cobra replicas:

- 427 KMS/SC: A beautiful re-creation of the Shelby Cobra 427SC

- 427 KMS/Lemans: This is a KMS/SC with a Le Mans-style hard top
- 427 KMS/Street: The fender flares are smaller, there is no hood scoop, and the tubular exhaust system runs under the car and exits the rear. There are no side pipes.
- 289 KMS/FIA: A faithful rendition of the Shelby 289 FIA race cars that helped team Shelby American win the World Championship in 1965 in FIA racing
- 289 KMS/Lemans: See the Kirkham Motorsports Web site for more information
- 289 KMS/Street: An accurate re-creation of the original 289 Cobra street car, also called the "slab-side."

Unique Motorcars

Unique Motorcars can build a 427- or 289-body-style turnkey car ($40,495) with the following standard features:

- Solid-color paint scheme (some dark colors cost more)
- Custom coil-over front suspension
- Jaguar-style independent rear

suspension
- Black-painted exhaust system
- Black competition Quickjack pads
- Chrome valve covers and air cleaner
- 3-inch lap belts
- Le Mans fuel filler cap, tires, and reproduction wheels

You add the engine and transmission, and you're ready for the road. Or Unique Motorcars can install the engine and transmission. Optional accessories are listed with the corresponding pricing on the Web site.

E.R.A. Replicas

E.R.A. Replicas builds turnkey cars of all of their authentic Cobra replicas. Pricing includes the engine and transmission. For example, a base-vehicle 289-FIA comp car that's completely finished sells for $50,000. E.R.A. also offers many optional components.

See E.R.A.'s Web site for more information.

Shelby American, Inc.

With the creation of that first Shelby Cobra 260 in 1962, Shelby American, Inc. came to life. Today, this company creates Shelby GT350 and Shelby GT500 Mustangs and also distributes the following continuation cars: 50th Anniversary Shelby Cobra, Shelby Cobra 427 S/C, Shelby Cobra 289 FIA, Shelby Cobra 289 Street, Shelby GT40, and Shelby Daytona Coupe. These cars aren't designated as replicas; they are all turnkeys needing just engines and transmissions to make them sing.

For more information on all of the Shelby American machines, visit the company's Web site.

Cobra/Ford GT40 enthusiast and Dan Gurney fan, Dean Lampe, purchased an unfinished Kirkham Motorsports 289 KMS/FIA from a friend. Lampe then finished the Kirkham by emulating one of the most winning Cobras of all time, a Dan Gurney–raced 289 FIA that in some races wore number 15 and had yellow stripes across the front fenders and hood.

Aeromotive Inc.
7805 Barton Street
Lenexa, KS 66214
913-647-7300
www.aeromotiveinc.com

Automotive Racing Products, Inc.
1863 Eastman Avenue
Ventura, CA 93003
805-339-2200
www.arpfasteners.com

BFGoodrich
P.O. Box 19001
Greenville, S.C. 29602
877-788-8899
www.bfgoodrichtires.com

Carlsbad Automotive Technology
2730 State Street
Carlsbad, CA 92008
760-729-9323
www.carlsbadautotech.com

Comp Cams
3406 Democrat Road
Memphis, TN 38118
901-795-2400
www.compcams.com

Dart Machinery
353 Oliver Drive
Troy, MI 48084
248-362-1188
www.dartheads.com

Energy Suspension
1131 Via Callejon
San Clemente, CA 92673
949-361-3935
www.energysuspension.com

Factory Five Racing, Inc.
9 Tow Road
Wareham, MA 02571
508-291-3443
www.factoryfive.com

Federal-Mogul Corporation World
    Headquarters
26555 Northwestern Highway
Southfield, MI 48033
248-354-7700
www.federalmogul.com

Holley/Weiand
1801 Russellville Road
Bowling Green, KY 42101
270-782-2900
www.holley.com

House of Kolor
210 Crosby Street
Picayune, MS 39466
601-798-4731
www.houseofkolor.com

HushMat World Headquarters
15032 W. 117th Street
Olathe, KS 66062
913-599-2600
www.hushmat.com

JE Pistons
15312 Connector Lane
Huntington Beach, CA 92649
714-898-9763
www.jepistons.com

Lokar Performance Products
10924 Murdock Drive
Knoxville, TN 37932
865-966-2269
www.lokar.com

MSD Ignition
Autotronic Controls Corporation
1350 Pullman Drive, Dock #14
El Paso, TX 79936
915-857-5200
www.msdignition.com

March Performance, Inc.
16160 Performance Way
Naples, FL 34110
239-593-4074
www.marchperformance.com

Melling World Headquarters
2620 Saradan Drive
Jackson, MI 49202 USA
517-787-8172
www.melling.com

Modern Driveline
25308 Arroyo Ct
Caldwell, ID 83607
208-453-9800
www.moderndriveline.com

Moroso Racing
80 Carter Drive
Guilford, CT 06437
203-453-6571
www.moroso.com

North County Powder Coating
2746 S. Santa Fe Avenue
San Marcos, CA 92069
760-727-4121

Powermaster
1833 Downs Drive
West Chicago, IL 60185
630-957-4019
www.powermastermotorsports.com

Optima Batteries
X-33 Optima Batteries
5757 N. Green Bay Avenue
Milwaukee, WI 53209
888-867-8462
www.optimabatteries.com

QMP Racing Engines
9530 Owensmouth Avenue
Chatsworth, CA 91311
818-576-0816
www.qmpracing.com

Redline Review
It's All About Speed
www.redlinereview.com

Rupe's Hydraulics
725 N. Twin Oaks Valley Road
San Marcos, CA 92069
760-744-9350
www.rupeshydraulics.com

Sharkhide Metal Protectant
P.O. Box 702
O'Fallon, IL 62269
618-624-4091
www.sharkhide.com

Summit Racing
P.O. Box 909
Akron, OH 44398
800-230-3030
www.summitracing.com

Tremec Transmissions
14700 Helm Court
Plymouth, MI 48170
734-456-3700
www.tremec.com

Warner's Muffler
190 Douglas Drive
Oceanside, CA 92058
760-433-2240
www.warnersmuffler.com

CPSIA information can be obtained
at www.ICGtesting.com
Printed in the USA
LVHW050809170120
643850LV00001B/26